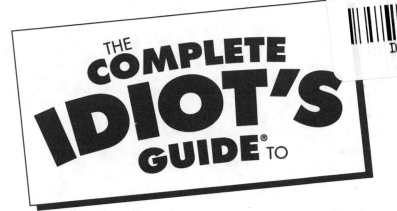

# THE COMPLETE IDIOT'S GUIDE® TO

# Market Timing

*by Scott Barrie*

ALPHA

A Pearson Education Company

# Contents at a Glance

# Contents

# Foreword

Now that the new generation has experienced a multi-year bear market of historic proportions, the buy-and-hold mantra preached by so many in the investment industry has lost its luster. Market timing is essential to investors of all levels for profitable investment results and the preservation of capital. And, as Scott Barrie details in this book, it's not only when you buy that is crucial, when you sell is just as important.

My firm, the Hirsch Organization, has published the *Stock Trader's Almanac* continually for 36 years. Though nothing is ever 100 percent perfect, we have used market timing since we first published the *Almanac* in the late 1960s to effectively capitalize on the market's major upmoves and avoid the bulk of the large declines. We make our business timing the market. Using nearly two centuries of historical market research into the recurring patterns, seasonalities, cycles, and trends, we study, analyze, report, and forecast the future course of the market with respect to current and changing market patterns, fundamental research, and technical analysis.

Mr. Barrie details some of our most reliable patterns in Parts 4 and 5 of the book, which focus on market seasonality and the symbiotic relationship between Washington and Wall Street. Most important are our Best Six Months switching strategy and the Four-Year Presidential Election/Stock Market Cycle. Using the Best Six Months has enabled us to cash in on the market's typical big moves from November through April while avoiding the abyss, May though October, where the market's worst months exist. The Four-Year Election/Stock cycle has proved invaluable in pinpointing major market bottoms. Many of these bottoms tend to occur in the second year of a President's term or the Midterm Election Year. Both our Best Six Months Buy Signal and Midterm Bottom Call coincided in October 2002.

In *The Complete Idiot's Guide to Market Timing*, veteran trader Scott Barrie provides market neophytes and seasoned professionals alike with the tools needed to time the market effectively. Starting with a solid understanding of market history, Mr. Barrie shows the reader what market timing is, how important it is to investment success and the preservation of capital, and how to apply it simply to current market conditions. He covers the essence of charting, economics, and valuation, which reveal some of the most simple and effective investment strategies out there.

As the famous American philosopher George Santayana said, "Those who cannot remember the past are condemned to repeat it." But as I like to say, "Those who study market history are bound to profit from it."

Scott Barrie has once again made understanding the stock market crystal clear and simple to understand by putting the core of market timing at the fingertips of the uninitiated and professionals. I encourage everyone with a dollar in the market to read and take to memory all the market wisdom within these pages.

Jeffrey A. Hirsch
President, Hirsch Organization Inc., and editor and publisher of the *Stock Trader's Almanac*

# Introduction

During the 1990s, the stock market was the best game in town and the rulers of the stock market during this bull market were the buy and hold crowd. However, the investment climate has changed. Surviving today's volatile markets and keeping your sanity requires a different and more flexible approach known as *market timing*.

This book will teach you how to spot the excesses of bull and bear markets and how to have a disciplined approach toward your investments through market timing. This is not another treatise on day trading, but a practical look at risks and rewards and how to move your investments between markets to get the maximum return on your money compared to the risks you are comfortable taking.

## How This Book Is Organized

The book is divided into eight parts:

**Part 1, "Understanding Market Timing,"** guides the reader through what market timing is and is not. It presents you with the different investment options you have and the risk and reward characteristics of each, so you have an idea of how good things can be, as well as the risks involved in investing so that you can make informed rational decisions.

**Part 2, "From the Chartists,"** introduces investors to the benefits and risks of "trend following." You will learn that market performance tends to fall into broad secular movements and how you can easily follow these long-term swings in the market without being glued to a computer all day trading in and out of the market. You will also learn how to spot warning signs of a market change and how to act ahead of the investing herd.

**Part 3, "Economically Speaking,"** explains the interaction between interest rates, the economy, and the stock market. It also guides the future market timer on how to spot changes in the investing climate and how this will affect different markets and your portfolio.

**Part 4, "Seasons in Securities,"** presents the market timer with the concept of the investment calendar. The best months and best years to invest are presented, backed up with plenty of historical examples to show how a calendar and a basic understanding of the flow of investment funds throughout the year can be used to get superior returns out of the market.

**Part 5, "Washington and Wall Street,"** analyzes the relationship between the power brokers in our government and the performance of your portfolio. Several myths regarding political parties and market performance are shattered as the reader is shown the best political environments and the worst political environments to invest in. Don't worry, this is not a crazy conspiracy theory, but an unbiased look at the relationship of Wall Street to Washington.

**Part 6, "Beating the Market from the Inside and Outside,"** presents the market timer with several different options for choosing either broadly diversified portfolios or narrow, carefully chosen portfolios to outperform the stock or match its performance with minimal time, and less risk.

**Part 7, "Putting It All Together,"** shows the market timer how to combine different market tendencies to create balanced portfolios to get a solid return from the market while minimizing the risks of investing.

**Part 8, "Be Your Own Financial Guru,"** guides the market timer through how to choose a qualified financial advisor as well as how to remain an independent thinker in the process. This section contains thoughts on the changing nature of the financial services industry and how to apply some common sense to your own personal finances to maximize the long-term benefits of investing.

## Extra Bites

The sidebars in this book offer tips, tricks, valuable knowledge, and definitions. Use these as road signs on the journey toward getting a good rate of return without undue risk from investing.

**Timing Tips**

This is a collection of little tips that are presented in a fashion similar to what you would get if you were surrounded by knowledgeable investors and traders as your learn to think independently about the markets.

**Trading Traps**

These are red flagged items that you should avoid in making decisions about your finances and investments. The number one rule of investing is not to lose money and these traps are presented to show you what you are trying to avoid.

**Wall Street Words**

The definitions of words and concepts in these boxes will demystify the concepts behind investing in various markets.

**Bet You Didn't Know**

These tidbits give you some background information on investing that you might not otherwise have known about.

## Dedication

To all those who seek a better life and more secure future; to my wife and children, who are the reason why I work; to my brother, Bruce, for being in the financial trenches every day helping people to have a more secure future.

## Acknowledgments

Having been involved in many aspects of the financial markets for a few years has taught me many things. But the most important thing is that a simple approach—quantified and tested, and rigorously based on sound logic—is the only way to hold on to your money and have it grow in the long run. This book serves as a collection of some of the ideas I have been taught by many over the years and I would like to thank them.

Though I am sure I will miss many, the following people were inspirational to me either personally or professionally, and instrumental in getting this book to market.

Bruce Barrie, my elder brother and his wife, Robyn, are both financial advisors with Morgan Stanley in Pleasanton, California. Their practical advice from years of working to help people achieve their financial goals has served both as an inspiration as well as a practical guide to helping people in the market place.

My friends at the Hirsch Organization, especially Yale Hirsch. His insight into the markets, gleaned from a lifetime of investment experience, have been instrumental in my own development as both an investor and analyst. The Hirsch Organization's *Stock Trader's Almanac*, in its thirty-sixth year of publication, has been an invaluable reference source for this book as well as in my own investing.

Michael B. O'Higgins, the author of *Beating the Dow* and *Beating the Dow with Bonds* for enriching the profession with his wonderful books. The originator of the Dogs of the Dow system, O'Higgins has proven through superior performance that a simple idea based on logic can help the average investor tame the ups and downs of investing.

Victor Niederhoffer, my mentor and author of *Education of a Speculator* for tirelessly sharing his knowledge and insights. He has instilled in me the basic necessity to measure the environment around you, for that is the basis for any rational decision, or the difference between speculation and gambling.

Finally and most importantly, I would like to thank my lovely wife and two beautiful children. Without their love and support I would not have motivation or confidence to achieve anything in life.

## Trademarks

All terms mentioned in this book that are known to be or are suspected of being trademarks or service marks have been appropriately capitalized. Alpha Books and Pearson Education, Inc., cannot attest to the accuracy of this information. Use of a term in this book should not be regarded as affecting the validity of any trademark or service mark.

# Part 1

# Understanding Market Timing

The stock market isn't always the best game in town, as sometimes markets do go down. This part lays out the beginning framework for making informed decisions regarding risk and reward by first presenting a broad history of stock market returns.

As Sigmund Freud said, "The less a man knows about the past, the more insecure his view of the future." These words are taken to heart in this part as the bulls and bears of history are examined so that you have a solid understanding of the potential risks and rewards of investing.

The concepts of risk and reward are then put together with history to act as a backdrop for the decision-making process of investing in stocks or other markets.

# Chapter 1

# Introduction to Market Timing

## In This Chapter

- ◆ What is the market?
- ◆ Why buy and hold may not work
- ◆ What is market timing?
- ◆ Why market timers have failed

Inside these pages I will show you how to move into and out of the stock market, hopefully enabling you to catch the bulk of the appreciation in the stock market and at the same time avoiding the bulk of the downside risk.

The goal of stock market timing is not to get the highest return possible—though that is nice—but to get a good return with minimal risk.

Part of this goal is achieved by being invested in the good times and avoiding the bad times, but part of it is achieved simply by having a plan for your investments. Most people fail to plan their investments; instead they rely on either just buying, because the time looks right, or continually buying and then selling when necessity forces them to. This is a sure-fire method for disaster.

The purpose of this book is to give you a disciplined plan for allocating your finances between various markets and the tools to make timing your movements between markets in an unemotional fashion, ignoring the conventional wisdom that has only served to increase the risks involved with investing and to lessen the returns associated with those risks.

# What Is the Stock Market?

Someone once said that the stock market is the world's largest casino, and it doesn't give complementary cocktails.

Usually when one refers to the stock market they are referring to an index. However, in the strictest sense of the word, the stock market is a market for the buying and selling of stocks.

A *stock* is an instrument that signifies an ownership position, or equity, in a corporation, and represents a claim on its proportionate share in the corporation's assets and profits. Stocks are also called equities or equity securities or corporate stock.

## Wall Street Words

A **stock** is an instrument that signifies an ownership position in a corporation, and represents a claim on its proportionate share in the corporation's assets and profits. When you buy a stock you are buying a piece in the ownership of that company. A **stock exchange** provides or maintains a marketplace where securities (stocks) can be traded. The largest stock exchange is the New York Stock Exchange. Another popular exchange is the over-the-counter market, where shares are traded on an electronic marketplace, known as the NASDAQ. **Stock indexes** are groups or baskets of stocks used to represent a segment of the stock market. For example, the S&P 500 represents the 500 stocks of leading industries and is said to be indicative of the entire stock market. A stock index is a proxy used to describe the behavior of the entire market.

The stock market is the general term for the organized trading of stocks through exchanges and over-the-counter. A *stock exchange*, like the New York Stock Exchange, is any organization, association, or group that provides or maintains a marketplace where securities, options, futures, or commodities can be traded; or the marketplace itself.

However, as I said earlier, when someone talks about the stock market, they are very rarely talking about an exchange for trading stocks, but instead they are most likely referring to a particular index.

For example, when you click on the news and hear that the stock market "soared 250 points today as signs that the economy may be rebounding and that corporate earnings are likely to increase as a result," they do not mean that the New York Stock increased, or even that every stock on it increased. What they are referring to is the stock market as represented by a stock index.

The Dow Jones Industrial Average or the Dow, the S&P 500, the NASDAQ 100, the finger next to your thumb—they're all *indexes*. An index is a group of stocks chosen to represent portions of the stock market (except for your index finger, of course). Most index investments are based on the Standard & Poor's 500 (the stocks of 500 leading companies in leading industries) and the Wilshire 5000 (all the publicly traded companies in America).

There are a myriad of different indexes to represent the stock market, but they can be broken down into a few main categories: broad- or narrow-based indexes and capitalization- or price-based indexes.

# Different Market Indexes

Probably the best known index in the world is the Dow Jones Industrial Index, because it was the first stock market index made publicly available. However as far as indexes go for the investor, the key market index is most likely the Standard and Poor's 500 Index, which is known simply as the S&P. The Standard and Poor's Index is a broad-based, value-weighted index.

Indexes are usually broken down by categories, as follows:

- ◆ Broad-based indexes, such as the S&P 500 or the NASDAQ 100 are used to represent a wide, or broad category of stocks.

- ◆ Narrow-based indexes usually key in on a specific industry or group. For example, semi-conductor stocks, or industrial stocks.

- ◆ Indexes usually represent company sizes as well. For example, the Dow Jones Industrial Average represents large companies as does the S&P 500, while the NASDAQ 100 represents smaller companies, in general.

The S&P 500 is a basket of 500 stocks that are considered to be "widely held." The S&P 500 index is weighted by market value, and its performance is thought to be representative of the stock market as a whole, hence when you hear on the news that stocks rose 1.5 percent today, or plummeted by –2.00 percent, they are usually referring to the S&P 500. It is said to be a value- or price-weighted index because each stock affects the index in proportion to its price per share. Thus, each stock is weighted by its market capitalization, or the number of shares outstanding multiplied by the price per share.

For example, if I had a stock selling at $40 per share with one million shares outstanding, it would have a *market capitalization* of $40 million. However, a stock selling at $20 per share with 2 million shares outstanding would also have a market capitalization of $40 million.

### Wall Street Words

**Market capitalization** is the market size of a company. Market capitalization equals the share price of the company multiplied by the number of shares outstanding. Most of the popular indexes are price- or market-capitalization weighted and targeted at specific capitalization groups. The Dow and S&P represent large capitalization stocks, while the NASDAQ represents small capitalization stocks.

The Dow Jones Industrial Average is the most widely used indicator of the overall condition of the stock market. It is a price-weighted average of 30 actively traded *blue chip* stocks, primarily industrial companies. Because this market average is based on only 30 stocks it is said to be a narrow-based index, as opposed to a broad-based index like the S&P.

### Wall Street Words

**Blue chips** typically refer to the stocks of large, national companies with solid records of stable earnings and/or dividend growth and reputations for high quality management and/or products. The term originated from gambling, when the blue chips were worth more than the red or the white ones, signifying quality and assurance.

A broad-based index attempts to mimic the movement of the market as a whole. Probably the broadest-based index around is the Wilshire 5000, which represents all U.S. exchange-traded stocks. Because the S&P 500 represents 500 stocks, which is a lot of stocks, it is also considered a broad-based index. A narrow-based index is designed to capture a small portion of the market as a whole, such as industrial stocks or blue chip stocks, like the Dow Jones Industrial Average.

Generally, the smaller the capitalization or the more specific an index is, the more volatile it is. In other words a narrow-based index representing small capitalization stocks will most likely be more volatile than a broad-based index representing big capitalization stocks.

Other narrow-based indexes include industry specific indexes, such as a high tech index, or an index of pharmaceutical stocks. Thus, when we hear on the news that stocks sank today, led by declines in petroleum stocks, they are usually looking at the performance of a broad-based index (stocks sank) as well as a narrow-based one—led by petroleum stocks.

The last of the popular indexes is the NAS-DAQ 100 index, more commonly referred to as the NASDAQ. NASDAQ stands for the computerized system established by the National Association of Securities Dealers (NASD) to facilitate trading by providing broker/dealers with current price quotes on over-the-counter stocks and some listed stocks, thus NASD stands for National Association of Securities Dealers and "AQ" stands for automated quote system. The NASDAQ, or NASDAQ 100 is said to represent over-the-counter stocks, which are usually smaller companies, with smaller market capitalizations.

> **Bet You Didn't Know**
>
> Fidelity Investments, www.fidelity.com, offers a lot of different industry-specific narrow-based indexes available for investors. In Chapter 9, I will highlight how different sectors react during the business cycle. Most business papers, such as *The Wall Street Journal, Investors Business Daily,* or *Financial Times* also cover specific industry groups in their market sections.

Security dealers also can make markets, establish prices, for smaller stocks that are not listed on a major exchange, such as the New York Stock Exchange. This market is said to be the "over-the-counter" market because trading used to be done via telephones and certificates were exchanged over a counter.

For example, the Dow Jones Industrial Average is said to be representative of large companies or blue chip stocks. Blue chips typically refer to the stocks of a large, national companies with solid records of stable earnings and/or dividend growth and reputations for high quality management and/or products.

Most sections of this book will only look at the Dow Jones Industrial Average, the S&P 500, and the NASDAQ. Though most investors will use the S&P 500 as their proxy for the stock market, in many places throughout this book I use the Dow Jones Industrial, because this index has a longer history. For example, I have data computed on the Dow Jones Industrial Average for over a century, while I have S&P 500 data starting from 1930 and NASDAQ 100 data starting from 1971.

Generally speaking, they are all proxies for the stock market. The most volatile, and the one that has seen the biggest gains and drops historically, is the NASDAQ. The next most volatile index most of the time is the Dow, followed closely by the S&P

500, as the Dow 30 stocks, all of which are in the S&P 500, account for well over half the market capitalization of the S&P.

Most investors when they think of the stock market and look at performance figures for the market are concerned with either the S&P or the NASDAQ, depending upon whether they are in large or small capitalization stocks, or both. Generally the NASDAQ has higher volatility, meaning when the market rises, this market rises more, but when it falls it tends to fall more. Volatility is a measure of potential risk and reward. If the market is extremely volatile, it can go up or down in a very short period of time, meaning you can make or lose money very quickly.

# Why Buy and Hold Doesn't Work

From the get-go, when we talk about investing, we are taught to buy quality stocks and forget about them. Just keep buying them and holding them until retirement and when we approach retirement, then we can sell them and live the easy life.

**Wall Street Words**

**Buy and hold** is the term used to describe long-term investing, as long-term investors are said to buy and hold a stock indefinitely. **Dollar cost averaging** is the term used to describe the method of continually buying a stock as its stock prices change. When prices decrease, you are able to buy more, and when they increase you buy less, thus the cost of the stock is averaged over time.

This strategy, known as *buy and hold* because it does not involve selling them, is probably the best way to amass wealth over a long period of time. In fact, in the last century, the stock market has offered roughly twice the rate of return of the bond market, and over three times the rate of return on short-term interest rate vehicles.

The basic premise of buy and hold is *dollar cost averaging*. When stock prices go down you are able to buy more stock and when stock prices go up, you enjoy the appreciation of your assets but you buy less.

For example, let's assume that a stock we are buying goes from 25 to 20 over three months and then from 20 to 30 over the next five months. We will invest $100 per month in the stock and ignore commissions on the stock purchases:

| Month | Price | # of Shares Bought | Stock Value | Average Cost |
|-------|-------|--------------------|-------------|--------------|
| 1 | 25.00 | 4 | 100 | 25.00 |
| 2 | 22.50 | 4 | 190 | 23.75 |
| 3 | 20.00 | 5 | 290 | 22.31 |

| Month | Price | # of Shares Bought | Stock Value | Average Cost |
|-------|-------|--------------------|-------------|--------------|
| 4 | 20.00 | 5 | 390 | 21.67 |
| 5 | 22.50 | 4 | 480 | 21.82 |
| 6 | 25.00 | 4 | 580 | 22.31 |
| 7 | 27.50 | 3 | 663 | 23.00 |
| 8 | 30.00 | 3 | 753 | 23.64 |

The first month, with prices at $25 per share, we are able to buy 4 shares. We have contributed $100 and we have $100 in stock. The next month, prices dropped to $22.50, and we buy another 4 shares with $90 and have $190 worth of stock and $10 left over. The shares that we bought the first month are worth $10 less than when we bought them, suffering a 10 percent drop in value, but our average price on the 8 shares is now $23.75, representing a loss of only –5.2 percent. In month 3, the stock is valued at $20 a share and we are able to buy 5 shares. So far, we have spent $300 and we have $290 worth of stock, for a decline of $10 or –3.3 percent because we are lowering our average cost. Get the idea?

At the end of this period, in month 8 we have purchased 32 shares of stock at an average cost of $23.64. With the stock at $30 a share, we have spent $753.00 on stock that is now worth $960.00, for a return of $207 or 21.6 percent.

**Timing Tips**

In the strongly upward-moving stock market of the 1990s the buy and hold strategy outperformed most market timers. It also outperformed most actively managed mutual funds. If you are going to practice buy and hold and dollar cost averaging, then you should consider doing it on a broad selection of stocks, because picking just one or two really bad stocks out of 10 and practicing this style can lead to very poor performance. After all, if most mutual fund managers can't consistently pick winning stocks, what are your odds? Most buy and hold or dollar cost averaging investors can learn a few tricks to improve their performance in these pages as well.

That is not bad work when you can get it. But don't confuse brains with a bull market. What would happen if stock prices didn't turn at $20 a share and go up to $30, but instead continued losing -$2.50 a share per month?

| Month | Share Price | # Of Shares Purchased | Investment | Average Cost |
|-------|-------------|------------------------|------------|--------------|
| 1 | 25.00 | 4 | 100.00 | 25.00 |
| 2 | 22.50 | 4 | 190.00 | 23.75 |
| 3 | 20.00 | 5 | 290.00 | 22.31 |
| 4 | 17.50 | 5 | 377.50 | 20.97 |
| 5 | 15.00 | 6 | 467.50 | 19.48 |
| 6 | 12.50 | 8 | 567.50 | 17.73 |
| 7 | 10.00 | 10 | 667.50 | 15.89 |
| 8 | 7.50 | 13 | 765.00 | 13.91 |

Well, at the end of 8 months, we would have spent $765, and we would own 55 shares of stock. The problem is that the stock would be worth only $412.50. In other words, we would be down -$352.50 or -46.1 percent.

But, hey the stock market will bounce back, right? As you will learn in the next chapter, that isn't always the case. How about a period historically when you started dollar cost averaging for a period of 3 years, and then stopped? It would have taken you 25 years to recoup your initial investment, plus a return of 11 percent. Not 11 percent per year, but a total return of 11 percent. During this period, you would have earned 0.44 percent on your money, or slightly beat putting the money in the bank Posture Pedic —your mattress.

**Trading Traps**

Buy and hold and dollar cost averaging are both very good long-term philosophies for investors to respect. However, they can require very long periods of time to pay off, as much as 25 years in some cases, historically. For most practitioners, they are better off practicing this method on either broad-based indexes, like the S&P 500, or on a narrow-based but large-capitalization index like the Dow Jones Industrials. Picking just a few stocks increases the risk of this strategy and increases the likelihood that more time will be required before you start to make money. This method is supposed to alleviate risk, not increase, so remember to practice it carefully and don't put all your eggs in only two or three baskets unless you are extremely comfortable with risk.

# Emotions and Timing

Buy and hold is a wonderful thing. Compounding your investments is a wonderful way to amass wealth, but it is not for everyone. There are several very long periods historically where buy and hold and dollar cost averaging would have been very frustrating.

For example, for much of the 1970s, dollar cost averaging would have had very little return. Ask yourself honestly if you can keep putting money into something, month after month, year after year, and get no return.

Deep down in your heart, or somewhere in the back of your mind, you may know this is the best thing to do, but could you? Could you do this for the better part of a decade, or two and a half decades, before you started to see a return?

What if the stock you purchased was Enron, Global Crossing, or any other number of once high-flying stocks that are now nothing more than scraps of paper?

What if you need the money? Typically the stock market and the economy move in a similar direction. If the economy goes into a recession, you may lose your job, and need your money. In fact, you most likely need that money at the absolute worst time for your portfolio.

**Timing Tips**

A common mistake many investors make is not to have a separate savings account or access to money quickly. They plow all their money into the markets and in tax-deferred accounts, not slating away a few bucks for a rainy day. Thus, when the rainy day comes, they have to liquidate their stocks, usually at a bad price, and also have to pay tax penalties. Put aside a little money in a savings account or a money market account. It won't grow very fast, but it will be available when you need it and won't force you to have to sell stocks in a panic.

Even if you don't need the money, your confidence may be shaky at the absolute worst time, and most likely if you are going to start investing now or have started investing recently, you have picked a bad time.

Historically, stock market participation by the public is the highest when prices are very near the highs and the lowest when prices are very near the lows. In other words, people who try this usually give up and they usually do so at the worst times.

Even if you are different, and you can buy and hold, this book will be helpful in that it can help you to make your decisions as to when to buy at a better time.

But, if you are like most of us, you do not have the intestinal fortitude for it, and as such would prefer a less emotionally trying way of participating in the markets. You are a market timer!

# What Is Market Timing?

*Market timing* is not about buying stocks at the exact lows and selling them at the exact highs. It is about moving your assets into the stock market when the time is right and moving them out when the risk outweighs the reward.

The goal is to both reduce risk and maximize returns.

### Wall Street Words

**Market timing** is the belief that you can improve upon long-term performance of investments by moving their investments between different asset classes, such as stocks and bonds (for example, switching assets from the bond market to the stock market). Market timing is the systematic movement of funds from one investment arena to another—such as from stocks to bonds—under the belief that in doing so you can increase your rate of return and/or lower your risk.

As you can tell by some of the rantings on the buy and hold approach or dollar cost averaging, it has been my personal observation that most people make the wrong investment decision at the wrong time.

For example, *Time* magazine declared the chairman and founder of Amazon.com its man of the year in 1999. The stock was a darling on Wall Street—everybody loved it. The Internet was going to change the world, and buying this company at $113 a share was considered a safe investment; after all, the marketplace rewards innovators like Mr. Bezos and those wise enough to invest in them. Well, in 2002 the stock is at $17! Try dollar cost averaging that one.

That is not the only example of such wrong thinking at the wrong time. Charles Dow, the founder of *The Wall Street Journal* and his predecessor, Mr. Hamilton, wrote of similar wrongful thinking at the turn of the century and in the 1920s and 1930s.

Thus, as a group, we the people tend to react to the stock market in the wrong way. This leads us to making the wrong decision at the wrong time, because we are basing our decisions on our emotions.

The purpose of this book, and of market timing, is to take some of the emotional guesswork out of your investing. You will be shown when the best times are to invest in the stock market, and safe alternatives in which to place your money when the risk is high or the potential rewards are minimal. You will learn to allocate your assets against the crowd, and have the madness of the crowds working for you instead of being one of the flock led to a sheering.

The fact that most people make the wrong decisions at the wrong time and have throughout history is a common theme in this book. It is so important we devoted an entire chapter to this subject ... see Chapter 6.

# Asset Allocation

Market timing is based on moving your assets between the stock market and other investments. The long-term goal is asset appreciation, as well as minimizing risk.

Straight *asset allocators* believe in putting a percentage of your assets into specific different asset classes, such as half in stocks and half in bonds. However, the market timer believes that during some periods, the weighting should be more heavily bent on stocks, while during other periods, the weighting should be more heavily in bonds or interest-bearing securities of a shorter term.

This is a slower and steadier way toward growth. The ups and down will not be as large, and hence you are more likely to be able to stick with your plan during times of adversity, because the pain will be less.

> **Wall Street Words**
>
> Asset allocators differ from market timers in that they usually try to keep a constant allocation mix, while market timers tend toward a more variable allocation mix.

# Why Have Market Timers Failed in the Past?

Market timing and asset allocation became dirty words, to be snickered at during the bull market of the 1990s and for good reason. Most market timers were bad at it, and had trouble keeping up with the stock markets tremendous gains, especially the gains of the smaller capitalization markets like the NASDAQ.

However, since 2000, market timers are looking a little smarter and the idea is gaining more merit and acceptance.

Many market timers failed for two basic reasons. One, many noticed that the stock market, especially the technology and growth stock laden NASDAQ market, was extremely overvalued. It remained overvalued much longer than it has in the past. Many of these market timers not only underperformed the market, but they placed stocks positions equivalent to bets that the market would drop—known as short sales.

---

**Bet You Didn't Know**

Whenever you see a report from an investment advisor or an investment company, you see a statement on it somewhere that says "Past Performance Is Not Necessarily Indicative Of Future Performance" or something similar. This is a fact of life in investing. What has worked in the past may not always work in the future. The markets change and reactions to the changes can affect the market and its performance as well. This is known as the "Theory of Ever Changing Cycles." Throughout this book we will be presenting ideas that have worked in the past. Most of these are based in part on logic, and we feel they will continue to work but cannot guarantee it. These cycles can change, and may change. One sure thing: What is popular and accepted as Wall Street wisdom now very seldom continues to work. Wall Street wisdom for the last four years has been that stocks will continue to go straight up ... but that has been proven wrong now, so maybe the wisdom that market timing does work will be proven wrong as well.

---

Thus, as prices advanced they not only underperformed the market but lost many in tandem with its advances.

Many others simply got out of the stock market too early, not believing in the power of the market to continue to extremely irrational levels. However, like many other investors, these professionals threw in the towel, getting tired of being ridiculed for missing the great party, and got back into the market at the wrong time. They got emotional and their emotions did them in.

Within this text we will show several different strategies, which take very little work and are very easy to implement, that you can use to move into and out of the stock market and hopefully earn a rate of return commensurate with the risk with confidence.

The move of the 1990s was also historically an extremely powerful and long bull market. In fact, in the twentieth century only one other period was stronger and only one other bull market lasted longer. However, over the long run, the stock market has displayed a normal behavior, and it is our feeling that the market will revert back to this norm.

# Why the Current Situation Is Different!

Normally, stocks rise and fall. Yes, the market can go down, and it can go up. It will go up again. Over the long haul, equities and the stock market will probably be the best investment, just as they have been in the past.

But, don't expect stocks to go straight up as they did in the 1990s. Many things have changed and many of these changes will affect the stock market.

In the days of yore, most stocks paid a dividend. However, with changes to the tax codes, more and more companies are no longer paying dividends, but instead opting to reinvest these moneys back into their business to produce more earnings. This is not a bad thing, but it does mean that the marketplace will more than likely be more volatile, increasing the need to plan your timing in the market more carefully.

Also, because we are in a global economy for good or bad, the cycles of the bull and bear will more than likely be exaggerated as stock prices are no longer just a reflection of the United States but of the world economy, which is slower to go into growth and slower to fall into recessions.

---

**Trading Traps**

Investors and Wall Street as a group usually make poor decisions. They react to the news, but the market tends to be priced off of future perceptions as much by, if not more than, the current situation. For example, stocks plummeted after the terrorist attacks on September 11, 2001. But, several days later the markets rebounded and rallied for several months in the wake of the attacks. Avoid making decisions based on fear, or greed, but instead take time and make rational decisions based on your analysis.

---

Currently, interest rates are at historically low rates, and inflation is under control. However, if either of these two things change, then the structure of the economy of the last decade will also change, again increasing the need to be able to move assets to different sectors to protect your money and to have it work for you.

In other words, we feel that the current environment is shifting, and as such the time is now for market timing to become a more important part of your financial planning.

## The Least You Need to Know

- When people refer to the stock market, they usually are referring to a specific measure or representation of the stock market, such as a market index.

- The most popular stock indexes are the Dow Jones Industrial Average (DJIA), the S&P 500, and the NASDAQ 100 indexes.

- The S&P 500 is a broad-based index representing large capitalization stocks. The NASDAQ 100 is a broad-based index representing small capitalization stocks, while the DJIA is a narrow-based index representing the 30 leading industrial companies, known as blue chips.

◆ Market timing is the movement of assets between various markets and market segments in an attempt to maximize returns and minimize risks. It usually means moving assets between the stock and bond markets.

◆ Most investors react to news, and as such make decisions that end up being the wrong decision. This is evident by the fact that public participation in the stock market tends to be extremely high at market tops and extremely low at market bottoms. One of the purposes of market timing is to avoid this mistake.

◆ Though stocks were the best performing asset class in the last decade, several factors point to an end to this cycle and the underperformance of the buy and hold strategy. The coming market cycle should then favor market timing.

# The Great Bulls and Bears of History

## In This Chapter

- ◆ Those who don't learn from history are bound to repeat it
- ◆ Bull markets
- ◆ Bear markets
- ◆ Behavior in both environments

This chapter is meant to give you a little history of the markets. Sigmund Freud, when he wasn't commenting about someone's mother or cigars, said, "The less a man knows about the past, the more uncertain his view of the future will be."

Just as history repeats itself, so do market moves in a large degree. We see large secular movements in the prices of stocks. Though the causes of these moves are unique each time, as is the general nature of these movements, they all tend to have the same basic underlying themes to them.

By understanding each of these and really looking at them in context, after reading this chapter, you will come away with a better perspective of the stock market. You will be less likely to be panicked or overenthusiastic about its movements, because it is these emotional responses to the market that are usually at the core of investing failures.

# Those Who Don't Learn from History Will Repeat It

The purpose of this book is to put stock price movements and those of other markets into perspective. We have all been taught over the last decade that superior investment results are achieved by being invested in the stock market. Though over the long term, this is decidedly true, we can't always invest over the long term.

It is often quoted that the annual return from stocks in the last century to the present have been roughly 11 percent per year including dividends, and 8 percent excluding dividends based on the returns of the Dow Jones Industrial Average from 1915 through 2001. Now 11 percent per year sounds wonderful, especially when the returns on a bank account, or even in the bond market are decidedly less. In fact, investments that grow at an annual rate of return of 11 percent will double about every six years.

**Timing Tip**

The miracle of compounding of money should be the eighth wonder of the world. A quick and dirty little trick to figure out how fast an investment will double is to divide the rate of return into 72. For example, stocks have averaged 11 percent return this century. Using the rule of 72, 72 divided by 11 is 6.5, meaning that an asset growing at 11 percent per year will double in six and a half years.

But the stock market doesn't just go up 11 percent every year. Some years it goes up 22 percent, and other years it goes down –22 percent, but in the end it has averaged 11 percent per year. Over time, in the long run, you may achieve the 11 percent annual return. But, as the economist John Kenneth Galbraith once said, "in the long run, we're all dead."

# Time and Risk

The power of investing in the stock market is that over time, returns tend to be higher than any other investment. However, in the short run, the returns of the stock market tend to vary considerably.

For example, the average return on a yearly basis is 8.0 percent, excluding dividends, based on the Dow Jones Industrial Average from 1915 to 2001. This is based on an equal investment at the end of each month, and looking at each investment one year later.

However, those returns have varied by 15.7 percent, as the *standard deviation* of stock returns each year during this period has been 15.7 percent.

Risk and reward are commensurate. Stocks have historically been the best performing asset in the long run. But in the short term they have also been the most volatile. Investing in bonds has seen less capital appreciation historically, but the returns are steadier.

As you will see in this chapter, very rarely does the stock market go straight up, but instead it moves "herky jerky," with brief periods of explosive prices to the upside as well as the downside.

**Wall Street Words**

**Standard deviation** is the statistical term used to describe the distribution of data. In the stock market, the standard deviation is about 15.7 percent historically, meaning that most price moves over a 12-month period of time will fall within +/- 15.7 percent of the average about 2 out of 3 years. Refer to the section, "Standard Deviations" for more information.

# Standard Deviations

Don't worry, I'm not going bore you with a statistics lesson. But understanding standard deviation is extremely important.

Think for a moment about a batting average. Let's say Sammy Slugger has been in the majors for 12 years and has had the following batting averages:

| Year # | Batting Average | Year # | Batting Average |
|--------|-----------------|--------|-----------------|
| 1 | .290 | 7 | .270 |
| 2 | .380 | 8 | .370 |
| 3 | .300 | 9 | .330 |
| 4 | .310 | 10 | .340 |
| 5 | .390 | 11 | .350 |
| 6 | .320 | 12 | .370 |

During Sammy's 12 years in the big leagues, he managed to hit an average 33.5 percent of the pitches thrown at him (.335). However, in years two and five, Sammy got real lucky and easy pitches were thrown at him. In his first year, Sammy had to get accustomed to the pitching in the "bigs," and in his seventh year, Sammy was plagued by injuries, and his batting suffered.

Now, in year 13 Sammy is going free agent and asking for a ridiculous sum of money. If you were looking for a batter for your team, and agreed to pay him $1 million dollars for every point above a .330 average, what are the odds he would make it?

Well, just like scoring in figure skating and gymnastics in the Olympics, you would throw out the highest and lowest scores. In this case, throw out the two highest and two lowest. As such, toss out his first year and his injury plagued seventh year, as well as years two and five when the league suffered from a lack of pitching talent.

We can now see that in the remaining 8 years, Sammy Slugger batted between .300 and .370, or his batting varied by .070 during these years. Now divide this number in half and see that though Sammy averaged .335 batting average, in no year did he hit exactly that. Instead, his performance varied by .035, thus you can say he averaged .335 +/- .035.

Thus, you now know that Sammy's average should range from .300 to .370 in the following years. Thus, our upside risk is a salary of $3.50 million to nothing.

This is the standard deviation. In other words, based on normal conditions—a standard bell curve for you math wizards—there is a 67 percent chance of paying Sammy Slugger $0.00 and $3.5 million dollars next year. Sammy gets $1.0 mil for every point above .33. The standard deviation is 0.035. With an average of .33, we expect 67 percent of the data to lie between .295 and .365, and at .365 we would have to pay this ball player 3.5 million as it is .035 above the average.

Thus, when we are deciding the club's budget, we can slate $3.5 million a year for Sammy Slugger, and feel fairly confident that in two out of three years, he shouldn't bat above that causing the club to lose money, which as we all know leads to disruptions in play. The same principles can be applied to stocks.

# Standard Statistics

Now, remember our batting average for stocks. Historically, the Dow Jones has returned roughly 11 percent a year this century. The monthly year-over-year standard deviation is 15.7 percent. Thus, we can expect the returns after one year to be 11 percent +/- 15.7 percent, or in other words we should expect two out of three years to have a standard return of –4.7 percent to 26.7 percent. Now obviously, we all want to catch those juicy 26.7 percent return years and avoid those –4.7 percent years, or worse. We will be presenting tricks for doing this later in the book, do not worry, but for now let's concentrate on the risk of investing.

We now know what range our investments should take, between –4.7 percent and up to 26.7 percent. In fact, 65 percent of all the monthly year-over-year returns from 1950 through 2000 did fall into this category.

However, what is interesting is that if we do the same procedure, except look longer term, say five years, we see that the average monthly five-year return—just as investing in March 1990 and selling in March 1995—is 53.3 percent total return, excluding dividends, with a standard deviation of +/- 49.6 percent. In other words, when we hold stocks for five years, our returns (two thirds of the time) should range between a gain of 3.7 percent and 102.9 percent. So our yearly return on stocks over a five-year period should range from 0.74 percent to 20.5 percent, with an average of 10.6 percent return.

If we look at 20 years, the standard deviation drops to roughly +/- 3 percent. Thus, as you can see, the longer you hold stocks, the lower the risks appear to be, based on standard statistics.

---

**Timing Tip**

With changes in the tax laws, and changes to corporate culture, many stocks no longer pay a dividend. Theoretically, the lack of dividends means that the company will plow that money back into the company, and stocks should see more appreciation due to this. However, these increases in prices due to lack of dividend payments should also make the market more volatile. More volatility means more risk, because although some companies may use the money effectively, some will not. The stock market is always changing—get used to it.

# Getting the Whole Story

Remember, in the long run, stocks have returned 11 percent per year. This sounds wonderful, and has enticed many people toward the buy and hold philosophy. Though this is true, it is a very misleading statistic.

Suppose you started investing when the economy was running extremely strong, and America was being transformed by new technology. Magazines were heralding a "new era" of economic prosperity, and the standard of living was increasing.

Everywhere you went new technology was buzzing around you, and millionaires were being made from the stock market on a daily basis. Analysts and those in the "know" were talking about how this new technology that had just begun would soon spread to every household in the United States and the world, and the boom had just begun.

We are not talking about the Internet age and the 1990s, but the 1920s with the automobile and electricity. The prophecies of a car in every garage (or almost every garage) and electricity in every home have come true. However, an investment in these sectors of the stock market at the beginning of 1929 would have taken over 24 years before it started to show a profit.

> ### Trading Traps
>
> Though stock returns have averaged between −4.7 percent to 26.7 percent per year, there have been prolonged periods where investments have not paid off, especially investments made at market highs. For example, buying at the market high of 1929 would not have paid off for about 25 years. The stock market does not have to return 11 percent per year and very rarely does it for several years in a row, despite the performance of the 1990s.

Though this is obviously a "cherry picked" example of the risks involved in investing, it does show the risk. It is not coincidental that public ownership and participation in the stock market increased substantially from 1927 through 1929. If an investor had starting investing in 1927 and continued all the way through 1929, investing an equal amount each month in the stock market—as measured by the Dow Jones Industrial Average—at the end of each month during this time period, they would have had to suffer from December 1929 to July 1951, before they saw their money grow by 11 percent—not 11 percent per year, but 11 percent total. In other words, by buying in the last three years of the 1920s, when public participation in the stock market had reached its highest levels, and holding those stocks for 21 years, they would have had an average annual return of 0.52 percent per year.

> ### Trading Traps
>
> The risk in the stock market isn't simply that prices will decline, but that they could go generally sideways as well. From 1966 to 1981, the Dow Jones Industrial Average traded between roughly 650 points and 1,000 points. The average buy and hold account would have seen little appreciation in prices during this time as they would have bought roughly around 825. It would not have been until the mid 1980s that they would have seen any appreciation in their portfolios even getting close to the 11 percent annual rate of return.

Now be honest. After buying stocks for three years, and then seeing your gains of 58 percent on your portfolio after three years (average return of +19 percent per year), and then seeing that portfolio plunge by 82 percent of its value over the next three years, would you be convinced that "buy and hold" is the secret to amassing wealth?

Guess what? Most other people agreed that this roller coaster ride was too much as well, and those millionaires created in the booming stock market of the 1920s, were standing side by side with the rest of the people in the soup lines of the 1930s.

So, though we know what to expect by statistics, the averages, we also know that they don't tell the whole story. Let's take a look at the great bull and bear markets of this century and see how prices have fluctuated.

# The Great Bull Markets

Despite recent history, stock prices do not go straight up and down. They tend to move in broad secular trends, which Wall Street has defined as a *bull market* and *bear market*.

Generally, a bull market is defined as a series of higher stock prices, punctuated by corrections. The standard Wall Street definition of a bull market is when prices rise by 20 percent or more from their lows and the market is in a bull market until prices correct by 20 percent or more from the highs.

Starting in 1915, which I chose because the stock market was closed down for several months in 1914 due to World War I, we have seen 26 bull markets in stocks (see the following table). In other words, during this time period, stock prices have increased from a low point by 20 percent or more 26 times, without suffering a decline of more than –20 percent from the peak in prices 26 times—based on the Dow Jones Industrial Average.

> **Wall Street Words**
>
> A **bull market** is a series of higher prices punctuated by a series of minor price corrections; a 20 percent increase in prices from a low point, without a subsequent 20 percent break in prices. A **bear market** is a series of lower prices, punctuated by a series of minor price advances; a 20 percent decrease in prices from a high point, without a subsequent 20 percent advance in prices.

| Start Date | Bottom Price Dow Jones | End Date | Top Price Dow Jones | % Change |
|---|---|---|---|---|
| Feb-15 | 54.22 | Nov-16 | 110.15 | 103.2% |
| Dec-17 | 65.95 | Nov-19 | 119.62 | 81.4% |
| Aug-21 | 63.90 | Sep-29 | 381.17 | 496.5% |
| Nov-29 | 198.69 | Apr-30 | 294.07 | 48.0% |
| Dec-30 | 157.51 | Feb-31 | 194.36 | 23.4% |

*continues*

*continued*

| Start Date | Bottom Price Dow Jones | End Date | Top Price Dow Jones | % Change |
|---|---|---|---|---|
| May-31 | 128.46 | Jun-31 | 156.93 | 22.2% |
| Oct-31 | 86.48 | Nov-31 | 116.79 | 35.0% |
| Jan-32 | 71.24 | Mar-32 | 88.78 | 24.6% |
| Jun-32 | 42.84 | Sep-32 | 79.93 | 86.6% |
| Feb-33 | 50.16 | Jul-33 | 108.67 | 116.6% |
| Oct-33 | 83.64 | Feb-34 | 110.74 | 32.4% |
| Jul-34 | 85.51 | Mar-37 | 194.40 | 127.3% |
| Mar-38 | 98.95 | Nov-38 | 158.41 | 60.1% |
| Apr-39 | 121.44 | Sep-39 | 155.92 | 28.4% |
| Jun-40 | 111.84 | Nov-40 | 138.12 | 23.5% |
| Apr-42 | 92.92 | May-46 | 212.50 | 128.7% |
| Jun-49 | 161.60 | Dec-61 | 734.91 | 354.8% |
| Jun-62 | 535.76 | Feb-66 | 995.15 | 85.7% |
| Oct-66 | 744.32 | Dec-68 | 985.21 | 32.4% |
| May-70 | 631.16 | Jan-73 | 1051.70 | 66.6% |
| Dec-74 | 577.60 | Sep-76 | 1014.79 | 75.7% |
| Feb-78 | 742.12 | Apr-81 | 1024.05 | 38.0% |
| Aug-82 | 776.92 | Aug-87 | 2722.42 | 250.4% |
| Oct-87 | 1738.74 | Jul-90 | 2999.75 | 72.5% |
| Oct-90 | 2365.10 | Jan-00 | 11722.98 | 395.7% |
| Sep-01 | 8235.81 | Mar-02 | 10635.25 | 29.1% |

# Bull Market Behaviors

The average bull market in stocks has lasted about 30 months, with an average gain of 109.2 percent during the bull run. In other words, in 2½ years, stock prices tend to gain roughly 43.7 percent annually during a bull market.

Some of these gains have been stretched out over longer periods of time, like the bull market from June 1949 to December 1961, which lasted 12½ years and gained 354.8 percent. Some of them have lasted a shorter amount of time, such as the two one-month 20 percent gains seen in the 1930s, or the most current bull market, which lasted just six months from September 2001 through to March 2002.

Over half of the bull markets have gained over 70 percent, and they have ranged from the phenomenally powerful market of the 1920s which gained 496.5 percent in total, producing roughly a 55 percent annual return during the period each year, to the short-lived May 1931 to June 1931 bull market, which gained a paltry 22.2 percent before dropping by 20 percent from its highs.

Half of these bull markets lasted 30 months or longer, taking roughly 2½ years before correcting by 20 percent, and half lasted less than 2½ years.

# Buying the Highs and Waiting for Redemption

Now, let's assume that we bought stocks at the exact high of each bull market. How many years on average would it take before our investment started to pay off?

Remember, in the stock market of the 1920s it wasn't until the latter half of the bull market that public participation in the markets started to increase dramatically. According to statistics, the same can be said for the great bull market of the 1990s, with public participation increasing dramatically in 1997.

Well, on average, had you started investing at the highs of each bull market you would have waited an average of 80 months for that investment to pay off. Investing in September 1929, at the highs of the Dow Jones Industrials would have seen an investor waiting 25 years. Buying in January 1973 at the highs, that investment would not have shown a gain until November 1982. Buying in August 1987, one would have had to wait a little less than two years until prices surpassed their pre-crash highs.

**Trading Traps**

Had you bought the market highs of the last bull markets, you would have to wait 80 months (on average) before you saw any price appreciation from that investment.

Looking at all these cases, had you invested at the highs, it would have taken a little over six years on average before the investment started paying off. If we exclude the 1929 period, as the largest and the 1990 shortest eight-month interval, the norm would be a little over 4½ years.

Thus, when the stock market reaches its peak value, we can expect the market to surpass that high between 4½ years and 7½ years later.

Unless you plan on investing for this time frame and not needing your money at any time during that period and can withstand holding losses in your portfolio for 7¹/₂ years, then buy and hold may not be for you.

# The Great Bear Markets

The stock market does not always go up. During the same period we have studied, the market has fallen by –20 percent from its peak and continued lower 25 times, and as we are writing this, is in the throes of its second official bear market in the last two years.

A bear market is broadly defined as a series of declining stock prices, punctuated by periods of rising prices. Generally, Wall Street defines a bear market as a –20 percent decline in stock prices from their highs. Thus, when prices decline by –20 percent from their bull market peaks, the press heralds it as a bear market.

We have witnessed 25 completed bear markets from 1915 through 2001, and from the March 2002 highs through July 2002, we are currently in the twenty-sixth.

The following table shows all the bull and bear markets from 1916 to the present. This information is presented to aid in understanding that secular bull and bear markets do happen, and will most likely continue to happen. Thus, by examining history we understand that prices do not go up or down forever.

| Start Date | Start Price Dow Jones | End Date | Bottom Price Dow Jones | % Change |
|---|---|---|---|---|
| Nov-16 | 110.15 | Dec-17 | 65.95 | -40.1% |
| Nov-19 | 119.62 | Aug-21 | 63.90 | -46.6% |
| Sep-29 | 381.17 | Nov-29 | 198.69 | -47.9% |
| Apr-30 | 294.07 | Dec-30 | 157.51 | -46.4% |
| Feb-31 | 194.36 | May-31 | 128.46 | -33.9% |
| Jun-31 | 156.93 | Oct-31 | 86.48 | -44.9% |
| Nov-31 | 116.79 | Jan-32 | 71.24 | -39.0% |
| Mar-32 | 88.78 | Jun-32 | 42.84 | -51.7% |
| Sep-32 | 79.93 | Feb-33 | 50.16 | -37.2% |
| Jul-33 | 108.67 | Oct-33 | 83.64 | -23.0% |
| Feb-34 | 110.74 | Jul-34 | 85.51 | -22.8% |
| Mar-37 | 194.40 | Mar-38 | 98.95 | -49.1% |
| Nov-38 | 158.41 | Apr-39 | 121.44 | -23.3% |

| Start Date | Start Price Dow Jones | End Date | Bottom Price Dow Jones | % Change |
|---|---|---|---|---|
| Sep-39 | 155.92 | Jun-40 | 111.84 | -28.3% |
| Nov-40 | 138.12 | Apr-42 | 92.92 | -32.7% |
| May-46 | 212.50 | Jun-49 | 161.60 | -24.0% |
| Dec-61 | 734.91 | Jun-62 | 535.76 | -27.1% |
| Feb-66 | 995.15 | Oct-66 | 744.32 | -25.2% |
| Dec-68 | 985.21 | May-70 | 631.16 | -35.9% |
| Jan-73 | 1051.70 | Dec-74 | 577.60 | -45.1% |
| Sep-76 | 1014.79 | Feb-78 | 742.12 | -26.9% |
| Apr-81 | 1024.05 | Aug-82 | 776.92 | -24.1% |
| Aug-87 | 2722.42 | Oct-87 | 1738.74 | -36.1% |
| Jul-90 | 2999.75 | Oct-90 | 2365.10 | -21.2% |
| Jan-00 | 11722.98 | Sep-01 | 8235.81 | -29.7% |
| Mar-02 | 10635.25 | Jul-02 | 7702.34 | -27.6% |

# Average Bear Market

On average, a bear market lasts about 10 months and sees prices drop by –34.5 percent based on the Dow Jones Industrial Average. Most bear markets range from 2 months long to 18 months long, and decline between –24.1 percent and 44.9 percent before a 20 percent gain in the Industrial Average is seen.

The worst bear market in history has been the March 1932 through June 1932 bear market, where in this short three-month period, the Dow Jones Industrial Average lost –51.7 percent of its value. This is closely followed by another short-lived bear market from September 1929 to November 1929, when stock prices plunged by –47.9 percent of their value, including the crash of 1929, which saw stock prices decline by –25.2 percent on October 28 and 29.

The longest bear market in history, using the Dow Jones as a proxy for the market was from May 1946 to June 1949, following WWII, when stock prices declined –24.0 percent over 37 months.

Roughly half of all bear markets have broken more than –33 percent, while less than half of them have lasted over nine months. Bear markets tend to be fast and furious. Look at all those that lasted only a couple of months, but wiped out more than a third of the value of the market.

It is this nature of the bear market, the fact that seems to inspire panic and fear that make them so deadly. They either seem to come in quickly and annihilate the markets gains in a short period of time, or they seem to be long and drawn out affairs.

# Behavior of Bulls and Bears

Thus far we have profiled a bull market and a bear market and shown you historical examples of both and their average behavior. This is akin to how the police investigate a crime scene. Now, let's take a look at the range of emotions and the feel of each, in much the same way the FBI profiles criminals.

## The Bull Market Profile

Every bull market starts off from the ashes of a bear market. In the early stages of a bull market, the public tends to be fearful of the stock market, and who can blame them? Only months earlier stock prices were either plunging, or slowly grinding lower.

Usually in the early phase of the bull market, the economy is in a recession or a slow-down. Companies are posting losses or earnings below the previous year, and many have suspended their dividend payments.

The early stages of a bull market are usually trumpeted by Wall Street as another chance to lighten up on your portfolio, as the rallies of the previous months would have served as excellent opportunities to sell off stocks to minimize losses.

Against this wall of worry, stock prices continue higher slowly but surely, plodding along. Eventually, the economy begins to turn the corner from recession and resumes its growth. Companies now are starting to post positive earnings, or at least meeting analysts expectations of earnings.

Prices are usually well off their lows, but still concerns about the economy rebounding are troubling and some companies are still laying off workers or going under. Eventually as the economy turns and starts growth, companies are expanding and stock prices are now more volatile but still going higher.

It is at this stage that investors start to pour into the stock market, especially as it is now well off its lows. Soon with people flocking to stocks again, prices are soaring. Analysts are ratcheting up earnings estimates, and companies are exceeding them. The economy is growing at a fast pace, and unemployment is low. Companies are coming out with new products or expanding production at an increasing rate.

At this point, the rising prices of stocks makes perfect sense. The future is looking brighter every day, and it is usually at this point that prices tend to peak.

## The Bear Market Profile

Usually by the peak in stock prices, public participation in the market is high, and companies are coming out with exciting new ventures. New stock is being issued, as new companies are coming to market. People are excited about the gains and the stock market is declared as the best game in town.

As prices soar, and along with them expectations of future growth, companies begin to fail to meet these growing expectations. Small setbacks are quickly snapped up, as buying dips in prices is a good idea and it is only a matter of time before new high prices will be seen. Usually at this point, small and aggressive stocks are way outperforming the larger companies.

However, the bulk of the stocks are failing to reach new highs after each sell-off. Companies, which are earning less due to higher wage costs and typically bigger debt loads, begin laying people off.

As more and more companies fail to reach expectations about performance, their stock is sold aggressively and prices are well off their peak. Usually about this time, a recession is looming and investors panic, sending prices cascading lower. Stocks bought in the latter half of the bull market, when most people started buying, are showing losses. People begin switching assets from the stock market to the bond market and prices look doomed to come crashing even lower. It is at this point when panic rules the day; then the cycle begins again.

## Avoiding the Emotional Roller Coaster of Investing

As we have tried to show in this chapter, investing is a long-term proposition. However, I will show in subsequent chapters, with a little effort and realizing that the market tends to move in cycles, known as bull and bear markets, that you can move into and out of the stock market and have a higher probability of success, unless you wish to hold stocks for 10 years or more.

Few people really have the discipline for the buy and hold style of investing. It is very easy in a bull market, especially the one like we saw in the 1990s that lasted an inordinately long amount of time. However, when the bear market hits, and a third of your gains are wiped out—and all of your recent purchases are worth a fraction of the value paid—people tend to panic and abandon the long-term thinking at just the wrong time.

**Timing Tips**

Your future financial security tends to be a very serious matter. As such, people often fret and worry about their investments and make decisions based on these feelings. It has been said that the stock market is driven by two forces: fear and greed. Greed reigns supreme in a bull market and fear in a bear market. Don't get caught in this vicious cycle; make decisions based on a rational plan, not on an emotional level.

The purpose of this book is to help people understand how the stock market moves, what the risks are as well as the potential rewards, and to show them that by having a plan that removes much of the emotion in making decisions regarding your finances, you will be better off.

## The Least You Need to Know

♦ The stock market has returned roughly 8 percent per year before dividends and 11 percent when dividends are included in this century and the last. This beats bonds or savings accounts, making stocks the best long-term investment vehicle.

♦ Long-term rates of return are averages, and as such they do not purport the truth about the risks in the market. Stock prices can go down as well as up. The shorter the amount of time one invests, the larger the likelihood of losses.

♦ The average bull market in the last century has lasted about $2^{1}/_{2}$ years and the average bear market has lasted about 1 year.

♦ Buy and hold investments, which are typically made in the later part of a bull market, can take several years before they show any positive returns. This is why most people lose money practicing this, as they start and stop at the wrong times.

♦ By using history as a guide, and using discipline, a person will probably be better off timing the stock market in the future as the market returns to a more normal pattern of trade.

**Chapter 3**

# Play the Market, Don't Try to Beat It

## In This Chapter

- ◆ Index funds versus stock picking
- ◆ Bonds
- ◆ T-Bills and money markets
- ◆ Risk and return profiles

In the last chapter, I mentioned the fact that stocks have outperformed other assets over the long term, but this increase in performance comes at a price, a higher risk. Ideally, the market timer will move from the best performing asset class to the next. However, this goal is far beyond our own abilities. What we should realistically aim for is not omnipotent performance, but a good balance of risk to rewards that we can personally live with.

In the classification of things, stocks have had the best performance long term, but as I showed in the last chapter, this is dependent upon either good timing or holding them for a long period of time.

Bonds have been the next best performer, with money market funds pulling a distant third. However, the risk associated with each of these decreases almost in lock step, thus each has a place in the timer's arsenal. Inside this chapter, I will highlight what each of these asset classes are and how you should use them.

# Index Funds Versus Stock Picking

As I explained in the first chapter of this book, the stock market is really the collection of all stocks. Currently there are more stocks in existence than you could count, when covering all the different exchanges and such worldwide.

However, what we normally think of when we say the stock market is a representative collection of some of those stocks. For example, if you watch the nightly news the commentator might say that stocks dropped 200 points today in active trading or that the market soared 225 points as positive economic news hit the market.

They are not talking about all of the stocks in the world, but a small sample, such as the Dow Jones Industrial Average, probably the best-known representation of the market in existence today. Perhaps they are talking about the S&P 500 Index when they say the market, or even the NASDAQ 100 Stock Index, which all can be referred to as "the market."

**Wall Street Words**

An **index fund** is a fund designed to track the performance of a specific index, such as the S&P 500 or the NASDAQ 100 index.

No matter which index we choose when we talk about the stock market, we are talking about an index, or a broad group of stocks. And now with the advent of index funds, or mutual funds designed to mimic the behavior of specific indexes, we can now invest in a specific index, buying a proxy of it—the *index fund*.

# Is the Market Random or Efficient?

When most people invest, they want to beat the market. If you are going to take the risks present in investing, should you not get the return to compensate you for those risks?

Ideally the answer is yes, but in practical application picking individual stocks to outperform the market is very difficult. This concept is known as the efficient market hypothesis and/or the *Random Walk Theory*, in layman's terms.

The Random Walk Theory, made popular in the best-selling book, *A Random Walk Down Wall Street* by Burton Gordon Malkiel (W. W. Norton & Company, 2000), states that market prices follow a random path up and down, making it impossible to predict with any accuracy which direction the market will move at any point.

Part of the Random Walk Theory is that the marketplace is efficient. This is not a new concept, but a concept that was written about at the turn of the century, known as the *Efficient Market Theory*. In essence, the Efficient Market Theory hypothesizes that stock prices are a reflection of all known facts. Thus, when somebody knows something that others do not, their own buying or selling of the security will drive prices up or down and back into line with everyone else.

This theory is partially supported by the fact that most investment managers cannot outperform the market, as measured by a similar index. However, several strategies—which will be presented in subsequent chapters—show that this theory may not be totally accurate.

**Wall Street Words**

The **Random Walk Theory** states that market prices follow a random path up and down, making it impossible to predict with any accuracy which direction the market will move at any point. The **Efficient Market Theory** holds that all market participants receive and act on all of the relevant information available as soon as it becomes available; if true, no investment strategy would be better than a coin toss.

Probably the greatest proof of an efficient marketplace is the fact that most professional stock pickers cannot "consistently" beat a similar market average. For example, if an analyst or money manager's specialty is small capitalization growth stocks, their performance would be judged against the NASDAQ 100 Stock Index. Over time, most of these financial geniuses do not outperform the representative index in their performance. In fact many statistics show that despite scores of research analysts—and high priced talent with more letters after their names than are contained in a can of alphabet soup—most of these people underperform the index that is representative of their style of investing. In other words, despite their immense brainpower and knowledge of the markets, by the time they discover something, it is already priced into the market.

The Efficient Market Theory is often cited as being true because Wall Street lore holds that 80 percent of all mutual funds underperform their corresponding index.

Now, as simple investors, we have to ask ourselves a question. Are we smarter than the average Wall Street MBA or Ph.D.? For many, the answer may be yes, which we will highlight later in Chapter 6. However, for many the answer will also be no. Part of this has to do with the fact that, just like this book not being free—but still a steal at the cost—those MBA's and Ph.D.'s come at a price. Now add their salaries and transactions costs to the equation, and these funds have higher overhead than those that simply buy and sell a standard list of stocks. In fact, this bias shows that in most cases, active stock picking has lower returns because of transaction costs.

However, there are exceptions. Some companies, which we will highlight when we get more specific on picking funds, have consistently beaten the stock market, proving that though the market is not totally efficient, it is efficient enough to discourage most of us from trying to beat it.

After all, as they say, if you can't beat them, join them. As such, when we talk about investing in the stock market in most sections of this book, we will be using an index as a proxy for those investments, and the proxy, when chosen well, should yield very similar results.

## Even the Market Has Risks

Stocks tend to move in broad cyclical movements, or bull and bear markets. Though not all stocks will move with the broad market, most stocks rise and fall with the indexes.

The variation, or standard deviation, on these returns is high, running about +/- 15.7 percent per year since 1950. Thus any year, in two out of three years we should expect the Dow Jones Industrial Average to gain about 8.8 percent before dividends, +/- 15.7 percent. In other words, stock market returns should range between –6.9 percent and 24.3 percent in any year.

As we stated in the previous chapter, this risk decreases the longer the investment is held, but the holding periods can be extremely long. An investment in simply picking a few stocks, or even using a professionally managed pick of stocks, in most cases will result in a lower average return with a similar or higher standard deviation. Thus, the risk is greater.

Hence, our advice is that most investors should look at index funds over stock picking for the bulk of their investments in the stock market. However, like all good rules, this one can be broken and we will list some of the reasons to break this rule in subsequent chapters.

## How About Bonds?

A *bond* is a debt security, similar to an I.O.U. When you purchase a bond, you are lending money to a government, municipality, corporation, federal agency or other entity known as the issuer. In return for the loan, the issuer promises to pay you a specified rate of interest during the life of the bond and to repay the face value of the bond (the principal) when it "matures," or comes due.

Among the types of bonds you can choose from are: U.S. government securities, municipal bonds, corporate bonds, mortgage and asset-backed securities, federal agency securities and foreign government bonds.

**Wall Street Words**

A **bond** is similar to an I.O.U. When you purchase a bond, you are lending money to an entity known as the issuer. In return for the loan, the bond issuer will pay the holder a specified rate of interest during the life of the bond and repay the face value of the bond (the principal) when it "matures," or comes due.

# Bond Market Returns

The bond market, especially when bonds are held to maturity, have a lower risk or standard deviation than an investment in stocks. Unlike stocks, which represent ownership, bonds represent an obligation. The biggest risk in bonds is default risk, or the risk that the issuer of the bond will not pay back the money lent. This is not the only risk in bond investing, unless you plan on holding the bond until maturity, as we will show you later.

Bonds versus stocks are similar to working for someone else and being self-employed. The self-employed person, if he or she is good at their job, can earn more money than somebody doing the same thing for a large company. Why? Because the self-employed person gets to keep all of the profits in most cases while an employee's compensation is determined on the merits of the amount of money they make for the company less a cut for the company. In other words, if you are an employee, and you make $100,000 for your company, they will more than likely pay you less than $100,000 because the company as a whole has to turn a profit. However, the self-employed person will make $100,000, less expenses.

But, over a course of five years, the employee may make more or at least has less risk. If one year his production falls, the company will probably not cut his salary. However, the

**Trading Traps**

Bonds are referred to as fixed income securities, because if they are held to maturity the rate of return is fixed. However, if you wish to sell a bond before maturity, the rate of return is subject to change. Yes, it is possible to take a capital loss in the bond market if they are sold before maturity and interest rates rise. For a more complete discussion on this see Chapter 16.

self-employed person, who is simply paid on performance only, will suffer during a bad year. It's the old commission versus salary paradox. Over the long run, the commission-based person will make more, but the variability of the money paid will be greater.

The bond market is very similar. Payments are made on a fixed schedule. Thus the returns are fixed, which is why they call them fixed income securities. However, the rewards are also fixed or stable—unless the bond is sold early, which entails risk and causes the risk and reward scenario to be variable, and is covered later in Chapter 16. Thus with risk being lower in bonds, the rewards are also lower.

It is similar to betting on a horse race. If you bet the favorite, the payout may be only $0.15 on the dollar. However, a long shot may pay $10 for every dollar bet. In the long run, if you are good at picking long shots, even only getting them right 20 percent of the time, the payout is sufficient to make this a better proposition. In the bond market you give up returns in exchange for a sure thing.

# T-Bills and Money Market Accounts

The surest returns come from short-term debt instruments like *T-Bills* and *money market accounts*. These investments pay a regular fixed payment like bonds, but have much shorter holding periods. Hence, the likelihood of holding one of these over a period of time until maturity, in the case of a T-Bill, is much greater so the returns have very small standard deviations.

**Wall Street Words**

A **money market account** is a savings account that shares some of the characteristics of a money market fund. A **Treasury bill**, or T-Bill, is a short-term debt instrument issued by the U.S. Treasury that will mature in less than two years.

Like other savings accounts, money market accounts are insured by the Federal government. A money market mutual fund is typically not insured by the Federal government and thus has default risk, which is usually extremely minimal and thus offers a slightly higher rate of return. A Treasury bill, or T-Bill, is a short-term debt instrument issued by the U.S. Treasury that will mature in less than two years. Basically, for all practical purposes, a T-Bill is just like a bond that will mature in less than two years.

These instruments have the lowest risk and the smallest standard deviations of returns. They also have the lowest returns, historically.

# Risk and Return Profiles

One of the inescapable laws of investing is that risk and return are commensurate. In the world of investing that means that when you have a larger risk of a loss you should be compensated for this risk by a higher rate of return.

Historically, the best performing asset class has been stocks. Stocks are also the riskiest asset. Bonds have the next highest rate of return, and they are the next most risky asset. Last, T-Bills and money market accounts have the lowest rate of return and they have the lowest rates of risk. For example, let's put these risks and rewards, and their holding periods, into perspective.

As we mentioned in this chapter and the last, the risk of equities or the stock market tends to decrease over time, at least historically. A classic and dramatic example can be seen by looking at investments on a particular day.

On October 19, 1987—also known as "Black Monday"—The Dow Jones Industrial Average declined by −22.6 percent. However, for the entire year, the Dow Jones Industrial Average increased by 2.0 percent in 1987.

For the year 1987, an investment in T-Bills would have returned 6.77 percent. In other words, the safest investment and the lowest yielding investment would have returned 4.77 percent more than the best investment long-term and the riskiest. In that same year, an investment in 10-year Treasury Bonds would have returned 8.39 percent.

However, if we would have held each of these investments for 10 years, the stock market return would have been an average of 28.6 percent over the 10-year period from the end of January 1987 to the end of January 1997. The return on a 10-year treasury bond would have been 8.39 percent if held to maturity and the return on T-Bills would have been 6.03 percent. Thus, the farther out in time you go, the more the market favors the stock market.

The goal of the market timer is to look for periods when the risks and rewards favor other assets besides stocks and to invest more heavily in them.

The bulk of the work presented in this book is on timing the stock market, hence the title emphasizing this point. As I mentioned in the first chapter, most market timers fail because they are out of the stock market during the key periods that account for the bulk of the gains in the market.

The fact that most market timers have failed in recent years is due to the phenomenally strong stock market in the 1990s. Remember in the previous chapter how we outlined all of the bull and bear markets from 1915 through 2001. Well, only one other period in history has outperformed that period, and that was 1929. Only one other bull market has lasted longer than the 1990s bull market and that was the Bull Market of 1949 to 1961.

Hence, it is our assumption that in the coming years, stocks will not be the only game in town. After all, over a period of 86 years, longer than most of us will live, only two periods have been comparable to the recent past.

It is time to look at the stock market once again as something that needs to be actively managed. In fact, if you assume you missed the three best periods of stock market performance, the returns associated with stocks is not much better than the return associated with that of bonds, which have significantly less risk.

Now that I have basically explained the mantra of market timing and hopefully shown why I think this will be the option of getting the most out of your investments in the coming years, the remaining parts of this book will highlight how to proceed.

## The Least You Need to Know

- ◆ Returns are generally a function of time and risk. The higher the risk, the higher the return should be. However, over the long term, risk tends to decrease with time as the higher returns of the past cushion future performance.

- ◆ In terms of return and risk, the stock market is the riskiest investment in the short term. However, over time, these risks are minimized because of its higher return.

- ◆ The next most risky asset is bonds, especially if they are not held to maturity. Because bond returns can be fixed over a period of time they are less risky than stocks, but their return has been less than that of the stock market over time.

- ◆ The least risky assets are T-Bills and money market accounts. However, the returns of these assets are minimal.

- ◆ With the stock market coming off of its second longest bull market in this century with its second greatest returns, market timing will become more and more important for your financial well-being in the coming years.

# Part 2

## From the Chartists

This part presents several different methods for viewing the stock market. The first presented is Dow's Theory, which was developed at the turn of the last century and has continued for the past hundred years to post impressive results.

From Dow's Theory, the concept of trends is developed and expanded upon by a simple mathematical method for moving with the major ebbs and flows of the marketplace.

From these concepts, we highlight one of the major themes of investing, that of contrarian thinking. Historically, investors have moved en masse into the stock market at the highs and retreated from the market at the lows. This cycle is presented, and the reader is taught how to spot the signs of excessive fear or greed in the marketplace, and how to exploit it for financial reward.

# Chapter 4

# The Dow Theory

## In This Chapter

♦ Oldest theory on market timing developed by Charles H. Dow

♦ The three movements of stocks

♦ Industry is tied to transportation, the averages must confirm

♦ Applying the Dow theory to your portfolio

Inside this chapter, you will learn about Charles H. Dow and the theory of stock market behavior that he developed. This theory is probably one of the oldest theories of stock market movement, having been originally penned by the founder of *The Wall Street Journal*, which is America's most read daily financial newspaper.

As we begin to explain the practical application of market timing, I think it's important to start with the Dow theory because it is one of the oldest. Though it was developed over a century ago, it is still practiced and followed today, proving its utility in the battle for market survival.

## Charles H. Dow and the Evolution of a Theory

Charles H. Dow was born in Sterling, Connecticut, November 6, 1851. The son of a farmer, Dow went to work in the newspaper industry at the age of 21, originally as a city beat reporter. Eight years later, his newspaper sent him to do a story on the discovery of carbonates in Leadville, Colorado. This trip changed the course of Dow's career from one of political and historical writing to the business writing he became famous for.

At the time, Leadville was the most famous mining town in the country. The paper felt Dow was the best equipped to write about it. In Leadville, Dow met prominent men in the financial community, and began to focus on the financial aspects of journalism. He reported extensively on the financial aspect of the mining boom.

By 1880, Dow had moved to New York City where he found a job on Wall Street reporting on mining stocks. He soon developed a reputation as a reliable reporter who was not only capable of expert financial analysis but also could be trusted with confidential information. During this time, Dow met up with an old friend and co-worker from New England, Edward D. Jones, who was also a reporter on Wall Street.

---

**Bet You Didn't Know**

At the turn of the twentieth century, the mining and railroad stocks were the high tech stocks of the day. Much as the rumor mill goes on today about the latest advancements in telecommunications, gene splicing, or software, the market of old traded furiously about new discoveries of ore reserves or rail lines. Dow covered this beat, giving stories and rumors better than most, which led to his success as a financial reporter … kind of the Maria Bartiromo of his day.

---

## The Forming of Dow Jones & Company

In November of 1882, Dow and Jones left their previous employers and formed Dow Jones & Company. The business of Dow Jones & Company was delivering "flimsies" or "slips" to financial institutions. Both Dow and Jones collected the news and messenger boys delivered the news. In the evening, Dow and Jones prepared the news for the next day.

Initially, the first office of Dow Jones & Company was located at 15 Wall Street—right next door to the entrance of the New York Stock Exchange—in the back room of a soda fountain. By 1884, still located behind the soda fountain, the company had grown in size. Dow and Jones no longer went out and collected the news themselves. There were now newsgatherers, manifold writers, and "lively boys" who delivered the news.

Every employee of the company solicited subscriptions to the news service and were paid a commission on each sale. And every employee would report news they came across—whether this was their job or not—so that the Dow Jones & Company "flimsie" became the most prominent and widely read market paper of its day. In 1883, Dow Jones & Company began printing a newssheet containing the news of the day. This was the precursor to *The Wall Street Journal*.

## The Forming of the Dow Theory

Through Dow's writings in *The Wall Street Journal*, several analysts derived what has become known as the *Dow theory*. Keep in mind that the Dow theory was never coined by Dow himself; he merely wrote his observations. Others decided that it was a valid theory. It has also gone through various interpretations. However, the basic points to the Dow theory are in regards to the three types of movements:

- ◆ Primary trend—Takes place over the course of years and can be either bull or bear trends.

- ◆ Secondary movements—Take place from weeks to months and run contrary to the primary trend.

- ◆ Day-to-day fluctuations—Can move in either direction (bull or bear); these are of slight importance other than the fact that they comprise the overall primary trend.

**Wall Street Words**

The **Dow theory** is similar to a barometer of business conditions. Just as barometric pressure can forecast the likelihood of rainfall, it does not attempt to measure the amount of rainfall. The Dow theory makes no attempt to predict the extent or longevity of a bull or bear market, only to diagnose the likelihood of a shift in the cycle.

The second part of the Dow theory is that the Industrial average and the Railroad average must corroborate each other's direction for there to be a reliable market direction signal. At the time of Dow's writing there was only the Railroad average. However, in 1969, Dow Jones & Company broadened this to include truckers and airlines so that today it would be confirmation by the Industrial average and the Transportation average that must corroborate each other's direction for there to be a reliable market direction signal.

The last leg of Dow's theory is that large active stocks will generally reflect the market averages. However, individual issues may deviate from the broad averages because of circumstances peculiar to them. The logic behind the makeup of the specific averages is that both the industrials and the transports are independent of each other. Yet, for the industrials to get their product to market, they must use the transports. When the industrials are doing well, the transports will do well. However, when one sector is doing substantially better than the other, a divergence is taking place. This demonstrates that one sector is much stronger than the other; and if it continues, without the other sector catching up, a major reversal in the market will take place, as market conditions are out of line with economic realities.

Following Mr. Dow's death in 1902, the next editor of *The Wall Street Journal*, William Peter Hamilton, continued Dow's work, often referring to previous editorials written by Dow to explain what was happening in the marketplace. Hamilton coined the term "Dow's Theory" in his editorials, which soon became the most popular feature in *The Wall Street Journal*.

Though Hamilton never made outright calls on the market, he would pen his thoughts on interpreting the Dow theory in such a manner to warn readers. His last forecast of a primary change in trend from bullish to bearish came in September 1929. In this precursor to his most famous editorial, which appeared in *Barron's*, Hamilton wrote that "Conceivably, its next move (the stock market) may be dictated by the floating supply of undistributed investment trust stock." In his own way, using the prose of the times, Hamilton warned readers that the market was looking overbought and to watch for a continued break.

A few weeks before his sudden death—due to natural causes—in 1929, William Peter Hamilton penned his most famous editorial on the Dow theory, "A Turn in the Tide." In this article, he told of the trend change after the major bull market and the coming bear market. Though Hamilton had no idea just how bad things would get, his sage advice, based on the work of his former boss, Charles H. Dow, helped him to foretell a change in the investment climate, well ahead of the depression and one of the greatest destructions of private wealth in history.

**Timing Tips**

The purpose of the Dow theory is not to pick the exact high or low of a market, as that task is probably impossible! The purpose of it is to spot major bull and bear markets and ride them. By this account, the Dow theory is a trend-following system hoping to get an investor to make a large commitment to stocks early in a bull move, and keep them aggressively invested throughout most of the move. It does not deal with day-to-day fluctuations, but longer term or primary bull and bear markets that can last for months or years. The basic idea is to get in after a bottom, ride the bull past its peak, and get out after it has completed its run, but before the primary bear market has taken its full toll.

Since this time, the Dow theory has helped others spot the timing of major bull and bear markets. Though the exact start of each is still a mystery, the Dow theory has been used as a good guide by market participants for a century, foretelling the major swings in the marketplace.

# The Dow Theory Interpreted

To an investor or stock trader, knowledge of the past movements in the market is as necessary as a record of the tides is to a ship captain, according to Robert Rhea, who formalized the writings of Hamilton and Dow into his 1932 book *The Dow Theory* (Fraser Publishing Co., 1994).

Rhea sought to define the Dow theory and came up with the following general assumptions that you have to take for granted. These laws of the marketplace are commonly accepted today, but at the time caused much uproar. The basic assumptions upon which Hamilton based his observations of Dow's writing and theory are as follows:

- The averages discount everything   The fluctuations of the daily closing prices of the Dow Jones rail (transportation) and industrial averages afford a composite index of all the hopes, disappointments, and knowledge of everyone who knows anything of financial matters, and for that reason the effects of coming events (excluding acts of God) are always properly anticipated in their movement.

- Manipulation   Manipulation is possible in the day-to-day movement of the averages, and secondary reactions are subject to such an influence to a more limited degree, but the primary trend can never be manipulated.

- The theory is not infallible   The Dow theory is not an infallible system for beating the market. It is intended only as a guide in timing purchases and to assess the general trend of the market.

---

**Bet You Didn't Know**

Though Dow, Hamilton, and Rhea all thought the day-to-day movements of the market were unimportant, each kept logs of daily movements. Predicting day-to-day fluctuations was difficult at the turn of the twentieth century, and it is just as difficult today. It is a full-time job, and as such we advise most readers of this text to avoid the matter, instead concentrating on longer, or primary, movements of the market. A study of day traders found that 80 percent of those who have attempted day trading have lost considerable amounts of money. Though it is not impossible to make considerable amounts day trading, you have to understand that it is difficult work.

---

Upon these basic assumptions, the Dow theory has been reduced to the following theorems that collectively are known as the Dow theory.

## The Market's Three Movements

There are three movements of the stock market, all of which are in progress at one and the same time working in and against each other. The first, and most important, is the primary trend, or those broad upward or downward movements known as bull or bear markets. These movements can last several months or several years, and are the movements that the Dow theory is used to attempt to predict.

The second movement is the most deceptive. This is the reaction or intermediate term trend of the market. These are important and semi-substantial movements counter to the primary trend, for example, large rallies in bear markets or sharp breaks in bull markets. These secondary movements usually last from several weeks to several months.

The third and least important movement is the short term, or daily fluctuations. Though daily fluctuations do make up all the larger movements, Dow thought the day-to-day fluctuations were unimportant, and highly unpredictable.

## Trends

Markets tend to move in a series or pattern, known as a trend. A bullish trend is defined as a series of successive rallies penetrating previous highs, with ensuing declines terminating above preceding lows. A series of successive breaks in prices that carry prices below previous low points, interrupted by rallies that fail to make successive higher highs is known as a bearish trend.

Hamilton and Dow both assumed that a trend was in place until a significant point is violated in the other direction.

## Both Averages Must Confirm

The movements of both the Industrial average and the Transportation average must confirm each other, and be considered together. Without both averages confirming each other, or setting trends in the same direction, reliable inferences cannot be drawn from the movement of the averages.

## Individual Stocks

All active and well-distributed stocks tend to generally break or rally with the averages. In modern portfolio theory, this is known as the stock's *beta*, or how much of the stock's price movement is correlated with—or can be explained by— the movement of a general broad-based stock index. Individual stocks are subject to their own unique circumstances, or company-specific items, therefore Dow and Hamilton both advised that investors trade in a diversified list of stocks when using the Dow theory, to mitigate the individual effect such matters may have on the application of the Dow theory.

One of the major criticisms of the Dow theory is that it does not help the investor pick which individual companies shares to buy or sell. This is a major obstacle in applying the Dow theory, since most of us either buy or sell individual shares of a company or buy mutual funds. As such, our interpretation of the Dow theory may be right, and the market may move in the predicted direction, but the individual components of our own portfolio may not. One way to avoid this is to buy shares that tend to rise in rising stock markets (high beta stocks) while investing in bonds and other asset classes during periods of predicted declining prices, or buying stocks that tend to rise in falling markets (negative beta stocks).

**Wall Street Words**

**Beta** is the degree of sensitivity of a stock in relation to swings in the market.

# Dow's Three Movements

Remember when you were first learning to drive how difficult it was to pay attention to the road, watch your speed, and move your foot from the gas pedal to the brake all at the same time? However, now when you drive, all these things are second nature and require very little thought. Distinguishing between Dow's Three Movements is very similar.

At first attempt, using the theory is similar. It is difficult to tell the difference between the secondary reactions and the primary movements or trends. However, with a little effort, the student of the Dow theory is able to spot these differences. Secondary reactions are able to be spotted, and as such allow the stock market participant to add to positions on downswings in the market with great confidence, especially in the early stages of bull markets.

Dow and many others since have felt that the primary movement of the market, or major secular bull and bear markets, are the most important factor in the successful speculation in the stock market. Though the Dow theory makes no attempt to forecast how high or low the markets will go, it does do an excellent job of foreshadowing changes in the major trend.

Think of the Dow theory as a tide table. It can't tell you how far up on the beach each and every wave will come. But, by knowing whether or not the tide is rising or falling, this knowledge can tell you whether to expect subsequent waves to come farther up the shore or that they are retreating. The Dow theory works in the same way by helping the speculator understand whether or not the general stock market should be rising or falling over the long haul.

The goal of the Dow theory is not to catch exact highs and lows in the market. Though being able to do so would lead to untold riches, so far this has proven impossible for everyone. The goal of the Dow theory is to inform practitioners of the art and science of the Dow theory that the market should be rising or falling over the long haul. The Dow theory tries to get its students into the market near the beginning of bullish trends; however, the entry of bullish signals are always late.

The true power of the theory is that it keeps the bullish investor in the market through the majority of the bullish primary trend, before warning of a primary bearish trend, before the declining prices have done too much damage. In other words, the Dow theory spots primary movements at their beginning stages, allowing the speculator to reap the major benefit of the bulk of its rise, and avoid or profit from the bulk of its decline. Not the exact highs or lows, but the majority of the move.

The Dow theory is designed to catch the "primary movement," and to ignore the secondary movements and the day-to-day gyrations of the marketplace. As such, it acts as a filter, sifting out these smaller moves and highlighting the major moves.

## Primary Bull Markets

Primary bull markets begin when a primary bear market ends. Usually at the bottom of stock prices, the news is the worst: current business conditions look horrible, unemployment is high, savings are low, and interest in the stock market tends to be low. Stocks are thought of as a risky investment—which they are—and predictions are rampant about the further downside seen due to the poor business conditions.

However, it is at this darkest point that prices are cheap. The market has discounted the worst possible. Usually following this environment, prices begin to retrace. Hamilton wrote that a reaction should retrace between 25 and 66 percent of the last major decline in a bear market. For example, assume the market drops from 2000 to 1500, a 500 point decline. A secondary reaction should see prices regain between 125 and 330 points or 25 to 66 percent respectively. Following this reaction, or intermediate rally, prices return to their downward ways. Business conditions are still slow, but usually improving slightly, and this reaction is still viewed as a reaction within a bear market.

The only notable thing about the return of the bear market is the fact that prices of both averages (the Industrial and Transportation averages) do not make new lows. As business conditions generally pick up slightly, though the economic news will most likely show the economy still slow, or inflation still running high, the market for stocks increases. At the point where and when both averages make higher highs than the preceding reaction high, a primary bull market is declared in force by the Dow theory.

Hamilton explained this quite eloquently in a June 25, 1923, editorial in *Barron's* magazine, "In the first stage of a bull market, then, there is a return to known values. In the second stage, and often the longest stage, there is an adjustment to these values as they become more stable with improving general business, and it is this period which most frequently sees the longest and most deceptive secondary reactions in a major bull market. The third is the stage where general confidence is discounting not merely present values but future possibilities."

In other words, the Dow theory declares a primary bull market in stocks when both the Dow Jones Industrial and Transportation averages make a new bear market low, followed by a rally usually lasting several weeks, followed by a break in which both averages do not make new lows. If the subsequent rally in the averages surpasses the previous rally's height, then the new highs are declared the start of a primary bull market.

Hamilton warned that the secondary reactions during this stage of the bull market could be treacherous. This is because at this time the news is extremely mixed. The economy has probably just started to turn, and general business conditions are improving but very slowly.

Hamilton warned his readers that the reversal of a primary trend is very seldom a sudden event saying that "The conditions which make for a big upward or big downward movement of the primary class practically never change themselves overnight, however encouraging the first recovery may seem."

---

### Bet You Didn't Know

A study was done years back correlating the stock market's performance versus major magazine covers (refer to the section "The Practical Contrarian and the Power of the Press" in Chapter 6). If the cover highlighted a company with a favorable bent, the study found that prices generally declined following the release of the magazine over the next several months. The same principle was applied to the general stock, with major business and financial magazines having pictures of bulls or dead bears, being a solid signal to some market timers that the primary trend of the market, or issue, may be changing. Though not always accurate, the results were impressive. It makes sense, because by the time everyone knows about something, the averages have already discounted it, according to the Dow theory.

It is usually after several tests of the bull market and substantially higher prices, that general business conditions are such that stocks are usually declared a "safe" investment and public optimism and interest in the stock market increases. This fits well with an old stock market saying, "It is time to sell and go fishing when the shoeshine and elevator guys start asking for stock tips."

It is usually at this time that the economy is strong, often with talk circulating that a new era (or age) of prosperity has emerged. Stock market valuations are such that they are not only discounting the current strong economy and good business environment, but also futures increases in both and excessive optimism.

Many market timers, Hamilton included, said that tops in the market are much more difficult to spot than bottoms. But the Dow theory gives a signal not of the exact high, but after the tide has turned.

Following an advance, a decline takes place. In terms of Dow's three movements, this break in prices would be classified as a secondary reaction, or bearish correction in prices, which is normal. However, following this reaction, the prices of the averages fail to make higher highs in both averages. The subsequent reaction to the downside carries the averages below the previous trough—or reaction lows—signaling a Dow theory primary bear market.

## Primary Bear Markets

A primary bear market begins when business conditions are favorable. Talk is of a new area, and companies are reporting strong earnings or improving earnings. However, typically stock prices have not discounted—or priced in—these favorable earnings, but also priced in future expectations of more favorable earnings.

This is usually a period of public optimism. Unemployment is low, and talk of the stock market and hot new public offerings dominates cocktail party conversations.

The first leg of the primary bear market dumbfounds many, as it is seen as merely another of the many corrections the previous primary bull market had already successfully weathered. However, the fact that the Industrial and Transportation averages are making lower lows and lower highs in conjunction, tells the student of the Dow theory that the tide has shifted. Though the Dow theory does incorrectly label the first downward leg of the primary bear market as a correction, subsequent lower prices are correctly labeled as being part of the primary downward trend.

Soon after this, the news begins to shift. Business conditions begin to slow, and many companies either suspend dividends or lower them. Earnings expectations are lowered or not met and prices continue to fall.

Sharp advances or corrections in the prices of the averages punctuate every primary bear market. Market pundits call each of these the end of the correction, or bear market, and herald the start of a new period of rising prices. However, the student of the Dow theory stays on the sidelines, or in defensive issues and cash or bonds, awaiting the end of the primary bear market to be signaled.

> **Timing Tips**
>
> Many critics of the Dow theory correctly point out that the Dow theory is always bullish at the top and bearish at the bottom. Again, the Dow theory is not a tool for picking market tops and bottoms, but a long-term indicator for forecasting the next major wave in prices.
>
> The true power in the Dow theory is in the fact that it keeps the investor in line with the primary trend, hopefully capturing the bulk of a primary bull move and avoiding the bulk of a bear market—or being short in a bear market.
>
> In order to ride the full extent, the Dow theory assumes a primary movement in the market is still in effect until the theory says otherwise. In other words, it does not capture the tops and bottoms, but is content with correctly allowing investors to catch the meat of the middle of the primary trend.

Usually after a course of time, prices of stocks are now beginning to discount the bad news and have factored in the increasingly poor business environment. Stock prices no longer seem to fall on "bad news" very much. Valuations tend to look cheap by historical standards in many cases, and public participation has dropped.

Cocktail party conversations, if about the stock market at all, tend to focus on losses and poor state of affairs of the economy. It is at this point that prices react upward on some good news, or brief signs of improving business conditions.

A sustained rally of several weeks or months occurs, then prices begin to drop lower again. Market commentators highlight the negative business environment, and tend to herald the recent advance in prices as another opportunity to sell stocks. However, as prices decline, both of the averages will not penetrate their previous low levels.

Though the economy is in dire straights, or looks to be in such a situation and earnings have been revised significantly downward, prices begin to advance again. Once the price of both the Industrial and Transportation averages score higher prices than the preceding rallies highs, the student of the Dow theory knows that the primary bear market has ended and the tide has shifted to a primary bull market.

Prices continue to rise, interrupted by only sharp corrections. Business conditions stabilize and begin to improve, and the tide shifts back to a primary bull market.

> **Timing Tips**
>
> One of the tenets of the Dow theory is that the averages discount future develop-
> ments. In other words, because a stock's price reflects all the known information
> as well as the hopes and fears of all market participants, the price of stocks often
> moves well ahead of the news.
>
> When taken to an extreme, though, this same theory has led academics to
> believe in an efficient market, which is impossible to beat or time. What the academics
> have failed to realize is that Dow's theory has been beating the market for decades,
> and hopefully it will continue to do so, as it is based on sound principles.

## Secondary Reactions

A secondary reaction is a movement against the primary trend for a prolonged period
of time. As is often said, nothing in the stock market goes straight up or straight
down.

These reactions against the primary trend are what make stock market speculation
extremely difficult. These are the result of excessive speculation, as well as a function
of *profit taking* and positioning by large traders and funds. Hamilton compared the
primary trend to a steam boiler, with the secondary reactions being the steam valve
that lets off excess pressure.

> **Wall Street Words**
>
> **Profit taking** is when
> holders of stocks sell their stocks
> to book profits. An old street
> adage is that a profit is not a
> profit until it is booked, or in
> other words you can't spend your
> chips until you cash them in.
> Profit taking, or the selling of
> stocks sometimes tends to over-
> whelm the market, thus driving
> prices lower.

These important declines in primary bull markets and
rallies in primary bear markets typically last from
between three weeks and three months. They often
retrace between 33 and 66 percent of the previous leg
of the market.

Typically, these reactions are seen as terminations of
the previous trend. However, unless both the Industrial
and Transportation averages both violate the secondary
previous reactions, the primary market direction last in
place is assumed in place. It is during these secondary
reactions, that investors in a bullish primary trend can
add to their commitments (purchase stocks), while
investors in a primary bear market can use them as a
means to exit stock positions (sell stocks).

# Both Averages Must Confirm

Though in Dow's and Hamilton's day it made sense that the Industrial and the Rail stocks should confirm each other, many pundits of the Dow theory have called this notion extremely antiquated. However, the basic theory it rests upon, and the very basic nature of the Dow theory, rests upon this assumption.

This idea makes sense. In order for industrial production to meet with consumer demand, it must be transported. For example, assume you make software. Each disk you sell is transported via a courier to your customers. Not only are you making money selling the software, but so is the courier company as it benefits from your increase in business.

In other words, for goods to reach the consumer, the transportation or freight hauling companies must benefit by increasing need for their services. It is one thing to make a product, but earnings are not realized until the product is sold, which typically requires transport.

> **Bet You Didn't Know**
>
> During the Internet boom in the late 1990s and into early 2000, United Parcel Services (UPS) and Federal Express (FedEx) were considered Internet stocks. Not because their websites allowed you to buy their services and track packages, but because the dot.com companies used them to ship their books, dolls, software, and pet food to clients worldwide.

Even the sale of services requires transportation. As the owner of a small financial consulting firm, I don't make any industrial products, but sell my knowledge and limited writing abilities. When business is booming, I typically have to travel for business more. In a strong economy, I have a harder time getting flights out late on a Friday, as many other business people are also traveling then and trying to get home to see their families for the weekend. Thus, even service industries need to transport their personnel around the globe, benefiting the transportation industry.

Sometimes transportation can lead the industrials. For example, before Ford Motor Company can realize the revenue on their car sales, they have to ship these vehicles across the country to the consumers. Before an increase in car sales is booked and reported, freight carriers may have already booked and reported the increase in freight volume.

Thus, when one major segment of the market is not moving in rough unison with the other, it may be a sign that the basis for the trend is questionable. The Dow theory states that the averages must confirm each other, not exactly at the same time, but both must make higher highs or lower lows to confirm the primary direction of the market. Hamilton even went so far as to say that "conclusions based upon the movement of one average, unconfirmed by the other, are almost certain to prove misleading."

## Individual Stocks

The Dow theory makes little reference to picking individual issues to speculate in. Though this is often seen as a shortcoming to its practical use, nothing could be further from the truth today.

> **Timing Tips** _____
>
> Though the Dow theory does not give people the signals to buy individual stocks, it does not have to in today's marketplace. Hundreds of mutual funds mimic the major averages, known as index funds. These allow investors to buy large groups of stocks based on indexes, such as the Standard and Poor's 500 stock index. You can also buy funds that mimic the Dow Jones Industrials, or industry specific funds, which highlight transportation companies. With more mutual funds in existence than individual listed stocks, it is fairly easy to find a fund to meet your needs.

The purpose of the Dow theory is to highlight the right environment in which to buy or sell stocks in. As the old saying goes, "All boats will rise and fall with the tide to a greater or lesser degree."

In a strong stock market, many issues of questionable companies will rise along with the general tide of higher prices. In a primary bear market, even stocks of exceptional value tend to fall along with the market. This makes sense as solid issues are often sold as business conditions deteriorate, because stocks are an easy asset to convert to cash.

For example, people are always looking for the next big thing. During the NASDAQ run-up of the late 1990s and into 2000, almost any stock which had a ".com" in its name seemed to rise, as the promise of the Internet seemed unending.

# Applying the Dow Theory

As we mentioned at the beginning of this chapter, the Dow theory has been practiced for more than a century. Many modern practitioners exist. Ned Davis Research Company compiled a study of Dow Theory Forecasts from newsletters, which we have included here.

This first chart shows how the leading Dow theorists of this day and age interpret Dow and Hamilton's work over the last several years:

| Market | Entry Date | Starting Balance | Exit Date | Ending Balance |
|--------|-----------|-----------------|-----------|----------------|
| Stocks | 08/02/78 | $ 1,000.00 | 07/02/81 | $ 1,085.68 |
| T-Bills | 07/02/81 | $ 1,085.68 | 10/07/82 | $ 1,246.36 |
| Stocks | 10/07/82 | $ 1,246.36 | 02/08/84 | $ 1,491.94 |
| T-Bills | 02/08/84 | $ 1,491.94 | 08/03/84 | $ 1,654.56 |
| Stocks | 08/03/84 | $ 1,654.56 | 10/15/87 | $ 3,241.59 |
| T-Bills | 10/15/87 | $ 3,241.59 | 03/21/88 | $ 3,461.04 |
| Stocks | 03/21/88 | $ 3,461.04 | 01/25/90 | $ 4,287.98 |
| T-Bills | 01/25/90 | $ 4,287.98 | 12/26/91 | $ 4,626.31 |
| Stocks | 12/26/91 | $ 4,626.31 | 03/25/94 | $ 5,664.38 |
| T-Bills | 03/25/94 | $ 5,664.38 | 07/10/95 | $ 5,965.72 |
| Stocks | 07/10/95 | $ 5,965.72 | 08/04/98 | $ 10,767.49 |
| T-Bills | 08/04/98 | $ 10,767.49 | 01/06/99 | $ 11,311.25 |
| Stocks | 01/06/99 | $ 11,311.25 | 09/21/99 | $ 12,559.70 |
| T-Bills | 09/21/99 | $ 12,559.70 | 12/31/01 | $ 13,197.73 |

*Note: Dow Theory Buy/Sell dates were compiled by Ned Davis Research and are based on a sampling of several different Dow Theory Investment Letters. Investments in T-Bills are assumed at the exit and the investor is assumed to get the 1 year T-Bill rate of return for 1 year, no matter if the holding period is longer or shorter. These factors will affect real performance, but is used for simplicity and illustrative purposes.*

The table shows a list of the Dow Theory Entry and Exit Dates. When the Dow theory flashes a buy signal, it is assumed that an investor went into "stocks" on that day as represented by the Dow Jones Industrial Average. So on the original buy date, the investor would have bought $1,000 worth of Dow Jones Industrial Average. When the Dow theory flashes a sell signal, the investor is said to then invest his entire account into one-year T-Bills. It is assumed that they will get the equivalent rate of return of the one-year T-Bill at that time, and the account is kept in T-Bills (or receiving the one-year T-Bill rate of return for the entire holding period) until the next buy signal from the Dow theory, at which time the entire account is put back into stocks.

As you can see, the Dow theory does not catch every wiggle in the market, but generally keeps the investor invested in stocks when the primary trend is up and out of stocks or in defensive issues when the market has tended to break.

If you would have invested $1,000 in the Dow Jones Industrials on the original buy date of August 2, 1978 and held through December 31, 2001, their initial investment would have been worth $10,184.11 —excluding transaction costs and dividends. However, the same investor starting his investing on the same day but switching between the stock market and a T-Bill equivalent would have made $3,013.62 more, before dividends and transaction costs.

The Dow theory has been around for more than a century and even in the bull market of the 1980s and 1990s, it has held up very well.

> **Timing Tips** _____
>
> Anyone interested in the Dow theory should consult the original text, which Robert Rhea compiled and interpreted from Dow and Hamilton's editorials in *The Wall Street Journal*. *The Dow Theory* by Robert Rhea is available from the Fraser Company, Box 494, Burlington, Vermont 05402 or by visiting www.fraserbooks. com. If you would like to see noted Dow Theorist Richard Moroney's thoughts, visit www.dowtheory.com and request a free copy of his *Dow Theory Forecast* newsletter. Or you may contact Horizon Publishing Company at 219-852-3200

## The Least You Need to Know

◆ The Dow theory has been in existence for more than a century and is a primary tool used successfully by many to forecast primary bull and bear markets.

◆ A primary bull market is defined as a long upward movement in stock prices that usually lasts from several months to several years, in which prices gain at least 20 percent in value.

◆ A primary bear market is defined as a long downward movement in stock prices that usually lasts from several months to several years, in which prices drop at least -20 percent in value.

◆ The Dow theory holds that as long as the Dow Jones Industrial and Transportation averages both make higher highs and stay above reaction lows, then the primary trend of the market is bullish.

◆ When the Dow Jones Industrial and Transportation averages both make lower lows and remain below previous reaction lows, then the primary trend of the market is bearish.

◆ Dow and his predecessor Hamilton correctly believed that though the short-term movement of the stock market, or what they called the day-to-day and secondary reactions of the market, can be manipulated, the primary trend of the market can not. Therefore, once a primary trend is in force, it is believed to remain in force until proven otherwise.

◆ The Dow theory is most useful in determining the long-term direction and environment for stock speculation. The system is not infallible, but correctly applied it should keep investors invested for the majority of a primary bull market and out of stocks or in defensive issues during primary bear markets.

# Chapter 5

# Averages, Trends, and 10 Percent

## In This Chapter

- A timer's friend is the trend
- Improving the averages
- It's all about money moving in and out
- Keep losses small, and ride the big ones

In the previous chapter we highlighted the Dow theory. The basic tenant was that markets have large primary movements or trends. These trends tend to last longer and go farther than most people expect. Inside this chapter, we will look at other ways to capture these broad moves in the market.

The first method we will examine is the simple moving average, which shows the primary trend of the market, then I will highlight some of the ways others have improved upon this basic tool. Because the stock market represents money, we will highlight how you can watch the flow of money into and out of the market, and how changes in these patterns can be useful in timing your purchases and sales.

Last, one of the key rules to successful investing or trading in any timeframe is to let your profits run and keep your losses small. We will examine a very simple and eloquent way of doing just that.

# An Introduction to Averages

In the previous chapter, we referred to the stock market as a series of averages, or representations of the market by the Dow Jones Industrial Average and the Dow Jones Transportation Average. These are simply a collection of stocks, which are weighted by their *capitalization*, and averaged together to give a proxy of their behavior. These "averages" are a little different from the averages we will be referring to in this chapter. A better name for these stock market proxies are indexes.

**Wall Street Words** _____

**Capitalization** is the total value of the company. Capitalization is the price per share multiplied by the number of shares outstanding. For example, assume a company has 10,000 shares issued and the stock is trading at $35 per share, the market capitalization of this company is $350,000. Measuring companies by capitalization makes sense as it allows one to see the total value of the company and not to fixate simply on the share price.

An index is defined as a list or something that serves to guide, point out, or otherwise facilitate reference. Stock indexes serve this purpose, as they are simply lists of stocks used to represent the whole universe of stocks. Generally, when someone asks, "How did the market do today?" they do not want to hear that XYZ was up $0.37 a share, and ABC was down -$1.20 a share. Instead what they are referring to is how one of the popular indexes did, like the Dow Jones Industrial Average, S&P 500, or NASDAQ.

For the market timer, an average is not a measure of the whole universe of stocks, but a measure of the price of one of the indexes. It is implying the average price of the index over a period of time.

These averages are used to judge the relative performance of the index. For example, when the price of an index is above its average price of the last X number of days, technical market lore holds that prices are bullish or more than likely to continue upward. On the other hand, when prices are below their average price of the last X number of days, technical market lore holds that prices are bearish or more than likely to continue lower.

**Timing Tips**

One of the early complaints about market timing is that it used to be impossible to buy or sell the index averages. However, now this is not the case. Just about every mutual fund company and brokerage firm has an in-house index fund or several that mimic the popular averages, like the S&P 500 or NASDAQ 100. Several other companies have indexes that mimic the Dow Jones Industrial, Transportation, and Utility averages.

To calculate the average of something is relatively easy to do. Simply sum up the total of all the data points and divide by the number of observations. For example, if we have the following closing prices:

| | |
|---|---|
| Day 1 | 50.00 |
| Day 2 | 51.00 |
| Day 3 | 53.00 |
| Day 4 | 52.00 |
| Day 5 | 51.50 |

Computing the average price would be accomplished simply by adding up all the five days, and dividing by five (or 50+51+53+52+51.50 = 257.50 ÷ 5 = 51.50), giving us a five day average price of 51.50.

If we add another day's data to the picture, we would calculate a five-day average by simply adding up days two through six, and dividing by five. For example, assume on the following day the price in question climbed to 53.00 again; then we would simply compute this by adding 51+53+52+51.50+53, yielding a sum of 260.50, and a five-day average of 52.10.

By recording each day's average price, we would have a running or moving record of these, known as a *moving average*. The number of days in the computation is usually referred to as the periodicity of the average, which is typically shortened to a five-day moving average in our example.

**Wall Street Words**

A **moving average** is simply the average price of the last X number of days, which is plotted on the chart alongside the most current data. For example, a five-day moving average would be the average price of the previous five days, plotted forward in time as new data is added. The longer the moving average, the less volatile it is.

# Averages and the Trend

One of the most popular moving averages for stock market timers is the 200-day moving average. The 200-day moving average represents the average price of the last 200 days, or roughly the last 10 months of price action. Most basic charting services on the Internet offer this functionality when plotting stock or index prices. The purpose of a moving average is to ascertain the general direction of prices. If prices are rising and above the moving average, then the trend is considered bullish. If prices are below the moving average, then the trend is considered bearish.

## The Upside

Proponents of using moving averages say that the stock market tends to act in the same way as the physical world around us. They then state Newton's First Law of Motion: "Every body continues in its state of rest or of uniform speed in a straight line unless it is compelled to change that state by a net force acting on it." In lay terms, "an object in motion will continue in motion." Since most traders and speculators in the stock market are not physicists or rocket ship scientists, traders have reduced this to mean that "the trend is your friend."

> **Timing Tips**
>
> One of the best features of a moving average is that it is impossible for the market to have a significant rally without prices crossing above the moving average. Therefore a moving average will always allow you to catch the really big moves. However, this is also a drawback. When prices rally, you can end up getting in at the top of a trading range, because moving averages are lagging, as such by the time the price rises up to the moving average signaling a buy, the upward move may be over.

Dow defined an upward trend as a series of higher prices, where the market made higher highs and higher lows. He defined a series of lower highs and lower lows to be a downward trend. As such, interpretation of the Dow theory regarding the trend of the Dow Jones Industrial and Transportation indexes is somewhat subjective.

However, using moving averages is not so. As I mentioned earlier, many industry professionals watch the 200-day moving average of stocks and the market indexes for clues as to the trend. If the price is above the 200-day moving average, the trend is said to be up, while when the price of the issue or index in question is below the 200-day moving average.

Though this is not a perfect system, it does make sense. Basically, what this tool does is help the speculator to get into stocks when they are rising, and gets one out of stocks when they are falling. The real beauty of it is that once it puts someone into stocks, it tends to keep them in during periods of rising stocks. This is because the average will always be slower than the market. For example, let's look at a series of numbers: 2,4,6,8,10. The average would be 6. Now if we added 12 to this, the average would be 8, increasing by an equal amount to the increase, but still trailing behind the series.

During a period of strong stock market performance, the moving average will remain below the price of the issue being studied. Thus, when the markets enter into a primary bullish trend, the moving average will eventually be below the index, signaling a bullish trend, and the speculator will have an idea that the future direction of stocks is up.

> **Trading Traps**
>
> The major flaw with a moving average system is that it needs higher prices to get you in, and requires a breaking price to get you out. In other words, it will get you into equities only after a run-up in prices, and signal you to exit your position only after falling prices. The other major problem with moving averages is that during periods of little change, they can cause you to jump into and out of the market, excessively, causing lots of small losses, which after multiple times can and do line up to be large losses.

## The Downside: Number One

However, there are some large potential problems with using moving averages. First, moving averages lag the market. Just as the Dow theory did not try to catch the exact high or low of the market, neither do moving averages. In fact, moving averages require people to buy when prices are rising, and hoping for continued higher prices. They also require people to sell their issues after they have declined, on the presumption that prices will decline further.

For the market timer, this first issue of lag should not be of terrible concern. The purpose of market timing is to attempt to ride the primary trend of the market: Buying into bullish environments and selling before bear markets wipe away all of their gains from the preceding period. In order to get the bulk of the market's rise, you have to accept riding out some dips. Some of those dips will be minor reactions, while others will end up being the start of a bear market.

For most of us mere mortals, we cannot tell the difference between the two. As such, we are forced to wait for evidence that a bull market has begun before buying, and wait for evidence that a bear market has begun before liquidating our stock portfolios, or investing in defensive issues such as bonds or money market accounts.

## The Downside: Number Two

The second major problem with a moving average system is the frequency in which it can trade. It is very possible for the market to close above its 200-day moving average one day, and below it the next. This can result in a constant purchasing and selling of positions, until a major trend develops. In the trading world, this is known as *whip sawing* and can be devastating to an account, and to a person psychologically. Also, because the average lags, the short in and out will cause the speculator to lose several times in very small amounts. However, these small amounts do add up!

### Wall Street Words

**Whip sawing** is frequent in and out trading. The major draw back of whip sawing is that transaction costs can mount—commissions. For example, if you trade in and out of a stock 10 times, making $0.50 per share, but you pay $75 every time you do this, you will end up losing $250, because transaction costs eat up your meager gains.

For example, examining the period from 1991 through mid 2002, a follower of a simple 200-day moving average system would have entered and exited the market a total of 36 times, or roughly every 120 days on average. Though this doesn't sound so bad, roughly 20 of the most recent 36 signals had you switching into and out of the market in less than 20 days, with 12 of the signals lasting less than one week (or five business days).

Despite this shortcoming, a simple 200-day moving average system would have had you invested in stocks 76 percent of this time. During this period, a simple buy and hold approach would have seen the S&P 500 increase from 334.78 to 931.86, or a gain of +597.08 points, assuming you bought on the original moving average cross over and held until the last day of the study. Following the moving average system of simply buying the S&P 500 whenever it crossed above its moving average and exiting the market when it crossed below its moving would have yielded +801.98. Though the moving average system yielded less results, for being invested in the market 76 percent of the time, it did manage to garner 76 percent of the total gain.

|  | **Buy and Hold** | **200-Day Moving Average** |
|---|---|---|
| Start Date | 01/24/91 | 01/24/91 |
| Starting Price | 334.78 | 334.78 |
| Ending Date | 08/20/02 | 04/02/02 |

|  | **Buy and Hold** | **200-Day Moving Average** |
|---|---|---|
| Ending Price | 931.86 | 1136.76 |
| Points Gained | 597.08 | 560.10 |
| Days Invested | 4,226 | 3,233 |

You will notice in the table that the exit dates for the two systems (buy and hold vs. the 200-day moving average) are different. This is because from April 2, 2002 through August 20, the S&P 500 remained below its 200-day moving average. Also, because the moving average system is sometimes wrong, yielding a negative trade performance. In fact, during this sample period, 10 of the 36 moving average buy signals yielded negative returns. The bulk of the signals were profitable, and produced rather large profits, while at the same time the average false signal proved to be small.

One of the major drawbacks of this type of approach is transaction costs. However, by investing in the proper type of funds or by using special account types—both of which are explained in later chapters—transaction costs can be cut way back and reduced to be only a minor drag on performance. However, the problem of whip saws is still present, thus we need to modify the simple moving average.

This is one of the key points of market timing. In many cases, you are not trying to beat the market; you are simply following a methodical approach to your investing, which will allow you to make rational decisions, instead of panicky decisions based upon fear and greed. The purpose is to have a rational plan for holding on to profitable positions, and a plan for exiting unprofitable positions.

**Timing Tips**

One of the main purposes for market timing is to give the investor/speculator a disciplined framework to act within. Many speculators make their market decisions in the heat of battle, usually after sharp drops or rallies in prices … that often turn out to be the wrong time to adjust your portfolio.

By using a market timing framework, the speculator in the stock market already has a plan of action for entering and exiting the market, and thus can avoid emotional responses to sudden events that cause people too often to buy or sell stocks at the wrong time.

# Solving the Problems of Whip Saws

The most legitimate concern when applying a moving average system to your market timing is the issue of whip saws, or the frequent in and out trading. Not only does this make investing more work, but it also increases your costs, in terms of commissions and taxes. Short-term capital gains are taxed in most cases at a higher rate than long-term capital gains. As such, frequent in and out trading can increase your tax bill, as well as enrich your broker.

Because there are times when the stock market gyrates around in a trading range, and does not produce a long-term smooth trend to the market, these periods become the death of many who use moving averages in their market timing.

The purpose of a moving average is to filter out the larger, and longer term moves. As such, applying a filter to the moving average is extremely plausible. For example, let's take all buy signals in the S&P 500 index, when the price of the S&P 500 crosses over the 200-day moving average by 2.5 percent. The important point is not the 2.5 percent, as similar results can be achieved by using 2.0 percent or 3.0 percent. The important point is that the filter will make sure that prices move significantly above or below the average price, thus hopefully signaling larger trends in the market.

### Trading Traps

In this day and age of computers, it is very tempting to fit your decisions to what has worked in the past. For example, training yourself to speculate using past data and heavily adjusting market models to generate the perfect signals in the past. This is known in the analysis world as "curve fitting," and generally this practice of optimizing your results to the past often leads to less than stellar results in the future, when your money is on the line. Remember, just because something worked in the past doesn't mean it has to work in the future.

Using the same time period as before, we will compare buy and hold vs. investing in stocks (S&P 500) when the index settles one day 2.5 percent above its 200-day moving average. During the 10-year test period, buy and hold saw the S&P 500 increase from 334.78 to 931.86, or a gain of +597.08 points, assuming you bought on the original moving average cross over and held until the last day of the study. Buying on a breakout of 2.5 percent above the 200-day moving average and staying invested in stocks until prices crossed −2.5 percent below the 200-day moving average would have generated five signals, having you invested in stocks 77 percent of the time as buy and hold, and would have generated trading profits of 836.88 points in the S&P 500.

| Entry Date | Entry Price | Exit Date | Exit Price | Change in Pts. | Change in % |
|---|---|---|---|---|---|
| 01/30/91 | 340.91 | 03/30/94 | 445.55 | 104.64 | 31% |
| 08/26/94 | 473.80 | 12/08/94 | 445.45 | -28.35 | -6% |

| Entry Date | Entry Price | Exit Date | Exit Price | Change in Pts. | Change in % |
|---|---|---|---|---|---|
| 01/16/95 | 469.38 | 08/28/98 | 1027.14 | 557.76 | 119% |
| 11/02/98 | 1111.60 | 09/29/99 | 1268.37 | 156.77 | 14% |
| 10/29/99 | 1362.93 | 10/06/00 | 1408.99 | 46.06 | 3% |

Notice, that for some very long periods, you would have been out of the market. However, all of the major rises and falls during this period were captured by this method. Also, note that following the signals from this system would have produced a loss from late August 1994 through December 1994. This type of system tends to follow the flow of the market, just like a straight moving average. If the market enters into a sideways period, or switches trends radically fast, then it will deliver sub-standard results.

However, this trick to market timing is not meant as a stand-alone system or the only tool you need. It is a useful indicator, especially with a filter, but is just one of many. It has its drawbacks, which can readily be seen when the market goes through an extended sideways movement, like from the end of 1976 to March 1980. During this period, buying a +2.5 percent settlement above the 200-day moving average would have resulted in a negative return of –21 percent, while a simple buy and hold would have resulted in a much smaller loss of –2.7 percent during that period. In total, during this three and a half year period, you would have entered the stock market five times, and sold out at lower prices and a loss all five times.

# The Value Line 4 Percent Rule

One of the big benefits of moving averages is that they tend to keep you on the right side of the market for a long time and get you out of losing positions fairly quickly.

Along this vein, a popular market timing technique is the Value Line 4 percent rule. This system states that you buy the Value Line Composite Index whenever it rallies 4 percent off of its lowest closing value of the most current swing. You hold the position until the index declines 4 percent from the highest close of the period. After a 4 percent correction, you would sit in cash, bonds, or defensive issues, until the next 4 percent rally.

A 4 percent move is a rather small and very aggressive posture to take, much akin to what a shorter-term equity trader may use. This style of trade, which is suitable for many people, is not within the scope of this book, which is geared more toward attempting to catch the broad secular bull and bear markets. As such, we will look at a very similar style, but slightly different.

# A Different Twist to the 4 Percent Rule

Since we are looking at capturing bull markets, and avoiding bear markets, we thought we would test the same basic theory in the S&P 500 index, but instead of using 4 percent, we will play with 10 percent swings.

Whenever the S&P 500 declines by 10 percent or more, you could look to reestablish equity positions when the index closes at least 10 percent above this low level. The equity position is held until the index closes 10 percent or more below the peak value of the move. For example, if the index is trading at 100, we would look to be a buyer if prices rose to 110—which would be a 10 percent increase. We would hold this position until prices declined by –10 percent—or fell back to 99. However, the higher the index goes after we have established a stake in it, we will continue to move the exit point up as well. For example, if after buying the index at 110, it rose to 120, we would continue to hold our position until prices broke at least 10 percent from 120, or the index fell back to 108. If the index rose to 130, we would only exit if the index fell to 117. In other words, we would trail our exit point 10 percent below the peak value of the move, on a settlement basis.

Doing this since 1969, using the S&P 500 as a stock market proxy, investors would have made a total of 27 transactions, being invested a total of 9,284 days (roughly 25½ years). In total, the investor following this style of trade, would have reaped a total of 692.48 S&P points. A simple buy and hold during the same period, would have reaped a total of 833.50 points in the S&P, and would have been invested a total of 12,283 days (roughly 33½ years). In other words, being invested only after the market has rallied 10 percent and exiting on the first –10 percent break, an investor would have captured roughly 83 percent of the total gain in the index, and only would have been invested in the market, with money at risk, three out of four years.

However, this does have some drawbacks. Of the 27 different transactions, 15 would have resulted in losses equal to roughly 10 percent of your portfolio. Though this method did avoid the 1987 stock market crash, it would have had you buying directly after the crash, twice, which would have had one down roughly –21 percent in the two months following the crash.

| Entry Date | Entry Price | Exit Date | Exit Price | Change in Points | Change in % |
|---|---|---|---|---|---|
| 05/29/70 | 76.55 | 08/04/71 | 93.89 | 17.34 | 22.7% |
| 12/16/71 | 99.74 | 04/27/73 | 107.23 | 7.49 | 7.5% |
| 10/11/73 | 111.09 | 11/20/73 | 98.66 | -12.43 | -11.2% |
| 03/13/74 | 99.74 | 04/25/74 | 89.57 | -10.17 | -10.2% |

| Entry Date | Entry Price | Exit Date | Exit Price | Change in Points | Change in % |
|---|---|---|---|---|---|
| 10/10/74 | 69.79 | 12/03/74 | 67.17 | -2.62 | -3.8% |
| 01/10/75 | 72.61 | 08/08/75 | 86.02 | 13.41 | 18.5% |
| 10/21/75 | 90.56 | 05/25/77 | 96.77 | 6.21 | 6.9% |
| 04/24/78 | 95.77 | 10/26/78 | 96.03 | 0.26 | 0.3% |
| 01/26/79 | 101.86 | 10/25/79 | 100 | -1.86 | -1.8% |
| 01/10/80 | 109.89 | 03/10/80 | 106.51 | -3.38 | -3.1% |
| 05/22/80 | 109.01 | 08/24/81 | 125.5 | 16.49 | 15.1% |
| 11/02/81 | 124.2 | 02/09/82 | 113.68 | -10.52 | -8.5% |
| 04/23/82 | 118.64 | 06/18/82 | 107.28 | -11.36 | -9.6% |
| 08/20/82 | 113.02 | 02/13/84 | 154.95 | 41.93 | 37.1% |
| 08/07/84 | 162.71 | 10/15/87 | 298.08 | 135.37 | 83.2% |
| 10/21/87 | 258.38 | 10/26/87 | 227.67 | -30.71 | -11.9% |
| 10/30/87 | 251.79 | 12/03/87 | 225.21 | -26.58 | -10.6% |
| 12/16/87 | 248.08 | 01/30/90 | 322.98 | 74.9 | 30.2% |
| 05/21/90 | 358 | 08/17/90 | 327.83 | -30.17 | -8.4% |
| 12/04/90 | 326.35 | 10/27/97 | 876.98 | 550.63 | 168.7% |
| 12/01/97 | 974.77 | 08/14/98 | 1062.75 | 87.98 | 9.0% |
| 09/23/98 | 1066.09 | 10/08/98 | 959.44 | -106.65 | -10.0% |
| 10/16/98 | 1056.42 | 09/29/99 | 1268.37 | 211.95 | 20.1% |
| 11/08/99 | 1377.01 | 04/14/00 | 1356.56 | -20.45 | -1.5% |
| 07/12/00 | 1492.92 | 10/11/00 | 1364.59 | -128.33 | -8.6% |
| 04/18/01 | 1238.16 | 07/10/01 | 1181.52 | -56.64 | -4.6% |
| 10/03/01 | 1072.28 | 05/06/02 | 1052.67 | -19.61 | -1.8% |

Though the system has performed admirably—keeping an investor fully invested from 1990 to 1997—since 1997 the system has had its troubles. In fact, following this rule for the past two years, would have resulted in losses of roughly –16 percent to your portfolio, which may be less than buy and hold, but is still not really adequate.

The power of this style of trade was demonstrated during the large secular and extended stock market runs of 1984 to 1987 and the run from 1990 to 1997. Both of those moves were captured extremely well by such a percentage filter as this. Investors would have gotten in near the bottom of the market, roughly 10 percent above the bottom, and would have captured 80 percent of the total move. More than being a useful tool in positioning your portfolio, this shows that it is both possible to make money being wrong more often than right, as long as you let your winners run and cut your losers short.

# The Trend *Is* Your Friend

What I have tried to impress upon you with both the study of moving averages as well as the 10 percent break-out rule is that it is not necessary to pick exact market tops and bottoms to make money in the stock market.

Just as Dow postulated over a century ago, it is possible to trade the markets and adjust your risk under the assumption that longer secular moves in the market do take place. Understanding this concept, and cutting your losses at a reasonable level, will ensure longer-term financial stability to your portfolio.

Do not try to pick tops and bottoms, for even professional traders who watch the markets on a daily basis can't do this with regularity. What a speculator should do is watch for the broad based moves of the market and be content to move with the tide of the market, capturing the bulk of upswings and sitting patiently for market bottoms to appear.

## The Least You Need to Know

♦ A moving average is simply the average price of a security or index plotted along with prices. Generally, when prices are above their longer-term moving averages, they have a tendency to stay above those averages for extended periods of time.

♦ When a market tends to make a significant move over an extended period of time, it tends to continue in that direction, just as a body in motion tends to stay in motion.

♦ By increasing the size and length of filters, such as percentage moves from bottoms and tops and moving averages, it is possible to capture the bulk of bull markets and avoid the bulk of bear markets.

♦ By timing investments and equity market exposure, without even attempting to pick market tops and bottoms, you are able to match very closely the performance of constant risk, like you assume with a buy and hold market strategy.

♦ The key to any form of investing is to let your profitable positions continue and to accept losses in a timely manner. This is the basis of trend following, which provides speculators and investors with a tried-and-true methodology for doing so.

# Chapter 6

# Going Against the Crowd: The Art of Contrarian Thinking

## In This Chapter

- ◆ What is a contrarian?
- ◆ By the time it's known, it's priced in
- ◆ When the market guys are all bullish, be bearish
- ◆ Buy the rumor and sell the fact

In the previous chapters, we discussed market timing from the perspective of trend following. The Dow theory calls for investors to wait for lower corrections before selling out of their stock positions. Moving averages, breakouts, and Dow's theory require the market to move a good portion before entering and require the market to pull back before exiting positions. They rest comfortably on the theory that a trend, once established, will continue long enough to make a profit.

Though the general theory of trend following is a sound one—which is why we introduced you to it first—its does have its limitations. One way to combat these limitations, or at least be on guard in the later part of a trend, is to think against the crowd.

Thinking against the crowd is known as "contrarian thinking." Inside this chapter, we will highlight some different forms of contrarian thinking. From magazine covers to the different bets that the derivative guys are making, the contrarian looks for signs that the public and the marketplace is putting hope above reality.

# Learning to Think Beyond the Crowd ... Being a Contrarian

An old market maxim is the investors should "buy when they are scared to death, and sell when they are tickled to death." Just as Dow observed a century ago, markets tend to be their highest when business conditions are the best, and at their lowest price when business conditions are at their worst.

It has been said that the stock market is a discounting mechanism, meaning it does not react to the news today, but perceptions about business activity, and the earnings of tomorrow, or the immediate future. In other words, when you buy a stock, it is usually not priced to reflect current earnings and conditions, but future earnings and conditions discounted back to the present.

This theory of market pricing is widely accepted. In fact, the U.S. government uses the price change of the S&P 500 as one of its "leading economic indicators" to predict changes in the economy. This makes perfect sense, when everyone watches any of the financial news shows, the talk is constantly about companies making earnings estimates, or not. In fact, it is not uncommon for a stock to report higher earnings, but below Wall Street analyst estimates, and sell off sharply on the news. This has led to another often repeated market axiom "the news is not important, but the market's reaction to it."

The contrarian tends to think in these terms, looking for situations where the marketplace has already priced in good news, and is vulnerable to realistic expectations, or a situation where the marketplace has already priced in "bad news," and may be ready to turn around.

A contrarian is someone who takes a contrary view or action. When applied to the financial markets, it is generally an investor who makes decisions that contradict prevailing wisdom. The key word here is "prevailing" as applied to wisdom. For example, a contrarian will see business conditions as fantastic, and hear that the markets and business have entered into a "new era" and then think how much of this news has already been factored into prices.

Remember one of the tenets of the Dow theory, "The fluctuations of the daily closing prices of the Dow-Jones Rail (Transportation) and Industrial averages afford a composite index of all the hopes, disappointments, and knowledge of everyone who knows anything of financial matters, and for that reason the effects of coming events (excluding acts of God) are always properly anticipated in their movement." For the contrarian, this is accepted as a truism, however, not an infallible one because the knowledge reflected in the price is really a composite of everyone's opinion, which can be wrong.

**Timing Tips**

It has been said that the stock market is a discounting mechanism, meaning that the price of a stock, or the market, does not reflect today's environment, but the discounted stream of future earnings and dividends. In other words, when people are buying stock, they are expressing a positive view of the future. The higher the price they are willing to pay for a stock, the rosier their expectations for the future must be. However, there comes a point when nothing can live up to the expectations at certain prices. Typically stocks tend to go well beyond this point, but eventually come back down to earth, as "No tree grows to the sky."

The contrarian views the crowd as a hysterical mob. They overindulge, and the contrarian views these overindulgences as a sign that the market may be approaching an important top or bottom. Jean Jacques Rousseau, the Swiss philosopher who pondered that society is inherently corrupt while the individual is inherently good, summed up contrarian thinking quite eloquently by saying "Follow the course opposite to custom and you will almost always do well."

# The Practical Contrarian and the Power of the Press

It is difficult to be a contrarian, because as such you try to think opposite of what the general public is thinking and do the opposite. When you are wrong, usually your friends and neighbors are right, and they look at you funny when, in almost a belittling fashion, they tell you that it was obvious that that particular stock would continue to rise or fall, or the general market would such and such. This is because most people operate on conventional wisdom. To quote another old market axiom, "If it's obvious, it's obviously wrong" is the battle cry of the contrarian.

For example, if a stock is reporting great earnings and appears poised for growth, shouldn't the stock go up? Maybe not, according to the contrarians. If the news is already known, most people—professional market players—have already purchased the stock. The mutual funds already have bought it, because they have large networks of analysts who search out these very types of situations. The company insiders have already purchased the stock, because they are aware of the great opportunities ahead. Hence, by the time we—meaning you and I, the general public—hear about the company, who is left to buy it?

A classic example of this can be seen in the study of magazine covers and market performance. Paul Montgomery of Legg Masson, Inc.—a global financial services company—has done extensive study of magazine covers, newspaper articles, and feature news magazine stories on stocks and the markets, and their reaction to them. A common theme in his findings is that by the time we hear about such things in the press, they are already priced in.

For example, in December 1999, Jeff Bezos graced the cover of *Time* as the magazine's coveted "Man of the Year." His company, Amazon.com, was the darling of Wall Street and one of the leaders of the tech-stock boom that was sending Internet stock prices through the roof. Earlier that month, Amazon's price hit its all-time high at $113. By March, Amazon.com was headed in a different direction. Just four months after the *Time* issue, the stock had fallen from $113 to $60—a decline of almost 47 percent. By April, the stock slid to $46 and later in the year, it closed at $33—71 percent lower than its high in December.

Throughout this entire seven-month period, both Wall Street's and the public's infatuation with the company had been unbreakable despite the stock's horrible performance. According to Bloomberg, out of the 34 analysts covering Amazon on Wall Street, only *one* recommended the stock as a "sell" during this time.

---

### Bet You Didn't Know

Several who have studied the phenomena of magazine covers and market performance found that when Dow Jones' *Barron's Weekly* released its "most important issue ever" a common marketing ploy in financial magazine publishing, the market tended to break following it. *Barron's* reacted to these studies by stopping this marketing gimmick. It is important to remember that cycles, such as this one, can change. With increasing regulation of the securities industry and analysts, perhaps this indicator will go by the wayside as well. However, currently it does appear to have some basic predictive power.

---

This one situation does not stand alone. Mr. Montgomery of Legg Mason, Inc. who originated the "Magazine Cover Theory" back in 1971, came to the following conclusion: "When *Time*, *Newsweek*, *Business Week*, or other business periodicals have extremely bullish or bearish covers, especially featuring a picture of a bull or a bear, it pays to run in the opposite direction."

This lesson has not been lost on the press. Craig Shaw of *Investors Business Daily* wrote an excellent article in the paper's front Investors Corner highlighting the NASDAQ Index and news stories in the May 31, 2000, edition of the paper.

He highlighted the tendency for magazine covers to reflect conventional wisdom, which has typically been wrong at major market turns. The major magazines tend to be poor market timers because cover stories usually take months to weave their way to publication. He hypothesized that the process could run similar to this, "A business writer notices the market's growing weakness and pitches a story idea to his editor. That editor consults his bosses. The writer conducts dozens of interviews. Weeks and months may pass before the story gets the green light for the cover. By the time the magazine hits the shelves, the worst of the selling is usually over and the market's ready to rally."

> **Timing Tip**
>
> You can get two free weeks of *Investor's Business Daily* by visiting www.investors.com. The *Investors Business Daily* Investors Corner article is typically a very good read, highlighting important points about the market often overlooked by investors. Try the paper free for two weeks—you just may like it!

He highlighted this theory covering the several months of trading in the NASDAQ Composite Index in 1998.

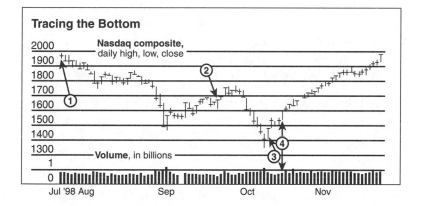

*NASDAQ Composite Index and contrarian thinking.*

Point 1 is the high, before concerns regarding a global economic meltdown sent prices plunging 27 percent in just six weeks.

Point 2 is the September 21, 1998, issue of *Forbes* magazine, where the cover asked the question "Is It Armageddon?" Inside, the magazine did warn readers that prices could plunge further, saying that "Bull markets don't last forever, not even in fairy tales." A week after the *Forbes* cover hit the newsstands, *Fortune* magazine had a front cover story called "The Crash of 1998." This article, in a similar vein to the *Forbes* article, warned readers of a continued, and extended drop in prices, stating that "This time the market won't be so quick to bounce back." A little over two weeks after the *Forbes* cover and a week after the *Fortune* cover story, the NASDAQ bottomed out and began the bounce back to new highs.

Point 3 is on October 9, 1998 the NASDAQ Index climbed 5.2 percent.

Point 4 is four days after that; the index scored another 4.5 percent rally in a day. Following this, the rally was broad-based in tech stocks, and the index nearly doubled over the next year.

The cycle started again, with Jeff Bezos's being on the cover of *Time* magazine, and the wonder boy of the new economy being voted as "Man of the Year."

Dr. Marty Zweig—noted fund manager, advisory service editor, and frequent guest on Louis Rukyser's old PBS Friday night show *Wall $treet Week*—used to count the number of bullish investment advisory ads in *Barron's* "to use as a bearish indicator when the number shot up." As the press is not the only ones who tend to get over excited about the market.

# Analysts or Cheerleaders?

Be on guard when you see enormous publicity about the prognosticating prowess of any analyst or investment advisor. He is likely about to fall on his face. Constant media attention is very seductive and may cause the recipient to feel invincible. One market guru even predicted an earthquake in Los Angeles back in 1981. In the market, this is known as the "Walking on Water Indicator."

Having been interviewed by the press a few times during my own career about financial matters, I have had to deal with extra media attention. In fact, one reporter said on his last call to me "Scott, thanks for the information the other day. It proved to be right on. However, you have to give me something that will make headlines, if I am going to continue to use you as a source." Thus, my own career as a market pundit was cut very short, but I am left to wonder how many understand the game of publicity better.

## Companies or Investors?

Wall Street is under fire for the lack of separation between analysts and investment banking functions. The job of an analyst is to help investors make informed decisions.

Investment bankers raise money and help companies. It has been alleged that when push comes to shove, Wall Street sides with the companies and not investors.

This might explain the rating system for stocks among major brokerage houses. Typically the system goes from sell to aggressive buy, but street knowledge says that anything lower than a buy is really a sell recommendation, as the analysts do not like to put out sell recommendations on a company, because that makes it hard for the investment bankers to do business with that company.

Though regulators are looking into the matter, investors should be aware of this and other potential conflicts of interest. Remember, it is your money, and your job to look after it!

> **Trading Traps** _____
>
> Most contrarians are too early. Do not blindly sell something, or establish short positions in it, just because everyone seems to be cheerleading for it. Sometimes stocks can go up, way up, without stopping. Many stock market bear funds went broke in 1999 and early 2000 just before the major top in the market, even though they were right that the next big move would be down … they were just too early. Remember, markets do not tend to top overnight, and very rarely do stock market crashes occur at the highs, they usually happen after the trend has shifted.

## Trust the Analysts?

Many analysts had been bearish toward the NASDAQ and the stock market in general for several years prior to the market top in 2000. Several of these financial gurus, who conveniently have services available for a small fee, have been bearish toward the stock market since 1990, or even 1987. Several of them had missed the great bull market, and now are crowing about catching the bear. Be warned.

Often analysts, especially in raging bull markets, become personalities themselves. With the popularity of CNBC, especially, these stodgy people have become like rock stars, basking in the public light. However, like most things in the market, this is not new.

Ralph Wanger—Chief Investment Officer, Acorn Fund—summed it up wisely by saying, "Analysts are supposed to be critics of corporations. They often end up being public relations spokesmen for them."

Thus, it is not uncommon for analysts to all agree on the direction of a particular stock. Several services rank advisory services and analyst expectations regarding companies and the general market. Several studies have been performed that show when all of these financial professionals agree on the future direction of a particular issue, or more telling, the general direction of the market, they are often wrong.

Remember our example concerning the drop in Amazon.com's stock? As the stock plunged from $113 to $33 during a seven-month stretch, only 1 analyst out of 34 tracked by Bloomberg had issued a sell signal.

## Track Institutional Ownership?

Another popular indicator on the stock market is the percentage of institutional ownership. Many professional fund managers like to buy companies well before the pack, thinking that even if they are wrong on the stock, the flock of other institutions buying the company in the future can drive the price up.

On a similar vein, many successful investors only like to buy stocks in which a large number of company "insiders" are buying, and buying recently. After all, who knows a company's prospects better than the people who work there on a day-to-day basis in senior positions?

# Market Sentiment from the World of Derivatives

The interpretation of magazine covers, news stories, and analysts' estimates and ratings is more of an acquired skill and an art form than not. However, it illustrates a point that is a general theme in the market. People are often wrong at major turning points in the market, market professionals included!

An interesting look at this is provided by the VIX indicator, which is Chicago Board Options Exchanges Volatility Index. VIX is the average of implied volatilities of short term, *at-the-money* index options traded at the Chicago Board of Exchange (CBOE). An option represents the right to buy (*call options*) or sell (*put options*) a stock or an index at a particular price.

## Wall Street Words

**At-the-money** refers to the strike or exercise price of the option, with "at the money" meaning this price is very close to where the option is trading. A **call option** gives the buyer the right, but not the obligation, to purchase a particular stock or index at a specific price anytime during the life of the option. A **put option** gives the buyer the right, but not the obligation, to sell a particular stock or index at a specific price anytime during the life of the option

Dr.'s Black and Scholes won a Nobel Prize in economics for formulas that describe an option's fair market value. The core of this complex mathematical model is volatility, or how much the market will move over the next several days, weeks, and months. The VIX shows the level of variability that the market would have to demonstrate over the next month to make current option prices fair. In other words, VIX shows the amount of variability that the derivatives market is expecting in the future. The higher the VIX, the greater the volatility of the market, and the lower the VIX, the lesser the volatility being priced into options.

Volatility is akin to risk, so a high VIX means that the options market is pricing in increased risk, while a low VIX equates with lower risk. We have all been taught to look for low risk investments, so basically what the VIX implies by being high is that it is a good time to sell, while a low VIX and risk should be a good time to buy.

Normally, you might think that the derivatives market is for rocket scientists and Wall Street *quants*. Well, guess what? These guys and gals are no better at timing the markets and picking tops and bottoms than the analysts, newsletter writers, or magazine editors.

In other words, when the VIX is high, meaning that the options traders are pricing in an inordinate amount of risk, it is akin to hearing cocktail chatter or magazine headlines declaring the end of the world ... a contrarian buy signal. However, when VIX is low, implying the options traders are paying scant attention to risk and are overly optimistic, it is akin to hearing bullish tips when getting a shoe shine, or receiving hot stock tips by the score at a cocktail party ... a contrarian sell signal.

> **Wall Street Words**
>
> **Quants** are quantitative analysts—I'm one—or the math gurus, rocket scientists, and physicists who took their fancy math and modeling to Wall Street in the 1970's and 1980's to beat the market.

Remember, the contrarian moves against the crowd. If conventional wisdom says buy, you sell or vice versa. Thus, one may time the market by looking for periods of high implied volatilities in the options market as buy signals and periods of low volatility implied by the options traders as a sell signal.

# Using VIX to Time the Market

In the last five years, the VIX index has had a normal value of around 25 percent. Thus when the VIX gets above 30, it is high. Conversely, a reading of around 20 percent is low. For our use of the VIX in this book, we draw upon a study done by Victor

Niederhoffer and Laurel Kenner in their MSN Money column, the Speculator, which is available weekly on www.moneycentral.msn.com.

Niederhoffer and Kenner looked at VIX and tested the hypothesis that a VIX above 30 represented a good contrarian buy signal. They tested this hypothesis with the assumption that you would buy the S&P 500 Index the first time the VIX settled above 30 and hold the position until VIX declined to 25 or lower.

| Buy Date | VIX | S&P Close | Sell Date | VIX | S&P Close | S&P Change in Points | %Change in S&P |
|---|---|---|---|---|---|---|---|
| 10/27/97 | 39.96 | 876.99 | 12/1/97 | 24.88 | 974.77 | 97.78 | 11.1% |
| 12/24/97 | 30.47 | 932.70 | 12/30/97 | 24.93 | 970.84 | 38.14 | 4.1% |
| 1/9/98 | 34.46 | 927.69 | 1/14/98 | 24.21 | 927.94 | 0.25 | 0.0% |
| 8/4/98 | 33.10 | 1072.12 | 11/5/98 | 24.80 | 1133.85 | 61.73 | 5.8% |
| 12/14/98 | 32.47 | 1141.20 | 12/18/98 | 24.66 | 1188.03 | 46.83 | 4.1% |
| 1/13/99 | 31.26 | 1234.40 | 3/8/99 | 24.98 | 1282.73 | 48.33 | 3.9% |
| 9/23/99 | 30.28 | 1280.41 | 10/6/99 | 23.53 | 1325.40 | 44.99 | 3.5% |
| 10/15/99 | 31.48 | 1247.41 | 10/21/99 | 24.77 | 1283.61 | 36.20 | 2.9% |
| 4/5/00 | 30.59 | 1487.37 | 6/1/00 | 24.74 | 1448.81 | -38.56 | -2.6% |
| 10/11/00 | 30.95 | 1364.59 | 1/23/01 | 23.86 | 1360.00 | -4.59 | -0.3% |
| 2/28/01 | 31.00 | 1239.00 | 5/1/01 | 24.51 | 1258.00 | 19.00 | 1.5% |

*Compliments of Niederhoffer and Kenner's Speculator article dated May 3, 2001 available at http://moneycentral.msn.com/articles/invest/extra/6693.asp.*

From October 2, 1997 to May 1, 2001 the VIX indicator has crossed above 30 eleven times. Following a buying an S&P 500 Index on each of these higher than 30 VIX signals and holding the index until the VIX went to 25 or lower would have yielded nine profitable trades and two unprofitable trades, for an average gain of 3.1 percent over an average holding period of roughly 29 days.

Three percent in 29 days does not sound that impressive at first glance. However, if you were able to capture this rate of return for one full year, it would be roughly a whopping 27 percent rate of return.

In total during the period studies, the S&P 500 Index gained roughly 43.5 percent, over a total of roughly 900 trading sessions. Using the VIX timing method, a market timer could have captured a total return of roughly 34 percent and only been exposed to market risk about one third of the amount of time. In other words, the VIX timing method captured over 80 percent of the total gains in the market, but only had the speculator invested 33 percent of the time.

# A Final Word on Being a Contrarian

It has been said that to be successful you need to either do things much better than the average person, or much differently. The contrarian looks at the world and the markets from a different vantage point, and when applied properly, this can be quite beneficial to their investing bottom line.

Many people consider the true value investors to be contrarians, because though they may not look at magazine covers, or watch the VIX, they do tend to seek out invest ments that are currently being shunned by the marketplace, which is why they are "values." The most famous members of this club of market contrarians are Warren Buffet and his infamous Berkshire Hathaway company, and Fidelity Magellan Fund manager, Peter Lynch.

However, being a contrarian can be a lonely endeavor. Though the professionals and the press are often wrong at major market turning points, as we hopefully demon-strated in this chapter, they are often right for the bulk of a long term trend.

**Timing Tips** _____

Contrarian investing is one of the general themes throughout this book. It does not have to be limited to looking at magazine covers, or esoteric indicators like the VIX, but can also be applied to looking at industry groups and such. Value invest-ing is one form of contrary investing, in that value investors buy stocks that are being avoided by others. The value investor believes that these stocks are under-priced, meaning that others who are selling it to them are wrong. If that is not a con-trarian act, I am not sure what is.

## The Least You Need to Know

♦ Markets tend to make tops on excess enthusiasm. When everyone is buying stocks—not on current business conditions, but expectations of improving busi-ness conditions from already remarkable conditions—a warning flag should be flashing at you.

♦ By the time something is common knowledge, it tends to be already priced into the marketplace for stocks. This is evident by the fact that major business peri-odicals that run front cover stories, especially those proclaiming a bull or bear market with no end in sight, tend to hit the newsstands just as the market is about to turn.

◆ Stock market professionals are very good at catching the bulk of the market's major trend. However, they tend to be extremely wrong at major turning points. They do not have crystal balls to foretell the future, so be sure to take great enthusiasm from them with a grain of salt.

◆ A major sign of a market top is when buying stock becomes the only prudent thing to do according to conventional wisdom. The exact opposite mass mood is prevalent at market bottoms; when all shun the idea of the stock market, it is typically a good time to buy.

◆ The VIX indicator is the Chicago Board Options Exchanges Volatility Index, which is the average of implied volatilities of short term, at-the-money index options traded at the Chicago Board of Exchange (CBOE).

◆ Even the Wall Street gurus or derivatives traders tend to get caught up in this enthusiasm and tend to be wrong at major market turning points. By watching indicators such as the CBOE's VIX index, the marketplace's attitude toward risk can be gauged, and prudent speculators tend to do the opposite of this crowd mentality when it is at an extreme.

# Part  3

## Economically Speaking

Most of the large day-to-day moves in the stock market are trumpeted by the press and Wall Street as being reactions to expectations of changes in policy by the Federal Reserve.

Inside this part, we examine the Federal Reserve (the Fed), its origins, and how this institution attempts to guide the economy and ultimately the stock market. We look at different Fed policies and how when they change, the stock market reacts, explaining whether Fed actions should be followed or ignored, and which segments of the stock market tend to perform the best as the economy moves from growth to recession.

# Chapter 7

# The Almighty Federal Reserve

## In This Chapter

- The economy and stocks
- The bankers' bank, the Federal Reserve
- The purpose of the Fed and its tools
- Don't fight the Fed

In the previous chapters we looked at the stock market from strictly a chart- or price-based viewpoint. Though, much of this work—especially the Dow theory and contrarian thinking—deal with the psychology of the market, we have not touched upon the relationship between the stock market and the economy.

In this chapter, we will begin to examine this relationship, by looking at the Federal Reserve, how it functions, and what effects this institution has on the markets and the economy.

# The Economy and Stocks

One of my own mentors and a very well-known speculator once put the relationship of the markets and the economy into perspective for me. Instead of thinking of the relationship as a "hodgepodge" of economic statistics and numbers, he said to think of the economy as an ecosystem and the markets as different flora and fauna within this system.

**Timing Tips**

In the next chapter, we examine the stock market under various conditions, and explain in more detail the relationship between stocks and the economy. But, generally speaking, the stronger the economy, the stronger the stock market. However, the stock market tends to move several months ahead of the actual economy, so it tends to reflect not current conditions, but perceived future conditions.

This example can best be illustrated using a conversation between two animated lions that took place in the animated Disney movie, *The Lion King*. The king lion (Mufasa) explains to his cub (Simba), the future king, that he is a part of the great circle of life. He points out that lions eat antelopes and when the lion dies, his body is consumed by the grass, which the antelopes eat. As such, each animal from the lowly grasshopper to the great lion is connected.

In an ecosystem, all the components are in some way connected. For example, if grasshoppers get too plentiful and eat too much grass, the antelopes will suffer, which in turn will eventually cause the lion prides to suffer. So even though the grasshopper and the lion are not directly associated with each other in the food chain, they are connected.

Companies operate within the economy in a similar fashion. Though a cement company may not seem to be directly connected to a software company, they both operate in the same business environment, known as the economy. Thus, an economic drought or recession will probably hurt them both even though their products are radically different. The software company will sell less software due to the trying economic times and the reluctance of businesses and consumers to buy new or upgrade software, while the lack of new construction will most likely hurt the cement company as well.

At the core of the circle of life on the plains of Africa is rainfall, which is the main dictator of the supply of grass, barring other factors. For the economic ecosystem, the core factor is interest rates, or the cost of money. Though money can't buy love and happiness, it surely does make the economic world go 'round.

# Phases of the Economy and Interest Rates

Interest rates are simply the cost of money. Interest is the cost of borrowing money, or the benefit received for lending it. For example, assume you deposit $10,000 in the bank. For the privilege of using your money, the bank pays you interest, usually expressed as a percentage, such as 3 percent.

Now, if you wish to borrow $10,000 from the bank, you have to pay them interest—which is almost always higher than the rate you would receive depositing the money in the bank. Thus, the level of interest rates is a reflection of the cost of money, whether you are a borrower or a lender.

Interest rates are a function of the supply and demand of money. When the demand for money (the need for borrowing) exceeds the supply of money available to lend, the lenders demand a higher rate of interest. Thus, if the borrower really wishes to borrow, then he must pay the asking rate. However, when the supply of money exceeds the demand for it, interest rates tend to decline as borrowers may opt not to borrow money if the rate being charged is too high.

When interest rates are put into economic per-spective, they tend to reflect the general level of economic activity, as borrowers tend to drive the interest rate market.

**Timing Tips**

Interest rates reflect the price of money. Under this theory, businesses will bor-row en mass when they perceive opportunities that will give returns well in excess of interest rates, or borrowing costs. However, when no such opportu-nities are perceived, they will refrain from borrowing and rates will go lower. Thus, just as stocks are a reflection of future eco-nomic activity, so are interest rates.

# Interest Rates and the Economy

During periods of economic distress, interest rates tend to be lower, as the demand for money is less. Thus, during recessions and such, the supply of money tends to outstrip the demand for money, and interest rates decline. During periods of eco-nomic growth, interest rates tend to rise, as the demand for money outstrips the demand for it.

Think about it this way. During bad economic times, I may be less apt to borrow money. First, because my income is probably lower and thus the payment of interest creates an additional expense. Secondly, the investment environment is in such bad economic times that businesses can't pencil out a profit from borrowing the money and investing it in more productive areas, such as plant and equipment. Thus the demand component of money dries up, sending interest rates lower.

During strong economic times, many companies will stand in line to borrow money, as they can borrow money at 10 percent, and invest it in plant and equipment and make a return of 20 percent. When the environment is good, and businesses foresee this continuing, they gladly borrow money to invest in more profitable ventures.

> ### Bet You Didn't Know
>
> Generally, low interest rates tend to encourage economic expansion, while higher rates tend to discourage economic expansion. The 1970s are the exception that makes the rule. High interest rates in the 1970s were due to inflation, which is covered in Chapter 16 on bonds. Basically, prices were rising so fast that the repaid dollars from debt instruments would buy less, thus rates had to be high to compensate for the loss of purchasing power.

But eventually this cycle feeds upon itself, and causes its own change. For example, at the bottom of a recession, rates get so low that more and more businesses find it attractive—even with the difficult economic climate—to borrow money and invest in a higher returning asset. This causes the economy to grow and be lifted out of recession.

However, eventually the rush to borrow and invest creates both heavy debt burdens and drives up the cost of money, making fewer and fewer investments profitable. As costs increase, reducing returns, businesses slow down on borrowing money and the economy turns, back toward recession.

Of course this is an idealized version, but it serves to demonstrate how the economy in general, and the fortunes of businesses and their stock prices in particular, are affected by interest rates.

Besides the supply and demand for money, the greatest influence on interest rates and the economy comes from a government institution, the Federal Reserve Board. This is our national bank and is trusted with insuring the soundness of our national banking system. It is very important for all market participants to understand the Federal Reserve and how they operate.

# The Federal Reserve: Creation and Purpose

Just prior to the founding of the Federal Reserve, the nation was plagued with financial crises. At times, these crises led to "panics" in which people raced to their banks to withdraw their deposits. A particularly severe panic in 1907 resulted in bank runs that wreaked havoc on the fragile banking system and ultimately led Congress in 1913 to write the Federal Reserve Act. Initially created to address these banking panics, the Federal Reserve is now charged with a number of broader responsibilities, including fostering a sound banking system and a healthy economy.

---

| Bet You Didn't Know |
| --- |

It appears that the Federal Reserve may not be totally beyond politics. As a way of staying apolitical, the Federal Reserve has tended to strongly avoid raising interest rates in election years or very closely to presidential elections. This may be part of the reason why the year prior to elections and election years tend to be some of the better performing years for the stock market historically.

Congress oversees the entire Federal Reserve System. And the Fed must work within the objectives established by Congress. Yet, Congress gave the Federal Reserve the autonomy to carry out its responsibilities insulated from political pressure. Here are the Fed's three parts:

◆ The Board of Governors

◆ The regional Reserve banks

◆ The Federal Open Market Committee

Each operates independently of the federal government to carry out the Fed's core responsibilities. The goal of the three parts is to guide the economy at sustainable growth with low inflation.

## Board of Governors

At the core of the Federal Reserve System is the Board of Governors, or Federal Reserve Board. The Board of Governors, located in Washington, D.C., is a federal government agency that is the Fed's centralized component. The Board consists of seven members—called governors—who are appointed by the president of the United States and confirmed by the Senate. These governors guide the Federal Reserve's policy actions.

Governors actively lead committees that study prevailing economic issues—from affordable housing and consumer banking laws to interstate banking and electronic commerce. The Board also exercises broad supervisory control over certain state-chartered financial institutions, called member banks, as well as the companies that own banks. This ensures that commercial banks operate responsibly and comply with federal regulations and that the nation's payments system functions smoothly. In addition, the Board oversees the activities of Reserve banks, approving the appointments of their presidents and three members of the Reserve banks' boards of directors.

## Regional Reserve Banks

The Federal Reserve System is divided into 12 districts. Each district is served by a regional Reserve bank, most of which have one or more branches. Reserve bank activities serve primarily three audiences—bankers, the U.S. Treasury, and the public. Reserve banks are often called the "bankers' banks," because they store commercial banks' excess currency and coins and they process and settle their checks and electronic payments. Reserve banks also supervise commercial banks in their regions.

*Twelve Reserve banks and their branches.*

| 1 BOSTON | 2 NEW YORK | 3 PHILADELPHIA | 4 CLEVELAND | 5 RICHMOND | 6 ATLANTA |
|---|---|---|---|---|---|
| | Buffalo | | Cincinnati<br>Pittsburgh | Baltimore<br>Charlotte | Birmingham<br>Jacksonville<br>Miami<br>Nashville<br>New Orleans |
| 7 CHICAGO | 8 ST. LOUIS | 9 MINNEAPOLIS | 10 KANSAS CITY | 11 DALLAS | 12 SAN FRANCISCO |
| Detroit | Little Rock<br>Louisville<br>Memphis | Helena | Denver<br>Oklahoma City<br>Omaha | El Paso<br>Houston<br>San Antonio | Los Angeles<br>Portland<br>Salt Lake City<br>Seattle |

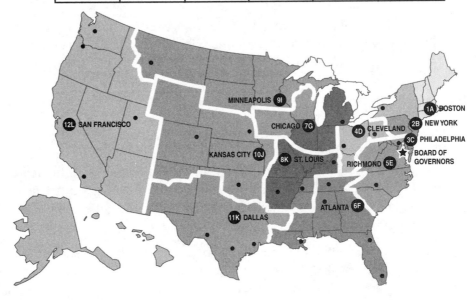

As banks for the U.S. government, Reserve banks process the Treasury's payments, sell its securities, and assist with its cash management and investment activities. Finally, Reserve banks conduct research on the national and regional economies, prepare Reserve bank presidents for their participation in the Federal Open Market Committee (FOMC) and disseminate information about the economy through publications, speeches, educational workshops, and websites.

**Timing Tips**

The most important Federal Reserve Bank in the country is the New York bank. Not only because New York is the financial capital of the world, but because the Federal Reserve Bank of New York is charged with conducting the Fed's Open Market operations, or the buying and selling of treasury securities designed to increase or decrease liquidity in the banking system and affect interest rates.

## Federal Open Market Committee

The Federal Open Market Committee, or FOMC, is the Fed's chief body for monetary policy-making. Its voting membership combines the seven members of the Board of Governors, the president of the Federal Reserve Bank of New York and four other Reserve bank presidents, who serve one-year terms on a rotating basis. The chairman of the FOMC is also the chairman of the Board of Governors.

The FOMC typically meets eight times a year in Washington, D.C. At each meeting, a senior official of the Federal Reserve Bank of New York discusses developments in the financial and foreign exchange markets, as well as activities of the New York Fed's domestic and foreign trading desks. Staff from the Board of Governors then present their economic and financial forecasts. In addition, the Board's governors and all 12 Reserve bank presidents—whether they are voting members that year or not—offer their views on the economic outlook.

Armed with this wealth of up-to-date national and regional information, the FOMC discusses the monetary policy options that would best promote the economy's sustainable growth. After all participants have deliberated the options, members vote on a directive that is issued to the New York Fed's domestic trading desk. This directive informs the desk of the committee's objective for "open market operations"—whether to ease, tighten, or maintain the current policy. The desk then buys or sells U.S. government securities on the open market to achieve this objective.

**Timing Tips**

Federal Open Market Committee (FOMC) meetings are closely watched and may cause extreme volatility in the markets. Interest in watching the Fed has become so intense that often the market will sell off on interest rate decreases and rally on increases, short term, when the rate changes fail to live up to expectations. For example, the most recent Fed cut of $1/4$ point was greeted with a sharp market break, as the market was expecting $1/2$ point. Treat expectations of the Fed like earnings expectations— they'd better be met or there will be heck to pay.

# Chairman of the Fed Board

Heading the Board is the chairman. As the head of the nation's bank, when the chairman speaks, Wall Street and the public listen!

The Chairman of the Federal Reserve Board is appointed by the U.S. president to serve four-year terms. The chairman of the Board of Governors has a highly visible position. He reports twice a year to Congress on the Fed's monetary policy objectives, testifies before Congress on numerous other issues, and meets periodically with the Secretary of the Treasury. Other Board officials are also called to testify before Congress, and they maintain regular contact with other government organizations as well.

> **Trading Traps**
>
> Remember the old E. F. Hutton commercials that said, "When E. F. Hutton talks, people listen!"? Though E. F. Hutton has long since merged with another Wall Street firm, this same sentiment can apply to the Chairman of the Federal Reserve's speeches and testimonies to Congress. Watch for extreme market volatility on these days and the days preceding such events. Though Fed Governors are aware of the influence their mere words can have on the international markets, they speak in cryptic fashion, which is carefully rehearsed. This "Fed speak" may be part of the problem. Be careful, but usually the effects are short-lived.

Probably the Chairman's most important responsibility is participating on the Federal Open Market Committee (FOMC), the committee that directs the nation's monetary policy. As head of the institution that is charged with guiding the world's largest economy, Wall Street closely monitors all of the Chairman's speeches and public comments for clues as to how the Federal Reserve will guide the economy in the future.

# Tools of the Federal Reserve

The Fed uses three main tools to carry out its monetary policy goals:

◆ Reserve requirements

◆ Open market operations

◆ Discount rate and discount window

All three tools affect the amount of funds in the banking system.

## Reserve Requirements

Reserve requirements are the portions of deposits that banks must hold in reserve, either in their vaults or on deposit at a Reserve bank. The Board of Governors has sole authority over changes to reserve requirements.

All banks must hold a certain percentage of their money on deposit in reserve. This is necessary to meet depositors' cash needs, as most deposits in banks are demand deposits, meaning the funds are available upon request, as opposed to time deposits, like CD's, which are available only after a certain period of time without penalty.

Because banks make money by loaning out money, to ensure their liquidity they must hold reserves. The amount of reserves held is dictated by the Federal Reserve. If the Federal Reserve wishes to tighten the reins on monetary expansion, it will increase the reserve requirement, thus restricting the amount of money available to lend and drive up interest rates. If they wish to loosen the supply of money and lower interest rates to foster economic growth, they decrease the reserve requirement, increasing the available supply of money to lend.

**Timing Tips**

The Federal Reserve compiles its economic outlook, statistics, and thoughts in a report known as the Beige Book, due to the color of the original report. For more information on the Federal Reserve visit www.federalreserve.gov.

This tool has been little used in recent decades, as the reserve requirement has stayed relatively stable. However, be aware that the Fed has this tool to guide the economy and may use it.

## Open Market Operations

By far, the most frequently used tool is open market operations, which involve the buying and selling of U.S. government securities.

After each FOMC meeting, the committee issues a directive to the domestic trading desk at the New York Fed. This directive reflects the committee's policy goals: easing, tightening, or maintaining the growth of the nation's money supply.

Several times a week, the domestic trading desk buys or sells Treasury securities on the open market. The term "open market" means that the Fed doesn't decide on its own which securities dealers it will do business with. Rather, various securities dealers compete on the basis of price. When the Fed wishes to increase reserves, it buys securities; when it wishes to reduce reserves, it sells securities. Because open market operations greatly affect the amount of money and credit banks have on hand, they ultimately affect interest rates and the performance of the U.S. economy.

## Discount Rate and Discount Window

The discount rate is the interest rate that Reserve banks charge banks for short-term loans. Discount rate changes are made by Reserve banks and the Board of Governors.

One of the most important ways that the Fed ensures safety and soundness of the banking system is acting as lender of last resort. Through its discount window, the Fed lends money to banks so that a shortage of funds at one institution does not disrupt the flow of money and credit in the entire banking system. The rate of interest charged at the *discount window* is known as the *discount rate*, and is closely watched by Wall Street for clues as to the Fed's bias for longer-term raising or cutting of interest rates.

Typically, the Fed makes loans to satisfy a bank's unanticipated needs for short-term funds. But the Fed also makes longer-term loans to help banks manage seasonal fluctuations in their customers' deposit or credit demands. Agricultural banks, whose customers need funds for spring planting and can repay these funds after the fall harvest, often take advantage of the Fed's seasonal borrowing program.

### Wall Street Words

The rate that the Federal Reserve charges from its discount window is known as the **discount rate**. The **discount window** is often referred to as the window of last resort, and most banks will avoid routinely borrowing from it for fear it could give the impression that they are in trouble. As such, the discount window is rarely used and the discount rate is considered largely symbolic.

When Congress established the Federal Reserve, it charged the Fed with the critical task of providing a safe and efficient method of transferring funds throughout the banking system. Reserve banks and their branches carry out this mission, offering financial services to all financial institutions in the United States, regardless of size or location. Hand in hand with that mission is the obligation to improve the payments system by encouraging the use of efficient procedures and technology.

Essentially, a Reserve bank serves as a bankers' bank, offering a wide variety of financial services. It distributes currency and coin, processes checks and offers electronic forms of payment. The Fed competes with the private sector in its financial services to foster competition in the marketplace and promote innovation and efficiency in the payments system. It does not seek to make a profit from its participation; it sets prices only to recover costs.

Though the discount rate is largely symbolic, as most large banks do business in the Federal Funds market to meet their short-term liquidity needs, changes in the discount rate often go hand in hand with changes in the federal funds rate, and the general level of interest rates.

In fact, there is an old Wall Street saying, "Don't fight the Fed," which shows how much Wall Street respects the power of the Federal Reserve and the influence they can exhibit on the economy.

# Don't Fight the Fed

Given that the Federal Reserve is charged with guiding our economy, and the economy is the environment in which companies conduct business, it is no wonder there exists a relationship between the Federal Reserve and Wall Street.

Though the Federal Reserve can only affect the interest rate paid by banks to other banks (the fed funds rate) or the rate charged at the discount window (the discount rate), these changes have a ripple effect throughout the entire banking system.

When the federal funds rate is increased, the Federal Reserve does this by providing less money to the banking system. It does this by not buying U.S. Treasury securities from banks. This lack of payments for the securities decreases the bank reserves (money in their safes). However, banks must keep some money around in reserve, the minimum amount that is set by the reserve requirement. After all, they have people to pay. So banks then raise short-term interest rates to decrease lending of their reserves in reaction to an increase in the federal funds rate or a change in the discount rate.

When the Federal Reserve lowers the federal funds or discount rate, it does so by injecting money into the banking system. It does this by buying U.S. Treasury securities from banks. The payments for these securities increase the bank reserves (money in their safe). Since banks make money by lending money, the extra money is set to be loaned out so they can make a profit. To encourage borrowing, the banks then cut short-term interest rates to spur lending of their reserves.

When interest rates are rising, people are spending less and it is more difficult to attract clients and market products. Thus companies' sales suffer, which usually corresponds to lower earnings and thus, lower stock.

# Fed and Market Performance

It has been well documented that in the past, changes in Federal Reserve policy have led to changes in the stock market. For example, it is generally well-accepted Wall Street wisdom that lowering of the federal funds and/or discount rate led to higher stock prices over the course of the next year, while higher rates are bearish, leading to substandard returns or lower stock prices.

**CAUTION** **Trading Traps**

Though the Chairman of the Federal Reserve has often been described as the most powerful man alive and the Federal Reserve as the most powerful institution, even they cannot seem to halt a market movement bent on happening. Following the last five cuts in the federal funds rate and discount rate in 2001, the stock market still finished lower a year later. Don't fight the Fed may be good Wall Street wisdom, but it isn't necessarily always right, either!

However, in this most recent bear market, which started in 2000, the Federal Reserve, which had been aggressively lowering rates, has been ineffectual in changing the course of the bear market.

For example, in January of 2001, the Federal Reserve lowered the discount rate three times, dropping it from 6.00 percent to 5.00 percent and the federal funds twice, dropping it from 6.50 percent to 5.50 percent, yet the market was still –8.9 percent lower as measured by the Dow Jones Industrials on a year-over-year basis.

The following table shows changes in the discount rate and federal funds rates and the effect it has had on the Dow Jones Industrial Average over the course of the year following changes in interest rates.

|  | Discount Rate (%) | Federal Funds Rates (%) | Dow Return 1 Year Later |
|---|---|---|---|
| January 1996 | 5.00 | 5.25 | 26.3% |
| March 1997 | 5.00 | 5.50 | 33.7% |
| September 1998 | 5.00 | 5.25 | 31.8% |
| October 1998 | 4.75 | 5.00 | 24.9% |
| November 1998 | 4.50 | 4.75 | 19.3% |
| June 1999 | 4.50 | 5.00 | -4.8% |
| August 1999 | 4.75 | 5.25 | 3.6% |
| November 1999 | 5.00 | 5.50 | -4.3% |
| February 2000 | 5.25 | 5.75 | 3.6% |
| March 2000 | 5.50 | 6.00 | -9.6% |
| May 2000 | 6.00 | 6.50 | 3.7% |
| January 3, 2001 | 5.75 | 6.00 | -8.9% |
| January 4, 2001 | 5.50 | 6.00 | -8.9% |

|  | Discount Rate (%) | Federal Funds Rates (%) | Dow Return 1 Year Later |
|---|---|---|---|
| January 31, 2001 | 5.00 | 5.50 | -8.9% |
| March 2001 | 4.50 | 5.00 | -3.7% |
| April 2001 | 4.00 | 4.50 | -7.3% |
| May 2001 | 3.50 | 4.00 | -9.0% |

This is surprising, given that generally in past cycles, the Federal Reserve has been a pretty good indicator for timing the market.

However, the more modern history you look at, the less effectual this indicator becomes. As I have mentioned and will mention throughout this book, these cycles can be fleeting and ever changing, so even when considering the Federal Reserve, it is best to look for a confluence of indicators and studies before investing too heavily in the stock market.

Part of the reason why the Fed may have been ineffectual is that changes in the Federal Reserve target rates (fed funds and the discount rate) are now widely anticipated, with many traders and fund managers acting ahead of the news. Also, the Greenspan Fed, though quite effective, has taken a role of following commercial interest rates, instead of changing them. Thus, the market is less taken by surprise and therefore less susceptible to changes in these key rates.

However, despite its current poor performance, investors should still watch closely for changes, as many on Wall Street respect the power of the Fed, and as such, so should we.

## The Least You Need to Know

- The stock market and the economy are closely tied together. Economic conditions make up the environment in which companies do business, and as such it affects their earnings, which will eventually affect their market performance.

- Interest rates are a reflection of the cost of money. During a strong economy, interest rates tend to be increasing, as the demand for money outweighs the supply. During a weak economy, rates tend to be low or falling as the demand for money dries up.

- The Federal Reserve is charged with guiding the United States Economy toward sustainable growth with low inflation. The Fed uses reserve requirements, open market operations and the discount rate to steer money supply and interest rates to help guide the economy toward its goals.

◆ Though the Fed does not control interest rates in the private sector, they do set the federal funds rate—the rate that banks charge each other for overnight transactions, as well as the discount rate. Both of these rates affect the banks' cost of capital, and therefore affect the general level of interest rates.

◆ Changes in interest rates affect the economy, which is why the Fed targets to influence rates. Generally high interest rates slow down economic growth, while low interest rates encourage growth.

◆ Wall Street lore holds that when the Fed lowers rates, the stock market benefits. Though this observation, which has been coined as "Don't fight the Fed," has historically been very accurate, in recent years its performance has been mediocre at best. Perhaps this cycle is changing, but due to the Fed's enormous influence on the economy, it is still worth noting and respecting.

# Chapter 8

# The FED, the Economy, Rates, and the Market

## In This Chapter

- ◆ Reviewing the Fed, the economy, and interest rates
- ◆ Three steps and a stumble
- ◆ Two steps and a jump
- ◆ The current environment

In the previous chapter we highlighted the Federal Reserve and how it attempts to guide the economy and inflation by controlling interest rates. We then saw how interest rates can help guide the economy through a regular cycle of contractions and expansion, or recession and growth. As the economy ebbs and flows, the stock market is gyrated. Not by what is going on today, but on perceptions of what will happen in the future.

We also noted how different sectors of the economy tended to lead and how that leadership changed as the economy rose out of recession and into growth, and then heated up and moved back toward recession. In this chapter, we will start off with tying together the Fed and the business cycle a little more completely to really drive home the point that the two are very interconnected, and put that into the perspective of the general stock market.

Along the way, I will show you two highly watched indicators, which are easy to track, based on Fed action, and finally finish up with a discussion as to why the old rules are not working and whether or not this cycle will change.

# Reviewing the Fed, the Economy, and Interest Rates

The Federal Reserve System was established in 1913 as a reaction to financial crisis. The purpose of the Fed is to provide the United States with a safer, more flexible, and more stable monetary and financial system.

Over the years, its roles have evolved and expanded. Today, the Federal Reserve's duties include conducting the nation's monetary policy by influencing money and credit conditions in the economy in pursuit of full employment and stable prices. The Federal Reserve is also responsible for promoting the stability of the financial system, as well as providing banking services to depository institutions and to the federal government. The Fed is also charged with ensuring that consumers receive adequate information and fair treatment in their interactions with the banking system.

---

**Bet You Didn't Know**

During the crash of 1913, the famous financier JP Morgan acted in a fashion very similar to the Fed; he staved off a bank panic by lending money to other competing banks. The Fed was established in reaction to panic and still serves this role in times of panic. Typically following a financial panic, such as the crash of 1987, the failure of Long Term Capital Management, or the sharp break in dot.com stocks in 2000, the Fed usually lowers interest rates to stave off panic and restore faith in the banking system. Sometimes their actions work, sometimes they don't, as far as stock averages are concerned.

---

## The Fed Guides the Economy

Though providing banking services to depository institutions (banks) and the Federal government as well as ensuring that consumers receive adequate information and fair treatment in their interactions with the banking system are important parts of the Federal Reserve's duties; as investors and market timers we are concerned with their role in conducting the nation's monetary policy by influencing money and credit conditions.

As discussed in the previous chapter on the Federal Reserve, the Fed influences the economy through monetary policy.

The Federal Reserve conducts monetary policy using three major tools:

♦ Open market operations—The buying and selling of U.S. Treasury and Federal agency securities in the open market.

♦ Discount rate—The interest rate charged depository institutions on loans from their Federal Reserve Bank's lending facility (the Discount Window).

♦ Reserve Requirements—Requirements regarding the amount of funds that depository institutions must hold in reserve against deposits made by their customers.

Using these tools, the Federal Reserve influences the demand for and supply of balances that depository institutions (banks and savings and loans) hold on deposit at Federal Reserve banks (the key component of reserves) and thus, the federal funds Rate—the rate at which depository institutions trade balances at the Federal Reserve.

**Timing Tips**

The most commonly used tool by the Fed is open market operations, or the buying and selling of U.S. Treasury and federal agency securities in the open market. The most highly publicized tool is changes in the fed funds target rate or discount rate. Usually changes in these levels cause great cheer or panic in the stock market. For the last several years, the Fed has kept reserve requirements very static. However, should they decide to change reserve requirements, look on lower reserve requirements as bullish and increased reserve requirements as bearish.

Changes in the federal funds rate trigger a chain of events that affect other short-term interest rates, foreign exchange rates, long-term interest rates, the amount of money and credit, and, ultimately, a range of economic variables, including employment, output, and prices of goods and services.

## Fed Stimulation

When the Federal Reserve wishes to increase economic activity, seeking its goals of full employment and stable price, it works to increase the amount of money in circulation, thus paving the way for economic growth.

To stimulate the economy the Fed lowers its target rate for federal funds. As the laws of supply and demand dictate, by lowering the cost of money the demand for it will increase. If people have more demand for money, they will use that money to buy things, which will cause corporations to produce more, increase employment, creating a chain reaction under ideal circumstances that end up with the economy expanding and stock prices going up as earnings increase.

**Wall Street Words**

The **law of supply** says that prices move in the opposite direction of supply: increases in supply equal lower prices while decreasing supply should result in higher prices. The **law of demand** says that demand moves opposite price as well. Higher prices lead to lower demand and lower prices lead to more demand.

The *law of supply* dictates that the price of a given product is a direct function of the availability of the product. Under the law of supply, as price increases sellers are more willing to provide large quantities of their product to the marketplace, and when prices are low sellers are less willing to provide product to the market.

The *law of demand* dictates that the price of a given product is a direct function of the demand for it. Under the law of demand, as price decreases the demand for the product increases as buyers are more willing to purchase it; as the price of a product increases, buyers are less willing to purchase it according to the law of demand.

Thus, by decreasing federal funds interest rates, the banks that deposit their excess reserves with the Federal Reserve will look to get a better return by lending that money out. The banks, or depository institutions will lend money more freely to the consumers and corporations, who in turn will spend it on goods and services, or on increasing their production capacity.

They will increase their use of money and borrowed money because it is cheaper. Rework the law of demand for a moment. If demand for a product is a function of the price of that product, then is the price of that product not a function of the demand?

A corollary to the law of supply and demand is that the cheaper a product is, the higher the demand for it will be. Though, like many things in economics this is not always true; it is true with regards to money, and the cost of money is interest rates.

As any first-year MBA student can tell you, if you can borrow money at X percent and get Y percent on it, then by all means you should do it. Now think for a moment about interest rates. If a company can borrow money for a new factory and increase production by 15 percent and decrease costs by 15 percent, and borrow that money at 5 percent, then they will.

**CAUTION**

### Trading Traps

Economists and people fresh out of school assume that if you can borrow money at X percent and get Y percent you should as long as Y percent is less than X percent. However, the reality of the marketplace doesn't always offer a stable return on an investment. For example, a popular play on this in recent years has been to borrow money in Japan at very low rates and invest it in the United States in stocks. With stock prices falling, the interest rate differential was outdone by falling stock prices, and losses have been incurred. There is no such thing as a guaranteed rate of return on anything but Treasury securities, and the rate is only guaranteed on them if you hold to maturity.

Thus, by lowering interest rates, and repeatedly lowering interest rates, the Fed is stimulating the economy, as eventually the cost of money will become cheap enough to stimulate investment.

Investment in plant and equipment also serves the Fed's other goal, that of insuring maximum employment. In order to build a new factory, or even to buy a new accounting system or any other investment, jobs are created or retained.

For example, if a company decides to build a new factory, then a construction company will get the contract to build that factory. The construction company will then hire plumbers, electricians, carpenters, and other craftsmen to build that factory. These people, having a good job for the next several years, may then in turn buy a new television set from the local electronics store, which in turn may have to hire additional sales help.

Thus by reducing the cost of money, the Federal Reserve is able to increase employment as well as stimulate the economy.

However, the law of supply also plays a role in this. When the price of money drops (interest rates) then lenders are less willing to lend, because their returns are lower. However, this is not always the case, because most lenders are in the business of lending money.

Banks look at money as a good. In essence, they have two basic options of what to do with their money. They can hold it and deposit it with the

### Timing Tips

Investment in plant and equipment or expansion of a business creates more wealth in the economy in a ripple effect fashion, known as a Keysian Multiplier effect. Building creates jobs. Jobs create demand for goods and services, which in turn creates more building. The driving force behind this under certain conditions can be Fed action, but changes in rates usually take six to nine months to begin to take effect.

Federal Reserve and get a declining rate of return because the Federal Funds rate is decreasing, or they can lend it out and get a better rate of return. Well, their cost of money, the amount that they pay on deposits, decreases along with interest rates, so even as interest rates decline, their profit margins to a certain extent remain the same. Thus, decreasing interest rates do not cause diminished returns in the short run, and hence they are apt to loan money.

**Timing Tips**

The Fed also has to manage the money supply or liquidity of the financial system when trying to influence the economy. The Fed may lower its target rate, but if banks have few qualified borrowers or the demand for money is scarce, prices (interest rates) may have to fall by a lot to entice borrowers to take the risk. This is why the Fed usually raises or lowers rates several times in a row.

## Fed Contractions

The Federal Reserve has two main responsibilities that affect investors the greatest, the goals of full employment as well as the goal of price stability. These two goals can be mutually exclusive at many points.

When employment is running high, people have more money and they are apt to spend it—after all what is money for. People have more money when employment is running high, or unemployment is low, because labor—which is what all of us are in one sense of the word or the other—is in tight supply.

**Timing Tips**

Employment is a key factor of the economy. People spend more when they have money and jobs, and less when they are fearful of losing either. Thus, employment levels are important to the stock market and the economy.

Don't take our word for it, though; just watch the stock market on the first Friday of the month, when the monthly employment report is released. Historically, this is the most volatile day of the month.

Think of an employee as a bushel of corn. If you need 50 bushels of corn every month, you go to your local farmer or grain elevator and buy those bushels. However, when a drought hits, and the farmer does not produce a very big crop that year, the price of corn will go up because it is in tight supply. So if the farmer or grain elevator only has

200 bushels of corn and you, as well as many other local users, are demanding those bushels, they will raise the price because they know they will run out of supply and have to buy more at a higher price.

Labor works the same way. It is easier to demand a raise from your boss when there are few qualified people who can do your job available in your boss' eyes. As the law of supply dictates, the price of a given product is a direct function of the availability of the product. Thus, when employment is full, the cost of labor increases.

**Timing Tips**

When unemployment is low, labor costs tend to be high. When unemployment is high, labor costs tend to be low. This is simple supply and demand at work. Labor is a cost of business and negatively affects earnings. However, high employment also means strong demand from consumers, which is usually positive for earnings. The trick is seeing whether labor costs or earnings increase faster. If costs rise faster, profits and stock prices fall. If earnings increase faster, stock prices rise. It is this relationship that turns markets from bullish to bearish and bearish to bullish.

Part of the goal of the Federal Reserve is to ensure price stability. This in actuality means to control inflation, or widespread price increases across the economy. A key component of this is the labor market, as labor is involved in all aspects of the production of goods and services.

When the labor market gets tight, the cost of labor increases. As the cost of labor increases, the cost of production increases. Eventually, as the costs of production increase, as well as the costs of raw materials (which also take labor to produce), companies begin to raise prices.

As prices increase, workers demand more money, as their paychecks don't go as far. With the supply of labor restricted, companies grant the raises and raise prices to keep profit margins in line.

But the law of demand states that as the price of a product increases, buyers are less willing to purchase it. Hence, under inflation, companies are faced with rising costs (labor and raw materials) and decreasing demand for their product if they raise prices, and decreasing profit margins if they don't.

Thus, as the economy increases its growth and the labor market becomes tighter, inflation is more likely to increase. The Fed controls inflation by raising interest rates.

> **CAUTION**
>
> **Trading Traps** _____
>
> The Fed has two goals, to ensure price stability and full employment. These goals at times can be mutually exclusive or contradictory, as full employment can be inflationary, while a deflationary course of action can hurt employment. They weigh both of their goals and try to reach a happy medium between them, which is why the Fed doesn't always appear to act in a logical manner, as they are trying to have their cake and eat it, too.

When the cost of money increases, people are less likely to borrow money for purchases because it is more expensive—remember, the law of demand states that as the price of a product (money in this case) increases, buyers are less willing to purchase (borrow) it. So as interest rates increase, consumers curtail purchasing on credit and investments in plant and equipment look less profitable, due to higher costs of money and labor, and companies do not expand.

Faced with increasing costs, profit margins decrease, and companies begin looking for ways to bolster profits. Profits can be increased by either increasing sales, or by decreasing costs. Two of those costs are debt and labor. Thus by restricting debt, and laying people off, they can reduce their costs and bolster their profits.

However, as people begin getting laid off, they curtail their spending. Others, fearful of possibly losing their jobs down the road, curtail their spending as well. Sales decrease, and companies lay more people off and postpone investment in their businesses and the economy slows.

As you can see by these examples, as the Fed raises and lowers interest rates, it affects the entire economy. Their goals of price stability and full employment can be contradictory, but they manage the dichotomy of these often-conflicting goals very well.

Since, as we explained in previous chapters, stock prices are directly related to expectations regarding future earnings, which are a function of the economic future, the power that the Fed has over the economy, and hence, the stock market is enormous.

In fact, according to many, changes in interest rates and the possible effect these changes will have on the economy are a driving force in the stock market.

# Three Steps and a Stumble

If stock prices are a function of future earnings expectations, and future earnings expectations are a function of future economic conditions and future economic conditions are a function of future interest rates, then the Federal Reserve and their monetary policy should have a tremendous effect on the stock market. Guess what? History shows that it does.

> **Trading Traps**
>
> The phrase "Don't fight the Fed," is often taken as gospel at brokerage firms. Analysts will take Fed action as the end all and be all, ignoring all other factors. Before simply blindly following the Fed, you should think if the events that caused the Fed to change its course of action will help or hurt earnings. If they are raising rates to slow the economy, will that work? Look for other things to back up your thoughts as well as Fed action, because even the Fed makes mistakes and can't change the course of a market that is bent on a direction.

As we learned in the previous chapter on the Federal Reserve, the economic policy-setting branch is the Federal Open Market Committee (FOMC). Despite feelings to the contrary, the FOMC is not omnipotent. The FOMC, as we learned in the previous chapter, is made up of people, mostly economists and bankers, but people nonetheless. They base their decisions on their own feelings toward the economy. If they feel that inflationary threats abound, then they will raise interest rates. If they feel that employment levels are too low and the threat of inflation is minimal, then they ease rates.

These highly knowledgeable people are not above mistakes, and changing their minds. After all, future economic activity is more difficult to predict than the weather. Sometimes they see the economy as being too strong and inflationary and will raise rates, and several months later will view it as too weak with little threats toward inflation, and thus lower rates, or vice versa.

As such, Wall Street and the marketplace look for consistent trends in changes toward the key Federal Funds and Discount Rate as an indication that the Fed has set policy and it will continue.

## Runs in Rate Changes

From 1946 through 2001, the Fed has changed its key interest rates—the discount rate prior to 1993 and the fed funds target rate post 1993—137 times over the 55 years that we are studying. In other words, the rates are manipulated about $2^{1}/_{2}$ times per year, which seems quite frequent.

However, the Fed has changed the direction of interest rates, known as the bias, only 30 times. In other words, over the 55-year period studied, the Fed has been on 15 consistent campaigns to lower interest rates and 15 campaigns to raise interest rates.

**Timing Tips**

In 1993, the Federal Reserve changed its policy to start announcing a target fed funds rate. Prior to this, the marketplace used the discount rate as a fed funds target. Thus prior to 1993, one can look at changes in the discount rate as showing a Fed bias. But after 1993, the target fed funds rate is the important rate to watch now.

**Timing Tips**

When the Fed decides on a direction to move interest rates, they tend to stick with it. Of the last 137 interest rate changes, only 30 have been in the opposite direction of the previous rate change. In other words, the Fed has only changed its mind 20 percent of the time. But the Fed can also go a long time between rate changes, and tends to cluster their successions in groups.

Of the 15 times the Fed has been trying to stimulate the economy, it has lowered its key interest rates a total of 67 times. The Fed has slowed the economy by raising interest rates a total of 70 times.

When the Fed embarks upon a mission to manage the economy they tend to have to repeat their actions. The economy does not readjust to changes in interest rates instantaneously. In fact, when the Fed has attempted to change the course of the economy, by lowering interest rates, it has had to do so, on average, four times to get the economy to respond. When the Fed is trying to squash inflationary pressures by raising interest rates, it has had to raise interest rates an average of four or more times before achieving the desired result.

Thus, when the Fed changes its bias, as is evident when they either raise rates after a period of decreasing them, or decrease them after a period raising them, history shows that further monetary action is not far behind. Thus, the stock and bond markets pay very close attention to the Fed especially when biases change.

If this is true, then when the Fed raises interest rates to slow down the economy, the stock market should perform poorly, because the economic environment will not be conducive toward earnings growth.

This is evident by the Wall Street saying "sell stocks after three steps and a stumble."

## Three Steps and a Stumble Examined

If the Fed guides the economy and the economy affects the stock market, then when the Fed raises interest rates to slow down the economy and decrease inflationary pressures by raising interest rates, then stock performance should suffer.

This general idea is captured in the *Three Steps and a Stumble* market sell signal. This signal is generated following three interest rate decreases, when the Fed raises interest rates.

This observation has turned out to be quite accurate, especially in the short term. In the post–WWII environment, following a Three Steps and a Stumble signal, the Dow Jones Industrial Average has decreased six of the nine times this signal has occurred losing an average of –2.7 percent:

**Wall Street Words**

After lowering rates three times and then a rate hike, Wall Street says the market will stumble; this is known as the **Three Steps and a Stumble** sell signal and is a popular observation about the relationship between the Fed and the stock market.

## Three Steps and a Stumble Sell Signals

| Date | DJIA | 3 Months | 6 Months | 1 Year |
| --- | --- | --- | --- | --- |
| 09/12/58 | 519.43 | 8.4% | 17.7% | 22.7% |
| 07/16/71 | 888.51 | -1.1% | 2.5% | 3.8% |
| 08/30/77 | 858.89 | -2.2% | -12.0% | 2.5% |
| 09/26/80 | 940.10 | 2.4% | 8.0% | -12.3% |
| 04/09/84 | 1133.90 | -1.0% | 4.3% | 10.6% |
| 09/04/87 | 2561.38 | -30.6% | -19.1% | -19.8% |
| 02/04/94 | 3871.42 | -4.5% | -2.0% | 1.5% |
| 03/25/97 | 6876.17 | 10.6% | 15.1% | 29.0% |
| 06/30/99 | 10970.80 | -6.3% | 3.8% | -5.2% |

*Signals based on three decreases in the discount rate followed by a rise in the discount rate, prior to 1993. Following 1993 the fed funds target rate is used. In 1992 both rates stood at 3.0%*

*Stock market data compliments of www.chartbook.com*

This indicator tends to be a better indicator for shorter-term duration than longer-term duration, as six months following a Three Steps and a Stumble signal, the market has generally been higher six of the nine times both six and nine months following the signal. Despite the gain in prices, it is worth noting that the average performance during these periods, +2.0 percent and +3.0 percent respectively, are well below the average gains during those time periods.

In other words, following a rate hike after three cuts in the Fed's key interest, the stock market has tended toward weakness, showing the power of the Fed.

**Timing Tips** _____

The two big errors for the Three Steps and a Stumble sell signal both occurred during the two largest bull markets of the post–WWII era—1958 and 1997. In both of these cases, productivity was rising, and thus corporate earnings were rising faster than inflationary pressures. It is interesting to note that subsequent changes from raising to lowering rates following these signals were also ineffectual.

The Fed isn't simply the slayer of bull markets, but quite often the Fed can be a savior in a bear market by lowering interest rates.

# Two Steps and a Jump

As we showed in the previous discussion on Three Steps and Stumble, when the Fed decides on a policy direction, and shows commitment toward it, they tend to stay on course. Of the Fed's 67 decreases in its key interest rate, over half of them have been in successions or runs of five or more.

**Wall Street Words** _____

After two rate hikes, followed by a rate decrease, the stock market is said to rally. This is known as a **Two Steps and a Jump** buy signal as is widely followed amongst Fed watchers on Wall Street.

In fact, as I write this book, the Federal Reserve, under the wise guidance of Chairman Alan Greenspan, has lowered the Fed Funds Target rate a whopping 11 times in succession to attempt to stimulate the economy.

Historically, following the Fed lowering its key rate two or more times in succession, the economy has revived and the stock market has soared.

Wall Street, ever the diligent Fed watcher, for obvious reasons, has caught onto this with a cute little saying to describe this phenomena ... _Two Steps and a Jump_.

## Performance Signal

A Two Steps and a Jump signal is generated after the Fed lowers its key interest rate two times without an intervening raise in the rate. The two cuts in the key rates can be months apart and do not have to occur in successive FOMC meetings, but they do have to occur with a raise in between them.

In the post–WWII environment, we have seen this occur 12 times, and market performance following these signals has been impressive:

## Two Steps and a Jump Buy Signals

| Date | DJIA | 3 Months | 6 Months | 1 Year |
|------|------|----------|----------|--------|
| 02/05/54 | 293.97 | 9.0% | 19.0% | 39.1% |
| 11/15/57 | 439.35 | 0.2% | 3.7% | 26.9% |
| 06/10/60 | 654.88 | -6.6% | -7.7% | 7.4% |
| 04/07/67 | 853.34 | 1.3% | 8.0% | 0.9% |
| 08/30/68 | 896.01 | 9.0% | 1.1% | -7.2% |
| 11/13/70 | 759.79 | 16.5% | 23.4% | 10.2% |
| 12/09/74 | 579.94 | 32.8% | 44.8% | 43.0% |
| 05/29/80 | 846.25 | 11.4% | 16.1% | 11.8% |
| 11/02/81 | 866.82 | 0.5% | -2.1% | 14.3% |
| 12/19/90 | 2626.73 | 9.2% | 14.0% | 11.0% |
| 07/06/95 | 4664.00 | 1.6% | 11.0% | 21.2% |
| 01/03/01 | 10945.75 | -13.3% | -3.2% | -7.4% |

*Signals based on three decreases in the discount rate followed by a rise in the discount rate, prior to 1993. Following 1993 the fed funds target rate is used. In 1992 both rates stood at 3.0%*

*Stock market data compliments of www.chartbook.com*

The Two Steps and a Jump signal has happened 12 times, and in 10 of the 12 occasions, stock prices have jumped 3 months later. Following the last 12 Two Steps and a Jump signals, the Dow Jones Industrial Average has gained an average of 6.0 percent over the following three months.

### Timing Tips

Successive easing by the Fed after the first is widely heralded as a bullish factor for stocks, but data shows that the results historically following successive moves to lower rates really has very little predictive value for stocks. But, following more than rate easing, it may be time to look at the bond markets, as it shows the trend in interest rates is lower, and as such, bonds should benefit. See Chapters 16 and 19 for details about the bond market and investing in it.

Unlike the Three Steps and Stumble Fed observation, which did highlight weakness, but not that large of a weak tendency over the following year, the Two Steps and a Jump signals have posted gains much more often than losses (10 out of 12 times) in the following years, and posted impressive gains as well. On average, one year following a Two Steps and Jump Fed signal, the Dow Jones has posted an impressive 14.0 percent average gain.

If you watch the news or read a newspaper at all, you can't miss these Fed signals, as changes in the Fed key interest rates make front-page news.

## The Current Environment

As we mentioned earlier in our discussion on the Fed, during the writing of this book, the Federal Reserve embarked on a strong campaign to reinvigorate the economy in 2001.

Though this signal was widely touted, the most recent example of Two Steps and a Jump led to investment losses of –7.4 percent based on the Dow Jones Industrial Average.

In Chapter 7, we alluded that the Fed's effectiveness to guide the economy and thus the stock market may be diminishing.

After all, one of the things that market timers have to worry about is the changing environment and the fact that these cycles do change.

> **Timing Tips**
>
> The Fed lowered its key fed funds target rate 11 times in 2001, the most successive rate declines in the post–WWII period. However, as we all are aware, stock prices continued to plummet. The Fed does not control the stock market, but only influences it. Also adding to the stock market's woes was a mass exodus of funds from stocks to bonds. However, many people in coming years may be unhappy with bonds, especially in 2003 and 2004, as stocks may regain some of their luster.

The U.S. economy is growing more dependent upon world trade patterns and the economy of the world. No longer are American corporations strictly selling here, but most of the large companies and many small companies—mine included—can count clients on most continents. Thus, the actions of the Fed may be somewhat limited to guide the U.S. economy when so much of it is dependent upon factors that are outside its sphere of influence.

# Don't Count the Fed Out Yet

Though this logic makes sense, don't count the Fed out yet, or its influence on the economy of the United States, the world, and the stock market.

First, the Greenspan Fed has been a reactionary Fed, not a proactive Fed. Basically, Greenspan and his Fed have been following the interest rate market, and reacting to changes in those interest rates instead of leading them. The key interest rate for the Fed is the federal funds target rate. This is the rate that they would like to see rates trade at.

Instead of changing the target rate to change the rate funds are trading at in the federal funds market, the current Fed has consistently set the target rate to reflect that rate. Thus, the rate that the banks have been setting has been leading the Fed not the other way around.

At first glance this may seem like a bad thing, but one has to take the current Fed's track record into consideration. Greenspan has been at the helm of the U.S. economy for more than a decade, and his stewardship has lead to the longest post–WWII expansion in history. His policy also helped usher in the strongest stock market since the 1920s.

This may be part of the problem as well. Stocks going into the Fed easing were extremely overvalued. Stock ownership amongst the public was extremely high. Perhaps the failure of the Two Steps and a Stumble signal had more to do with the nature of the market and the need for prices to correct than with a change in the fundamental relationship between the Fed and the stock market.

Along these lines, we advise people not to count out these patterns, but to pay attention to the Fed. It is a powerful institution, and the words of "Don't fight the Fed" are sage advice, even if the most current signal did not work.

However, this should also serve as a reminder that just because the Fed has lowered rates an unprecedented 11 times in one year, it does not guarantee that stocks will be a safe investment. There is always risk, and the past never repeats itself exactly in the future.

## The Least You Need to Know

◆ The Federal Reserve's main purpose as far as investors are concerned is to encourage full employment and stabilize prices (inflation). They do this by adjusting interest rates, cutting rates to stimulate the economy, and raising rates to cool inflation.

◆ Stock prices are a function of earnings expectations. In a growing economy, or one perceived to be growing in the future, stock prices should increase. When economic growth is expected to slow or decline in the future, stock prices should decrease. Thus, Fed interest rate changes have an effect on stock prices.

◆ Following three interest rate cuts and then a rate hike by the Fed, typically stocks tend toward weakness, especially in the next quarter; this is known as Three Steps and a Stumble.

◆ Following two interest rate cuts without an intervening rate hike, stock prices tend toward strength. This is known as the Two Steps and a Jump buy signal.

◆ The Fed is fallible, despite the impression to the contrary, and at times other factors besides the Fed control market pricing. Do not buy or sell stocks based strictly on Fed action.

# The Business Cycle

## In This Chapter

- ◆ The four-year business cycle
- ◆ The modern business cycle
- ◆ The best stock market segments in an expanding economy
- ◆ Protecting your portfolio in a weak economy

In the previous chapter, we explained how the Federal Reserve attempts to control the economy, always looking to control inflation and at the same time, maximize employment. In other words, the goal of the Federal Reserve is to guide the economy along its cycle of growth and contraction.

The economy tends to experience periods of strength and weakness, with each period setting the stage for the next period, just as a pendulum swings back and forth. Inside this chapter, we will take a look at the business cycle, and how this cycle has evolved from almost regular clockwork in the 1950s and 1960s to one of extended periods of peaks and troughs in modern times.

Within this context, I will present how the stock market, and in particular, different broad industries, react within each stage of the economic cycle.

# Explaining the Business Cycle

The business cycle is usually defined as a movement in the general economy from periods of expansion followed by contraction and then expansion again.

Anyone who has ever lived in a manufacturing town has seen process play through. For example, the town in which I live, Grants Pass, Oregon, was primarily a logging town in the 1960s and 1970s, with the fortunes of the town fluctuating along with lumber prices.

> **Timing Tips**
>
> The business cycle is similar to many other naturally occurring cycles. The very part of the economy that causes the growth eventually leads to the destruction of the cycle. For example, increased investment in the Internet led to fantastic growth. But as more and more companies came into this field, eventually the productivity gains couldn't keep up and the expansion imploded on itself, much the same way that arctic fox populations increase after the lemming population increases. However, as the number of foxes increases the lemming population decreases.

In the 1980s, when environmental issues forced a slowdown in the logging industry, the local economy went to heck in a handbasket. Not only did logging companies go out of business, as well as mills and peripheral companies, such as trucking companies, but so did local shops and such. The local shops, which relied upon the logging dollars for sales shut their doors as well, as consumption slowed and unemployment was high.

> **Timing Tips**
>
> Legendary investor and hedge fund manager George Soros has been quoted as saying "the bigger the problem, the bigger the upside when it is turned around." This same principle can be applied to investing. Usually the hardest hit stocks going into a recession are consumer cyclicals, and they are usually the best performers going out of a recession.

However, during the next several years, new companies started to locate to Grants Pass, attracted by the natural beauty, as well as the small town charm and affordable cost of labor and real estate. As these new industries came in, new shops started, selling goods and services. These newfound entrepreneurs started building homes to house the growing population, which employed more people. These people then began eating out more, and new restaurants opened. The local logging mill reformulated itself to concentrate on different aspects of business, and further encouraged growth.

This growth continued for a long stretch in the 1980s, with eventually the supply of new homes on the market outpacing demand. More and more restaurants came in until they too had outgrown the demand from the local population. Eventually, the builders began cutting back on tradesmen, the shops began laying off people, and businesses again started to fail.

From growth, the town went into recession. Unemployment rose, tax revenues fell, and the city laid people off, causing more strife. Eventually, as Grants Pass became known as an excellent place to retire, Southern Californians began coming up, buying up the available housing cheap, and the builders again began hiring and constructing homes to meet this growing demand. New shops appeared, as large retailers like Wal-Mart and JC Penney came to town, and the growth began again.

## Business Cycle of Yesterday

For much of this century, the economy has followed a very similar cycle of economic growth and contraction. In fact, this cycle for a period was so regular, that many economists referred to it as the four-year economic cycle, by the fact that just about every four years from a previous economic downturn the economy would enter into a downturn.

From 1919 through 1945, we experienced six major business cycles. As measured from the bottom of the cycle to the top (through to peak) the average expansion lasted roughly 35 months, or almost three years. The average contraction last roughly 18 months, as measured from peak to trough during the same period.

From 1945 through 1991, we experienced nine complete business cycles, which saw expansion last an average of 50 months and contraction only 11 months.

**CAUTION** **Trading Traps**

The stock market and the economy are intertwined. Though both are cyclical in nature, you cannot be fooled by the fact that these cycles that have been static will continue to be so. Investors should always remember the Theory of Ever Changing Cycles, which states that many of these repeating cycles will change, or disappear. For example, the regularity of the business cycle was phenomenal up until the 1980s, when the standard cycle doubled in size.

Perhaps these changing cycles of the economy will change the cycles of the stock market? We won't know for a long time, but always keep that in the back of your mind ... nothing is a sure thing on Wall Street.

| BUSINESS CYCLE REFERENCE DATES | | DURATION IN MONTHS | | | |
|---|---|---|---|---|---|
| **Trough** | **Peak** | **Contraction** | **Expansion** | **Cycle** | |
| *Quarterly dates are in parentheses* | | Trough From Previous Peak | Trough to Peak | Trough from Previous Trough | Peak from Previous Peak |
| March 1919 (I) | January 1920(I) | *7* | 10 | *51* | 17 |
| July 1921 (III) | May 1923(II) | 18 | 22 | 28 | 40 |
| July 1924 (III) | October 1926(III) | 14 | 27 | 36 | 41 |
| November 1927 (IV) | August 1929(III) | 13 | 21 | 40 | 34 |
| March 1933 (I) | May 1937(II) | 43 | 50 | 64 | 93 |
| June 1938 (II) | February 1945(I) | 13 | *80* | 63 | *93* |
| October 1945 (IV) | November 1948(IV) | *8* | 37 | *88* | 45 |
| October 1949 (IV) | July 1953(II) | 11 | *45* | 48 | *56* |
| May 1954 (II) | August 1957(III) | *10* | 39 | *55* | 49 |
| April 1958 (II) | April 1960(II) | 8 | 24 | 47 | 32 |
| February 1961 (I) | December 1969(IV) | 10 | *106* | 34 | *116* |
| November 1970 (IV) | November 1973(IV) | *11* | 36 | *117* | 47 |
| March 1975 (I) | January 1980(I) | 16 | 58 | 52 | 74 |
| July 1980 (III) | July 1981(III) | 6 | 12 | 64 | 18 |
| November 1982 (IV) | July 1990(III) | 16 | 92 | 28 | 108 |
| March 1991 (I) | March 2001(I) | 8 | 120 | 100 | 128 |
| | | | | | |
| Average, all cycles: | | | | | |
| 1919-1945 (6 cycles) | | 18 | 35 | 53 | 53 |
| 1945-1991 (9 cycles) | | 11 | 50 | 61 | 61 |
| Average, peacetime cycles: | | | | | |
| 1919-1945 (5 cycles) | | 20 | 26 | 46 | 45 |
| 1945-1991 (7 cycles) | | 11 | 43 | 53 | 53 |

Figures printed in **bold italic** are the wartime expansions (Civil War, World Wars I and II, Korean War, and Vietnam War); the postwar contractions, and the full cycles that include the wartime expansions.
Sources: NBER; the U.S. Department of Commerce, *Survey of Current Business, October 1994*, Table C-51.

*Historical business cycles.*

Some of these cycles were very short, such as the 1980 to 1981 cycle, while others were much more extended, like the most recent business cycle of from March 1991 through March of 2001, which had been the longest post–WWII expansion in history.

## Phases of the Business Cycle

The business cycle has five phases:

1. The business cycle peak

2. The trough

3.  The recovery

4.  The expansion

5.  Back to a new peak

At a business cycle peak, corporate profits are usually exceptionally high and so is consumer confidence as employment is strong, and the labor market is tight. Generally interest rates are high, as consumers are spending freely.

However, all good things eventually come to an end. As corporate profits begin to sink, companies begin to lay off workers. Fearing potential job losses, consumers retrench, and spending is drawn to a close. Companies have trouble making profits and default on their loans, and banks tighten lending. This is typically when the Federal Reserve has stepped in and started lowering interest rates, to promote economic growth.

With interest rates falling, companies begin to borrow to improve their plants and purchase new equipment. This leads to growth in those sectors of the economy. People are hired, and they begin to save money as well as spend it.

Their spending picks up and other industries begin to benefit. As construction picks up, those employed in the construction industry may begin buying more new clothes, or television sets and other consumer goods.

At this point, the economy has bottomed out and is in its recovery stage. Other industries begin to benefit, and they too hire more workers, until the economy is lifted from recession and begins expanding again.

During the expansion phase, the consumer is still somewhat leery, but the improving economic climate and work prospects support him/her into spending and buying more goods.

Eventually, this causes more employment and the economy begins to accelerate and is strongly expanding. However, it is in this stage of development with high spending, that interest rates are rising also, and thus the seeds of the next contraction are being laid. Eventually, labor costs and interest rates hurt profitability, and the cycle begins again.

> **Timing Tips**
>
> A good trick for seeing the end of a recession is when the top-performing sector during a recession is the consumer cyclicals. Generally these companies tend to report the worst revenues during a recession, but are also the first to recover from a recession as the economy is rebuilt. For more information on sector performance, get a copy of the weekly investment paper *Barron's* that has industry sector performance tables each week.

Obviously, this cycle affects stock market prices, as stocks are simply a reflection of future expectations of the economy and a company's profits. Generally, the stock market runs a few months ahead of the business cycle.

### Timing Tip

Generally the economy tends to top out when there is little difference between long-term and short-term interest rates. The bond market calls this a flat yield curve, and it is usually indicative of a slowing economy or one poised to do such. At the end of a recession, generally long-term rates are much higher than short-term rates, making for a steep yield curve.

It is difficult to see all five stages of the business cycle, so most analysts think in terms of four main stages when looking at stock market performance: recovery, early recession, full recession, and early recovery.

Generally, as the economy is gripped in full recession, stock prices have usually bottomed out and are beginning to rise as many who have lived through the cycle before notice the value of the market and the prospects for improved earnings. Stock prices tend to accelerate in the early stages of recovery and tend to run very strong as the recovery takes hold. However, when the economy is at its strongest, usually stock prices have already topped out, in anticipation of the shift into early recession, and usually by the time the recession is in full swing, market prices are bottoming.

*Ideal business cycle.*

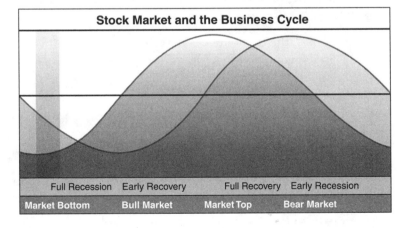

**Stock Market and the Business Cycle**

| Full Recession | Early Recovery | Full Recovery | Early Recession |
|---|---|---|---|
| **Market Bottom** | **Bull Market** | **Market Top** | **Bear Market** |

# The New Business Cycle

The U.S. economy has changed significantly in the last several decades. In the 1940s through 1960s, the United States was a manufacturing economy. We made things, like steel, and cars. However, starting in the 1970s, the U.S. economy has shifted from an emphasis on heavy manufacturing to service industries and light manufacturing.

This shift in the makeup of the economy forces us to think about the business cycle, and its effects on stock prices, in a different light. This shift in the cycle can be seen in the last two business cycles, which have both lasted over 100 months from peak to peak.

Under this new paradigm, the American economy revolves around technology and intellectual property. The massive Internet boom of the late 1990s was a result of this shift, or a symptom of it.

More and more jobs are going to computer programmers, and industry is adapting a

> ### Trading Traps
>
> As we mentioned in Chapter 6, beware when financial analysts and writers talk of new eras and new paradigms. This is usually a warning of an end of the cycle they are relying on. For example, during the late 1990s, many analysts said earning didn't matter for Internet companies, as it was all based on market share and revenues. However, as most dot.com investors know, eventually a stock will become what it is worth on future earnings. If it has no earnings in the foreseeable future, it will have no value. Beware of new eras and new rules!

high tech approach to manufacturing and whole service industries have sprung up to feed this process. This ever-changing nature of the economy makes it very difficult to predict the changes with the same regularity that we have seen in earlier times. However, though the duration of the business cycle may have shifted, the same basic tenets exist.

# The New Economy and the Business Cycle

The business cycle is much easier to understand when only a single industry is involved or location, like our Grants Pass, Oregon, example. But even in the high tech, Internet era, the same cycle can be seen. Think about the start of the 1990s. America was losing jobs to overseas manufacturers. Corporate cost cutting in the 1980s displaced many workers.

However, as the 1990s began to roll out, people got new job skills. Manufacturing, though, moved overseas for labor-intensive assembly line work; the work that remained became more skilled.

Companies began investing in computers for all employees. Companies like Microsoft, and its Windows product line, made spreadsheets and word processing extremely easy. This changed us from a manufacturing economy to an information economy, and may have changed the length of the business cycle.

Because information has such a different product life than manufactured goods, it only makes sense that the business cycle has shifted. Thus, it is understandable that the cycle shifted from one that averaged around four or five years to the last two business cycles, which have been twice as long.

However, it is interesting to note that even during these extended business cycles of the 1980s and 1990s, the stock market rewarded the same basic industry groups at similar places within these business cycles as it has in the past, shorter cycles.

# The Business Cycle and Sector Rotation

Obviously the stock market and the economy are closely related, as the economy is simply the business environment. However, as we mentioned earlier, the stock market tends to run on expectations, not current conditions, thus the stock market tends to lead the economy.

The stock market is made up of different companies, and each of these companies operates in a different sector of the economy. As their stock prices rise and fall, some industry groups will do better than others. This is known as *sector rotation*, or the switching of relative market performance from one industry group to another.

This sector rotation can be based upon the mass mood swings of the population during the economic cycle.

At the peak of the business cycle, consumers realize that times are good and have been borrowing heavily off of continued expectations for increased good economic times. This is usually when public participation in the stock market is high and the labor market is tight. It is usually at this point that industrial production is leveling off and increased raw material and labor costs tend to catch up with companies and earnings begin to falter. It is as the earnings peak and expectations for an earnings peak and public enthusiasm toward debt and the stock market are at their highest levels that the stock market tops out.

This sets the stage for the early stages of recession, or business slowdowns. At the beginning stages, the slowdown is not recognized as being across the entire economy as usually it is only a slowdown in one or two industries. Stock prices have started to retreat, but most analysts and market pundits think this is just another correction in the bull market. Industrial output has peaked and is now falling and unemployment is starting to increase as some layoffs are announced.

The early recession turns into a full-blown recession, with corporate layoffs and plant closures. Consumers begin tightening their belts, causing further economic weakness. Bankruptcies increase, and the economy eventually plunges into a full-blown recession.

At the darkest hour of the recession, the cycle begins anew. Though some market timers may wish to avoid the early and later parts of the recession and the ensuing bear market by switching out of the stock market and into bonds, bond funds, or money market accounts, other market timers look at this cycle as a guide to switching which specific industry groups they are in. These are the sector rotation players.

**Timing Tips**

Usually the stock market has reached its bottom about three to six months ahead of the worst part of a recession, based on historical studies. However, be aware that the stock market is not infallible. Many times in a severe economic downturn, intermediate corrections can be mistaken as bottoms, so wait for many signs of a bottom. Better safe than sorry.

## Sector Rotation Model

In a perfect business cycle, the best time to get into the stock market is during the recession. Remember, stocks tend to move ahead of the economy because stock prices not only reflect current conditions but future conditions as well.

Thus, in the later stages of a recession, market timers may wish to look at some broad industry groups, which have usually been hit pretty hard by the bear market. These include technology stocks and consumer cyclicals.

Consumer cyclicals are basics of our economy from airlines and automotive companies to consumer electronics, retailers, and recreational service providers. This makes sense that these would be the first group to bottom out in the stock market, as when the economy turns these will be the first companies to see their futures turn as the economy goes into recovery. Technology also benefits as the economy turns, for many non-technology companies, like manufacturers and industrial firms, cannot afford to buy new technology in the recession, but as their businesses start to improve, they have bigger budgets for getting new technology and software.

Technology bridges the gap, because as orders increase for technology, these orders are coming from industrial firms. Industrial firms include aerospace companies like Boeing, as well as manufacturing firms like 3M, as well as heavy machinery makers like Caterpillar and other companies that service these industrials, like trucking companies and railroads.

**Timing Tips**

The basis behind sector rotation is that the stock market moves ahead of the economy. If you understand which companies will have the biggest turnaround under slow, fast, and no growth, you can anticipate sector rotation. Remember, though, that market favoring of an industry group can be extremely fleeting, so if you play sector rotation, be sure to be nimble.

Usually the specialized industrial companies, such as those, which make components and specialized tools, go up first, followed by the more general or basic industry companies. At this stage, the economy is well into the early stages of recovery, and the stock market is usually well off its lows.

As industrial output increases, the economy's need for energy increases, and energy stocks of all shapes and sizes tend to be the market leaders, lifted from low valuations and brought into line with the rest of the market.

Now as the economy is going full bore, consumer staples, like food companies and such are making healthier products, as they introduce new innovations and the consumer is more willing to try higher-priced specialty items. Service industries, such as consultants, tend to do well in this environment as well, as the labor market is getting tighter and the need for such services is increasing.

### Bet You Didn't Know

It has been said many times on Wall Street that the news is not important, but how the market reacts to the news. Analysts' expectations have taken on a greater importance in recent years, and companies that fail to meet earnings expectations have been punished. Thus when earnings expectations are unrealistically high, requiring extended and ever greater economic growth, it is a sign that market valuations may be too high and due for a correction.

Usually at this point the economy is topping out. Corporate earnings are failing to live up to analysts' inflated expectations and the market has usually peaked. Money then begins to flow to more defensive sectors, such as utilities. Because public participation in the stock market is usually high near market tops, the financial services companies are doing well, such as brokerages, as well as banks.

At this point, the economy is close to, if not in full, recession and stock prices are plummeting, setting the stage for full recession and the start of another cycle.

The following graphic shows this industry sector rotation against the economy and the general stock market.

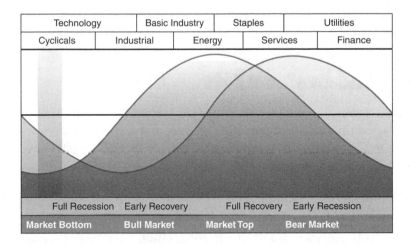

| Technology | | Basic Industry | | Staples | | Utilities | |
|---|---|---|---|---|---|---|---|
| Cyclicals | | Industrial | | Energy | | Services | | Finance |

*(continued)*

| Full Recession | Early Recovery | | Full Recovery | Early Recession |
|---|---|---|---|---|
| **Market Bottom** | **Bull Market** | | **Market Top** | **Bear Market** |

*Business cycle and sector rotation.*

## Rotation and Its Causes

Money in the stock market, at least on an institutional level, seeks out value. Wall Street fund managers are dominated by value investors, who seek out assets that should appreciate selling at fair or below fair values. This usually means they try to buy depressed companies before they turn around.

You will notice that in the previous section on sector rotation throughout the business cycle, the industries did well slightly ahead of what common sense would dictate. For example, in a full-blown recession, the cyclical stocks, such as heavy equipment makers, did well in the beginning of the market recovery. With the economy in bad shape, these companies probably have very poor current revenues and earnings. However, if the economy turns they will be one of the first to see improvements.

> **Timing Tips** _____
>
> Value investing is a form of contrarian thinking, as usually value investors buy stocks and industries that are out of market favor. Charles Dow once said, "To understand value is to understand the marketplace." However, value is a perceived commodity, so never buy a stock because it is cheap, unless you can clearly see a reason why it won't be cheap anymore. Many cheap stocks and industries can stay that way for a very long time.

It is along these lines that the money moves in. They buy these industry groups not because they see a turnaround right around the corner, but because in the current environment they are usually extremely beat up and selling at attractive prices, at least by their fancy balance sheet and income statement assessments and algorithms. They act almost as contrarians.

# The Business Cycle and Bear Markets

One of the goals of market timing is to avoid periods when the general stock market is declining, or at least try to smooth out the fluctuations in the stock market. By using the business cycle as a backdrop and watching the sector rotation, you can possibly get an idea of what to expect.

Though we often use the business cycle to predict the stock market, the relationship may work better in reverse, using the stock market to predict the business cycle.

For example, going into 2000, an astute student of sector rotation would have noticed that financial stocks, especially the stock brokerage firms, were topping the most active stocks list and posting impressive returns. Usually brokerage firms do well in the later, much later stages of a bull market when public participation is high. This should be taken as a warning sign, either to move to defensive issues like utilities, or move into other asset classes, such as bonds and interest rate vehicles, or even alternative asset classes such as hedge funds and managed futures programs.

# Interest Rates and the Business Cycle

As you will remember from the previous chapter on the bond market as well as the chapter on the Federal Reserve, interest rates tend to move in harmony with the business cycle. When the economy is strong, interest rates tend to rise, and when the economy is weak, interest rates tend to fall.

**Timing Tips** _____

Bond prices move in the opposite direction of interest rates. When interest rates rise, the price of bonds fall, and vice versa. Interest rates tend to move in the same direction as the economy. When the economy is strong, interest rates tend to rise; when it is weak, interest rates tend to fall. Thus, a strong economy tends to see poor returns from bonds, while a weak economy tends to see good bond returns.

Bond investors want to buy high interest rates and sell low interest rates, as bond values increase when interest rates are decreasing and decrease when interest rates are increasing. Thus, interest rates move in harmony with the business cycle.

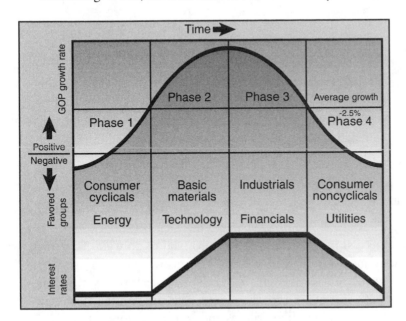

*Interest rates and the business cycle.*

Thus, during the expansion phase of the business cycle, and when it looks like the cycle may be topping out, market timers should look at moving more and more of their assets into bond funds and alternative investments. Anyone who was fortunate enough to do this in late 1999 or 2000 has considerably more wealth than those who stayed fully invested in the general stock market.

---

### Bet You Didn't Know

Fidelity, the mutual fund company, has several dozen different sector-specific funds, called select funds. Anyone interested in market timing and sector rotation may take a look at these funds as a vehicle to trade these. Standard and Poor's also lists many different sector indexes that also have depository receipts traded upon them. These SPDR's (Standard and Poor's depository receipts) are also a viable vehicle for industry-specific market bets.

---

During the bear market of 2000, the best performing asset class was bonds, which made considerable gains, thanks in large part to a friendly Federal Reserve, despite the low interest rates.

Thus, even if you are not going to use the business cycle to time the stock market and play specific industry groups, looking at the market in terms of the business cycle may help you to avoid bear markets and invest in bonds and alternative investments during times of recession.

## The Least You Need to Know

◆ The economy greatly affects the performance of the stock market. Generally, the stock market tends to move several months ahead of the economy, but by understanding this, and understanding the various stages of economic growth and contraction, you may do better in your investments.

◆ In the last century, the economy has followed a regular cycle of growth and recession covering about every five years. Though in the 1980s and 1990s these cycles lasted about twice as long; generally, specific sectors tend to do well during specific economic climates.

◆ Recovering from a recession, basic industry groups tend to do well. As growth picks up, technology and basic materials do well. As growth begins to slow, financial stocks and especially brokerages are the strong performers, which is a sign of a market top. Going into a recession and a bear market, the strongest stocks tend to be defensive plays, like utilities and consumer noncyclicals.

◆ Going into a recession, market timers may wish to look closely at investing in bond funds and other alternative investments. Generally, interest rates are lowered during these weak economic times, which adds to the return of holding bonds.

◆ Though the business cycle is difficult to predict, investors should remember that the stock market tends to lead the economy. Thus, when stock prices begin to rally after an extended recession, it may be signaling the end of the recession.

◆ When stock prices begin to break following a long rally, it may signal the start of a bear market. The market leads the economy as it anticipates changes in it, so don't get bogged down by the latest economic news as it may be changing.

# Part 4

## Seasons in Securities

The concept of the investment calendar is presented in this part. The best months of the year, as well as the best days of the month and of the week are highlighted so investors can take advantage of these changes in the market as money flows into and out of the stock market on a regular basis.

Particular emphasis is placed upon picking the best times to invest and how at other times the risks of the stock market outweigh the rewards.

# Chapter 10

# Seasons in Securities: Long-Term Calendar Anomalies

## In This Chapter

- ◆ A typical year in the market
- ◆ The best months to be invested
- ◆ The months that everyone should learn to avoid
- ◆ Invest in the best, forget the rest

In the previous chapters, we looked at the economy and how the business cycle and monetary policy affected the stock market. Though to many, this is the most logical explanation for stock market movements, it may not be as accurate as many believe.

First, the stock market is a forward thinking beast, or as the academics like to call it a "discounting mechanism." The market not only reflects today's conditions, but all the hopes and fears of tomorrow as well. As such, oftentimes it does not react rationally to news, as the full effect of many events is not known for months.

Inside this chapter, we are going to look at the performance of each month of the year. As you will be shown, a simple calendar can be an extremely useful market-timing tool. Because the stock market is a reflection of humanity, it only makes sense that its behavior, like our own, is dictated by the change of seasons.

# The Capital Behemoths

"The only thing for sure in the markets is that prices will fluctuate" is an old saying that is often said in jest, with a smile and a wink. Though said as a joke or with sarcasm, it is very true. However, several other things about the market may not be able to be stated with as much certainty as "prices will fluctuate," but they are certainly much more useful for the market timer.

Much of the information in this chapter is taken from the Hirsch Organization's *Stock Trader's Almanac*. In its thirty-sixth edition, this reference guide is not only a practical market-timing tool, but also a handy calendar and planning tool. It has sections to help you organize your investments, as well as scores of facts and market tendencies.

**Timing Tips**

The Hirsch Organization's *Stock Trader's Almanac* is so useful, that it is difficult to walk into a major investment house and not find at least one copy on someone's desk. For more information about the *Stock Trader's Almanac,* visit www.stocktradersalmanac.com or call the Hirsch Organization at 800-477-3400, ext. 1.

Yale Hirsch and the Hirsch Organization pondered about the typical performance of the market for many years. Mr. Hirsch sums up the driving force behind the markets for the last half century as being the institutions—those large organizations such as mutual fund companies, pension funds, banks, and hedge funds. The capital behemoths measure their equity portfolios in the millions and billions of dollars. When they move into and out of the market, the market moves under their size.

Though it is impossible to judge the extent of the movements of capital by these institutions, their actions are somewhat dictated by the investment calendar.

# The Investment Calendar

The investment calendar reflects annual, semiannual, and quarterly operations by institutions. Typically, during the end of the year and into the new year the market tends toward strength. This is evident from the fact that from November 1 through January 31 from 1950 through 2001, the S&P 500 index has gained 4.9 percent.

Considering that during this period the average yearly return was 11 percent, this three-month period captured almost half of the total return.

The drive up toward the end of the year and into the new year is attributed to public and private pension fund investments into the market. It is not uncommon for year-end bonuses to be invested into the stock market, nor is it uncommon for firms to fund their pension plans at the year's end—using the funds for other purposes during the year.

The following graph (compliments of the Hirsch Organization) shows the percent probability that the stock market has risen on any particular trading day in a normal month. The date or x-axis shows the number of trading days in the month.

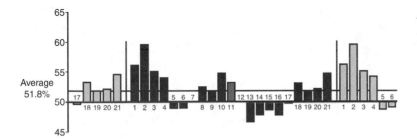

*DJIA chart for January 1, 1953 to December 31, 2001.*

This large influx of money at the end of the year tends to prop up stock prices. Couple this with year-end bonuses and people investing in stocks and contributing to their IRA's for tax purposes, and it makes sense that stocks tend toward strength this time of the year.

### Timing Tips

Calendar anomalies have been noted in the stock market by many famous and successful analysts, traders, and fund managers. These seasonal aberrations are usually sighted from recent memory, with scant attention paid to their accuracy or not. For example, the press often quotes the prospects for a "summer rally," which history shows is extremely rare and generally the weakest time of the year for the market. The seasons of the stock market are often misunderstood and misrepresented, thus the importance of this chapter to help set the record straight.

## Walking Through the Investment Calendar in a Normal Year

Typically, as January draws to a close, stock prices tend to consolidate in February. Often strong and sharp January movements are corrected in February as well. In the past 51 years, the S&P 500 has finished the month of February higher 28 times and lower 24 times, for an average change of –0.1 percent. During the 15 strong years from 1987 to 2001, the S&P 500 gained a paltry 0.6 percent in February.

March tends to be a stronger month, with the end of the first quarter. Usually March tends to start off strong, with enthusiasm toward earnings and prospects of a new and better year in the market and the economy. However, by the end of the month prices tend to decline as we enter into earnings season and tax time. From 1950 through 2001, the S&P 500 has rallied 34 times in March and lost ground 18 times for an average gain of 1.0 percent. This is the sixth best month of the year.

**Timing Tips**

Mr. Hirsch notes that "March often comes in like a lion and goes out like a lamb" as the typical trading pattern in March is for the strength of the month to be concentrated in the first half of the month. An example of this was seen in 2001, when the Dow Jones Industrials broke roughly 1,500 points in the last 10 days of March.

**Timing Tips**

April 1999, was the first month ever that the Dow Jones Industrial Average gained over 1,000 points during a calendar month. This feat had lifted April to be the strongest month historically for the Dow Jones Industrials. April also marks the end of the best six months of the year, which occur between November and April. Timers can improve upon April's performance by looking to exit the market near mid-month.

You would think as tax payment time approaches the market would sell off as funds are diverted from the private sector to the public coffers. However, nothing could be further from the truth. The first half of April tends to be one of the strongest periods for the stock market of the year, often outperforming the second half of the month. In the prior 51 years before the publication of this book, the S&P 500 has gained ground in April 36 times, and only lost value 16 times, for an average increase of 1.4 percent. If you measure stock market performance by the Dow Jones Industrial Average, April is the strongest month on record. However, when examining the broader-based S&P 500 index, April is the fourth strongest month on record.

Though April showers may bring May flowers in your garden, May is often thought of as a treacherous month for the stock market. The fourth worst month on record when measured by the S&P 500 index and the second worst month on record when measured by the Dow Jones Industrial Average. For the S&P 500, May has seen rallies in 28 of the previous 51 years, and declines in 23 years. The batting average for the Dow Jones is a more miserable 26 up and 25 down.

June tends to see some consolidation. Though market lore is full of the hope for a summer rally, market watchers are often disappointed by its performance. Typically, market volume tends to decrease during the summer months, as vacations and outdoor activities take precedence over the stock market. From 1950 through 2001, June has seen an average gain of only 0.3 percent on the S&P 500 and 0.1 percent as measured by the Dow Jones Industrial Average. May and June are often referred to as a "disaster area" for the market, as 15 of the 20 years between 1964 and 1984 saw market declines during this stretch. Even in the rosy market following the 1982 bottom in stock prices, May and June had seen poor performances.

July has historically been one of the better summer months for the stock market. The S&P 500 has rallied 31 times and broken 20 times in the 1950 to 2001 period. During this period, July has returned 1.1 percent on average in the S&P 500, and 1.2 percent on the Dow Jones Industrial Averages, making it the fifth best month on average for both indexes.

August used to be a great month in the stock market when America was an agrarian country. Money flowing from freshly harvested wheat fields would flow onto Wall Street. However, now that a mere 2.0 percent of the population lives on farms, August has been transformed into one of the worst months on record for the stock market. In the last 51 years, August has seen advances only slightly more than half the time, gaining a paltry 0.10 percent on the S&P and 0.3 percent on the Dow Jones Industrial Average. August is the third worst month of the year for both indexes historically.

### Trading Traps

According to the work of Hirsch Organization, the summer rally is a myth! Gains in the Dow Jones Industrial Average from the second quarter lows to the third quarter highs are the smallest of any of the seasonal gains. Thus, as market pundits pontificate about the prospects of a summer rally in your favorite financial publication, or on television, be sure to turn a deaf ear, as traditionally the summer is marked by dull trade and weakness.

As summer draws to a close, with vacations ending and the kids going back to school, September has been the worst month on record for the stock market, despite the fact that it has not born witness to the likes of the market crashes of 1987, 1989, or 1929. September is the only month on record in the last 51 years that has seen the market decline more often than rally. In the preceding 51 years, the S&P 500 has lost ground in September 29 times and only managed to rally 21 times, with September 1979 being unchanged. On the narrower average, the Dow Jones Industrials, September has seen declines in 32 years and rallies in only 19 years. On average, the S&P 500 index has declined –0.4 percent and the Dow Jones has declined –0.6 percent during September.

Though October has seen its share of fireworks to the downside, historically October has been a better performing month than September. October has seen its share of declines, such as the fabled crashes in 1929 and 1987, and the mini-crash of 1989. 1978 and 1979 saw severe market breaks in October as well, which were dubbed the "back to back market massacres" at the time. However, October has also seen several extended bear markets turned. The bear markets of 1946, 1957, 1960, 1962, 1966, 1974, 1987, 1990, and 1998 all bottomed and turned in October. Up 29 of the last 51 years, October has returned an average of 0.7 percent and 0.3 percent on the S&P 500 and Dow Jones Industrials, respectively. Historically, October is a middle of the road month for stocks, being the seventh best and sixth worst month on record. In other words, don't let the specter of October and those with selective memories scare you in October, as the month is about as scary as a jack-o-lantern.

**Timing Tips**

October has a bad rap! Though not a stellar month for the stock market it is not the worst month on record, despite crashes in 1929, 1987, and the mini-crashes of 1989 and 1997. Though we all fear market crashes, they are fairly rare events. More fear should be geared toward September than October, as September is historically the worst month on record. However, participants in the NASDAQ stock market should note that October is the worst month on record for this market measure. However, timers in this market segment are advised to be wary of September as well, as the two-month combination has seen an average decline of –0.80 percent from 1971 through April 2001.

November usually starts the year-end push higher for equity markets. Retail sales activity picks up with the impending holiday season, and institutional ownership begins to increase as well. This is evident by the fact that November is the third best month historically for the S&P 500 and the fourth best month for the Dow Jones Industrials. November has averaged 1.5 percent and 1.4 percent on the S&P 500 and Dow Jones Industrials, respectively, from 1950 through 2001.

Historically, the market tends to get caught up in the holiday cheer like the rest of us. After all, it is difficult to be pessimistic during a season whose motto is "peace on earth and goodwill toward all." Though it is only the third strongest month in terms of percentage gains as measured by the Dow Industrials, December has the distinction of being the month with the best batting average of the year. In 39 of the previous 51 years, the S&P has rallied in December, gaining an average of 1.8 percent. When market performance is measured by the broader S&P 500, December is the strongest month on record.

> **Timing Tips**
>
> The Hirsch Organization notes that "If Santa Claus should fail to call, bears may come to Broad and Wall." This trite little saying has a very good foundation and may serve as an early warning system of things to come. If the S&P 500 fails to rally in the last five days of December through the first two days in January, a severe break in prices may be approaching. For example, a −4.2 percent decline from the end of 1999 into 2000 foreshadowed the S&P's −10.1 percent drop in 2000. Though this little trick did miss the boat in 1985 and 1991, it does bear watching. Don't be grinched by holiday weakness.

December's charms, but not its warm pleasant feeling are carried over into January. The start of the new year has historically been rung in with higher stock prices, as hope for a better year and optimism rule the day. The second strongest month for the S&P and the third strongest for the Dow Industrials, January has returned an average of 1.6 percent on both indexes since 1950.

## Monthly Direction and % Change (January 1950 to April 2001)

|           | S&P 500 | | | Dow Jones Industrials | | |
|-----------|------|-------|----------|------|-------|----------|
|           | #Up  | #Down | Average% | #Up  | #Down | Average% |
| January   | 34   | 18    | 1.6      | 36   | 16    | 1.6      |
| February  | 28   | 24    | -0.01    | 29   | 23    | 0.2      |
| March     | 34   | 18    | 1.0      | 33   | 19    | 1.0      |
| April     | 36   | 16    | 1.4      | 33   | 19    | 2.0      |
| May       | 29   | 23    | 0.2      | 26   | 25    | -0.1     |
| June      | 28   | 24    | 0.3      | 26   | 25    | 0.1      |
| July      | 28   | 23    | 1.1      | 31   | 20    | 1.2      |
| August    | 27   | 24    | 0.1      | 29   | 22    | 0.03     |
| September | 21   | 29    | -0.4     | 19   | 32    | -0.6     |
| October   | 29   | 22    | 0.7      | 29   | 22    | 0.3      |
| November  | 33   | 18    | 1.5      | 34   | 17    | 1.4      |
| December  | 39   | 12    | 1.8      | 37   | 14    | 1.8      |

*Data compliments of 2002* Stock Trader's Almanac, *page 50. Thanks to the Hirsch Organization and www.stocktradersalmanac.com for allowing us to reproduce this.*

## Investment Time Not Real Time

As we attempted to explain in the previous section, the stock market does seem to follow a seasonal pattern. Part, if not all, of this pattern has to do with the behavior of the large institutions.

**Timing Tips**

Though the summer rally is often touted, the most bullish season for the market historically has been the winter months. From their fourth quarter lows, as measured by the lowest price in November or December, the S&P 500 index has rallied an average of 13.7 percent to its first quarter high.

Institutions tend to think in terms of quarters. Earnings are reported to Wall Street quarterly, and many investment managers receive bonuses based on quarterly performance.

A tie-in is evident from the fact that the best performing month of the first three quarters is the first month of each quarter, or January, April, and July, respectively. On average, these first months of the first three quarters have returned 1.30 percent from 1950 to 1990 and a whopping 2.03 percent from 1991 through 2001. By comparison, the second and third months of the first three quarters returned only 0.03 percent, 0.30 percent, 0.33 percent, and 0.46 percent from 1950 to 1990 and 1991 to 2001, respectively.

## Average S&P 500 % Change—First Three Quarters 1950 to 1990

|  | **1st Month** | **2nd Month** | **3rd Month** |
|---|---|---|---|
| 1st Quarter | 1.5% | -0.1% | 1.1% |
| 2nd Quarter | 1.3% | -0.3% | 0.3% |
| 3rd Quarter | 1.1% | 0.50% | -0.50% |
| Average | 1.30% | 0.03% | 0.30% |

## Average S&P 500 % Change—First Three Quarters 1991 to 2001

|  | **1st Month** | **2nd Month** | **3rd Month** |
|---|---|---|---|
| 1st Quarter | 2.12% | 0.50% | 0.46% |
| 2nd Quarter | 2.34% | 1.39% | 0.50% |
| 3rd Quarter | 1.43% | -0.94% | 0.42% |
| Average | 1.96% | 0.32% | 0.46% |

*Data compliments of 2002* Stock Trader's Almanac, *page 68. Thanks to the Hirsch Organization and www.stocktradersalmanac.com for allowing us to reproduce this.*

The last quarter of the year is unique and does not follow this pattern. However, this makes sense with it being the end of the year and the inflow of money into the markets driven by such an event. If taken in this context, then it makes sense that stock prices are the strongest in the final month of the final quarter, as money is invested at year end, as well as holiday bonuses, etc. Within this context, it is also not surprising that December is the strongest month of the year, at least as measured by the broad S&P 500 index.

This is further proof that Mr. Hirsch's observation of seasons in the security markets is extremely valid as well as his concept of the "Investment Calendar."

# Invest During the Best and Avoid the Rest

As we have shown in painstaking detail so far in this chapter, stocks do tend to follow a pattern associated with the "investment calendar."

The best six months of the year all tend to occur between November and April of the following year. Whether or not this bias is due to institutional control of the market or not, it is definitely worth noting.

In fact, investing in the best six months of the year, and avoiding the market and sitting in cash in the other six months has been a very successful strategy since 1950. This theory was first purported by the Hirsch Organization in their 1986 *Stock Trader's Almanac*, and despite their large following has continued to do well.

The following table shows the results of following the "investing in the best months and avoiding the rest" theory. It is based on investing $1,000 on October 31 and holding the stock position until April 30, when the proceeds are then switched to a money market fund the rest of the time. For simplicity's sake, commissions and fees are excluded and all proceeds are reinvested.

| Year | DJIA % Change Apr 30—Oct 31 | Investing $1,000 | DJIA % Change Oct 31—Apr 30 | Investing $1,000 |
|---|---|---|---|---|
| 1950 | 5.0% | $1,050.00 | 15.2% | $1,152.00 |
| 1951 | 1.2% | $1,062.60 | -1.8% | $1,131.26 |
| 1952 | 4.5% | $1,110.42 | 2.1% | $1,155.02 |
| 1953 | 0.4% | $1,114.86 | 15.8% | $1,337.51 |
| 1954 | 10.3% | $1,229.69 | 20.9% | $1,617.05 |
| 1955 | 6.9% | $1,314.54 | 13.5% | $1,835.36 |
| 1956 | -7.0% | $1,222.52 | 3.0% | $1,890.42 |

*continues*

*continued*

| Year | DJIA % Change Apr 30—Oct 31 | Investing $1,000 | DJIA % Change Oct 31—Apr 30 | Investing $1,000 |
|------|------|------|------|------|
| 1957 | -10.8% | $1,090.49 | 3.4% | $1,954.69 |
| 1958 | 19.2% | $1,299.86 | 14.8% | $2,243.99 |
| 1959 | 3.7% | $1,347.96 | -6.9% | $2,089.15 |
| 1960 | -3.5% | $1,300.78 | 16.9% | $2,442.22 |
| 1961 | 3.7% | $1,348.91 | -5.5% | $2,307.90 |
| 1962 | -11.4% | $1,195.13 | 21.7% | $2,808.71 |
| 1963 | 5.2% | $1,257.28 | 7.4% | $3,016.55 |
| 1964 | 7.7% | $1,354.09 | 5.6% | $3,185.48 |
| 1965 | 4.2% | $1,410.96 | -2.8% | $3,096.29 |
| 1966 | -13.6% | $1,219.07 | 11.1% | $3,439.97 |
| 1967 | -1.9% | $1,195.91 | 3.7% | $3,567.25 |
| 1968 | 4.4% | $1,248.53 | -0.2% | $3,560.12 |
| 1969 | -9.9% | $1,124.92 | -14.0% | $3,061.70 |
| 1970 | 2.7% | $1,155.30 | 24.6% | $3,814.88 |
| 1971 | -10.9% | $1,029.37 | 13.7% | $4,337.52 |
| 1972 | 0.1% | $1,030.40 | -3.6% | $4,181.37 |
| 1973 | 3.8% | $1,069.55 | -12.5% | $3,658.70 |
| 1974 | -20.5% | $850.29 | 23.4% | $4,514.83 |
| 1975 | 1.8% | $865.60 | 19.2% | $5,381.68 |
| 1976 | -3.2% | $837.90 | -3.9% | $5,171.80 |
| 1977 | -11.7% | $739.87 | 2.3% | $5,290.75 |
| 1978 | -5.4% | $699.91 | 7.9% | $5,708.72 |
| 1979 | -4.6% | $667.72 | 0.2% | $5,720.13 |
| 1980 | 13.1% | $755.19 | 7.9% | $6,172.02 |
| 1981 | -14.6% | $644.93 | -0.5% | $6,141.16 |
| 1982 | 16.9% | $753.92 | 23.6% | $7,590.48 |
| 1983 | -0.1% | $753.17 | -4.4% | $7,256.50 |
| 1984 | 3.1% | $776.52 | 4.2% | $7,561.27 |
| 1985 | 9.2% | $847.96 | 29.8% | $9,814.53 |
| 1986 | 5.3% | $892.90 | 21.8% | $11,954.10 |
| 1987 | -12.8% | $778.61 | 1.9% | $12,181.22 |
| 1988 | 5.7% | $822.99 | 12.6% | $13,716.06 |

| Year | DJIA % Change Apr 30—Oct 31 | Investing $1,000 | DJIA % Change Oct 31—Apr 30 | Investing $1,000 |
|---|---|---|---|---|
| 1989 | 9.4% | $900.35 | 0.4% | $13,770.92 |
| 1990 | -8.1% | $827.42 | 18.2% | $16,277.23 |
| 1991 | 6.3% | $879.55 | 9.4% | $17,807.29 |
| 1992 | -4.0% | $844.37 | 6.2% | $18,911.34 |
| 1993 | 7.4% | $906.85 | 0.0% | $18,911.34 |
| 1994 | 6.2% | $963.08 | 10.6% | $20,915.94 |
| 1995 | 10.0% | $1,059.38 | 17.1% | $24,492.57 |
| 1996 | 8.3% | $1,147.31 | 16.2% | $28,460.37 |
| 1997 | 6.2% | $1,218.45 | 21.8% | $34,664.73 |
| 1998 | -5.2% | $1,155.09 | 25.6% | $43,538.89 |
| 1999 | -0.5% | $1,149.31 | 0.0% | $43,538.89 |
| 2000 | 2.2% | $1,174.60 | -2.2% | $42,581.04 |
| 2001 | -15.5% | $992.53 | 9.6% | $46,668.82 |

Having followed this simple strategy since 1950, $1,000 invested in the Dow Jones Industrial Average would be worth $46,668.82 at the end of April 2001. By timing the market, you have actually gained $7.48. However, this also takes into account the terrorist attacks of September 11, 2001, which saw the stock market plummet initially in its wake. Ignoring this and ending the study in 2000, you would have sacrificed a gain of $174.60 by only investing during the best six months of the year.

**Timing Tips**

The performance of the Best Six Months strategy is even better in light of the September 11, 2001, terrorist attacks that sent markets plummeting. In reaction to this horrific act of cowardice and the system constraints imposed on the city of New York, America's stock markets were closed from the eleventh until September 17, 2001. In the following five days, the Dow Jones Industrial Average plummeted −1,369.70 points or −14.3 percent. However, a rush of patriotism coupled with tremendous value created by this led to an advance of 871.40 points or 9.6 percent during the following best six-month period. Following the Best Six Months strategy in 2001 and 2002 would have had a timer out of the market during the May through October drop of −15.5 percent in 2001, and would have allowed the timer to gain +9.6 percent from November through April 2002, avoiding the panic caused by the terrorists.

Only two years saw the market decline by more than –10 percent. The 1969 to 1970 period saw a decline of –14.0 percent during the best six months as the conflict (war) in Vietnam escalated with the Cambodian invasion, and the 1973–1974 decline of –12.5 percent caused by the OPEC oil embargo.

Over two thirds of the time, the best six month period trounced the rest of the year, or in 34 of the 51 years studied. Since the Hirsch Organization first published this study in their 1986 Almanac, the best six months have outperformed the rest of the year 12 times, or 80 percent of the time.

If you were to have invested $1,000 on October 31, 1985 following the best six month strategy and moved your money to a money market account for the other six months, you would have gained a total of $3,436.71 sacrificing only $355.39 in gains.

# Avoiding the Bad Months

Good things can and do happen to bad people and good things can and do happen during bad months in the stock market. However, looking again at the concept of best and worst months, the worst months may be a time to invest in alternative markets to the stocks market, such as bonds or even to park money in a money market fund.

If you are going to invest during the worst months, some industries to avoid are forest and paper products, oil and gas companies, airlines, and consumer industries. All of these sectors tend to have extremely poor performance from roughly May through September.

August and September have tended to be extremely good months for the volatile biotechnology stocks, with Internet stocks tending to do well in September, prior to 2000 and 2001, at least.

However, there is no shame in being in cash or bonds part of the year. The risks tend to be lower, as well as the volatility. This risk adjustment is what is the essence of market timing.

So don't be afraid to take the family to the beach or to Disneyland during the summer and forget about the stock market from May through October. Both your portfolio and your family may possibly benefit from it.

# Ever Changing Cycles

To quote Henry David Thoreau, "Live each season as it passes; breathe the air, drink the drink, taste the fruit, and resign yourself to the influences of each."

As a market timer, we must accept the cycles of the market, but also understand that these are averages, and are subject to change.

Events can shape the market environment just as events can shape our lives. Some events limit our choices, while others expand our choices. Just as in life, in the market it is much easier to look back and realize whether decisions were the right ones or not. Studying the seasonality of the marketplace it is easy to see in retrospect whether it has worked or not. However, as we go forward, we have to make the assumption that the future will act like the past, which is a big assumption to make.

As such, market timers should take studies, all studies, with a grain of salt. Just because something has worked in the past, does not guarantee it will work in the future. This same hubris has lead to the downfall of many great market personalities—as we detailed in the chapter on contrarian thinking—and could lead to our own downfall as well.

As such, we have to be adaptive to the cycles of the marketplace and not rigid. We are not talking about reacting to every economic announcement, or rumor, but watching the broader picture and then applying the tricks and traps we have learned within that framework.

Take a look again at the performance table of the best six months versus the rest of the year. Understand that it doesn't always outperform. In a strong secular bull market, sitting out the worst six months may not be a good idea, while though prices don't tend to drop as much during secular bear markets in the best six months, they do still drop, thus offering little condolence as your portfolio diminishes in value.

This may not work tomorrow if the fundamental structure of the markets does change, as the past does not have to repeat itself. Since I have quoted so abundantly from Yale Hirsch and the *Stock Trader's Almanac* in this chapter, it is only fitting to end it with more of his acquired wisdom.

"In the stock market, those who expect history to repeat itself exactly are doomed to failure ..." Yale Hirsch.

## The Least You Need to Know

◆ The stock market has a set pattern based off of the "Investment Calendar," which is dictated by the actions of large institutions. Their behavior tends to cause market strength at year end, as well as during the first month of every quarter.

◆ By understanding the market rhythm during the year, investors may be able to make more informed decisions about buying and selling stocks.

♦ Though we all fear the month of October, due to the stock market crashes in 1929 and 1987, September is actually the worst month historically for equities, as measured by the S&P 500. However, October is the worst month for the NASDAQ index.

♦ The best six months historically for the stock market have occurred from November through April. Investing in these months alone, and sitting in cash the rest of the time, would have allowed a market timer to catch almost the entire gain in equities that has occurred in the last half a century, with dramatically less volatility.

♦ The worst six months historically have occurred from May through October. Investing during these months only, a market timer would have captured only a small pittance of the appreciation in stock prices in the last half-century.

♦ Though investing only in the best six months of the year and avoiding the rest of the year would have allowed one to capture almost the entire appreciation, there is no guarantee that history will repeat itself. Longer-term secular bull and bearish cycles greatly affect the results.

**Chapter 11**

# Longer-Term Calendar Anomalies

## In This Chapter

- The incredible January effect
- The lame duck amendment and the market
- Numerology and the markets
- Even and odd years and the market

In the last chapter we highlighted the seasonal tendency of the stock market, walking you through the monthly historical performances to weed out the best and worst six-month periods. In this chapter, we will expand upon these calendar anomalies, again referencing some of the groundbreaking work done by the Hirsch Organization in their wonderful publication, *Stock Trader's Almanac*.

First we are going to discuss the January effect, a much touted and extremely well-known stock market tendency. From here we will show an incredible tendency for the market performance of one month to accurately predict the performance of the next eleven months. Following this, we will highlight market performance by year and offer insight into what are the best and worst years to invest in the market, which will be a brief segue into the following section on the relationship between Wall Street and Washington.

# Small Stocks Are Favored in the New Year

Any student of the market is vaguely familiar with the *January effect*. This is the tendency for small stocks to outperform larger capitalization stocks at the beginning of the calendar year.

Typically this bias is presented as a spread trade of sorts, or a risk arbitrage scenario, in which the investor buys small capitalization stocks and establishes short positions in larger capitalization stocks. For example, a popular way of showing this: subtract the S&P 500 from the NASDAQ or Value Line Stocks indexes.

### Wall Street Words

The tendency for small stocks to outperform larger capitalization stocks has been coined the **January effect**. This effect is usually demonstrated by the markets preference for NASDAQ stocks over blue chip stocks as represented by the S&P 500 index.

However, the plausibility of shorting stocks or even shorting index proxies is beyond the reach of many investors, so this market bias is often ignored, though it shouldn't be. The tendency for smaller capitalization stocks to outperform larger capitalization stocks is an important bias that can be used to help improve the best six-month timing strategy outlined in the previous chapter.

## Rationale Behind the January Effect

The market's tendency to favor small capitalization stocks over larger capitalization stocks has been theorized to be caused by several different factors.

First, many theorize that this effect is partially propagated by the dividend payment schedules of larger companies. Usually, only larger capitalization companies pay dividends. A much broader spectrum of companies in the S&P 500 pay a dividend than the NASDAQ companies. Typically when a stock pays out a dividend, the value of the shares decreases by almost an equal amount as the payout. This makes sense, as the dividend payment lowers the value of the company, which in turn should lower the price of the stock. Thus, with the preponderance of dividend payments at year end and the start of the new year, the S&P 500 is under a bit of pressure.

Secondly, many analysts have noted that year-end bonuses are usually invested, and typically invested in smaller capitalization stocks. Since many people think of bonuses not as income, but as "found money" they are more apt to buy riskier stocks in hopes of a bigger payoff than larger stocks. Thus after the holiday bills are paid off, this excess money is invested, and typically invested in the smaller capitalization NAS-DAQ stocks, supporting them and driving them higher, according to this theory.

> **Timing Tips**
>
> Stocks making new 52-week lows around the end of the year due to tax loss selling have tended to outperform the broader market in the coming weeks. These bargain stocks have returned an average of 12.7 percent in the 27 years (1974 to 2001) from December 15 through February 15. The broad-based NYSE Composite Index has returned an average of 4.5 percent during the same period. For more information on this market anomaly send an e-mail to service@hirschorg.com or call the Hirsch Organization at 1-800-477-3400.

Lastly, some theorize that investments for tax purposes at the end of the year and early in the new year are the motivation, as smaller investors who can take advantage of this tend to invest in smaller capitalization companies.

No matter what the reason, the prevalent pattern of the last several decades has been that smaller capitalization stocks have tended to outperform larger capitalization stocks strongly from mid-December through late February.

## The January Effect and the Best Six Months

As you will recall from the previous chapter, the best six months of the year for the stocks market occur between November and April. As many academic studies have shown, smaller capitalization stocks tend to outperform larger capitalization stocks in the first months of the year.

Though these two ideas appear to be mutually exclusive, they can be melded into a good market-timing trick. Instead of holding the S&P from November through April, market timers may wish to switch to the smaller capitalization NASDAQ index in January and February, and the S&P the other four months.

The following table shows the implementation of the idea of investing in the best months of the NASDAQ and S&P 500 index as outlined previously.

| | Best Six S&P Only | Best Six S&P and NASDAQ |
|---|---|---|
| 1971 | 13.6 | 19 |
| 1972 | -3.8 | -8.6 |
| 1973 | -17.3 | -13.5 |

*continues*

*continued*

|  | Best Six S&P Only | Best Six S&P and NASDAQ |
| --- | --- | --- |
| 1974 | 17.9 | 20.8 |
| 1975 | 14 | 19.1 |
| 1976 | -4.3 | -0.4 |
| 1977 | 5.3 | 10.6 |
| 1978 | 9.2 | 12.9 |
| 1979 | 5.3 | 4.6 |
| 1980 | 4.8 | 6 |
| 1981 | -4.2 | -4.9 |
| 1982 | 21.1 | 27.8 |
| 1983 | -2.2 | -7 |
| 1984 | 8.2 | 14.6 |
| 1985 | 22.2 | 25.3 |
| 1986 | 17.7 | 21.4 |
| 1987 | 4.6 | 7.2 |
| 1988 | 10.9 | 11.5 |
| 1989 | -2.5 | -2.7 |
| 1990 | 21.6 | 30.9 |
| 1991 | 6.4 | 15.3 |
| 1992 | 5.1 | 2.6 |
| 1993 | -3.4 | -1.7 |
| 1994 | 8.7 | 8.2 |
| 1995 | 11.9 | 12.4 |
| 1996 | 13.3 | 8.4 |
| 1997 | 20 | 24.4 |
| 1998 | 20.1 | 24.8 |
| 1999 | 7.2 | 30.3 |
| 2000 | -12 | -16.5 |
| 2001 | 8.3 | 8.3 |

The NASDAQ Index was officially started in 1971, hence we are restricted to using data from that date forward. If an investor had held the S&P 500 from November through April each year, they would have enjoyed a total return of 227.7 percent or an average return of 7.3 percent. In other words, being invested in the stock market for only six months, they would have captured an average return of 7.3 percent, or almost 80 percent of the total average yearly return of 9.3 percent.

> ### Trading Traps
>
> The NASDAQ market index is more volatile than the S&P 500 due to its smaller capitalization. As such, the strategy of adding the NASDAQ during January and February could increase your risk. Also, the switching of funds for a brief two-month period can result in tax consequences or commissions and fees, which far outweigh the advantage of doing this. Be sure to consult your tax advisor and financial planner for the suitability of this strategy in your portfolio before implementing it.

However, if the market timer stayed invested in S&P 500 during November and December and switched to NASDAQ stocks in January and February, then switched back to S&P 500 stocks in March and April, again only remaining invested in the market half the year, they would have scored an average return of 10.0 percent, or slightly better than being invested in the S&P 500 the entire time.

During the 31-year period studied, there were 23 years in which the market timer would have made money and 8 years when they would have lost money. Smaller capitalization stocks are thought to be more volatile, so this strategy may have increased risk over the simple six-month switching pattern only using the S&P 500.

However on examining the data in the previous table, this may not be the case. On average during those 8 losing years, the S&P lost an average of –6.2 percent during the six-month period. The combined S&P 500/NASDAQ switching system lost an average of –6.9 percent in those 8 years. It should be noted that this description of the relative risks is extremely limited, as another representation is that the modified S&P 500/NASDAQ switching strategy had larger losses in 6 of the 8 losing years. However, the system also produced larger gains in 18 of the 22 years that the strategy was successful.

It is also interesting to note that the winning and losing years for the Best Six Months strategy were the same for both variations of it.

# Yale Hirsch's January Barometer and Lame Ducks

The tendency for smaller capitalization stocks to outperform larger capitalization stocks is not the only noteworthy tendency for the stock market in January.

January also tends to be an excellent prognostication tool for predicting the performance of the rest of the year. According to the Hirsch Organizations *Stock Trader's Almanac*, January's direction—based on the monthly change in the S&P 500—has predicted the annual major trend of the stock market with amazing accuracy. Based on January's change—up or down—the rest of the year has followed this directional bias in most years.

> **Trading Traps**
>
> January is historically the second strongest month of the year producing an average gain of 1.6 percent for the month. Thus, waiting for this month to completely finish can result in a lot of lost opportunity.

The prognosticating power of this simple observation is pretty powerful. In the last 52 years, this indicator has correctly predicted the closing direction for the entire year an amazing 41 times, or almost 80 percent of the time! Many of the errors were minor, or generally flat years. The only three significant errors in the January barometer's batting average occurred in 1966, 1968, and 1982.

> **Timing Tips**
>
> Instead of waiting for the entire month of January to pass by, a little trick is to watch the first five days of the month. As goes the first five days, so goes the rest of the month. As we now know, as "goes January, so goes the year!" But, remember five days is a very brief period of time and major events can sidetrack this indicator as it did in 1986 and 1998.

If you'd waited to invest in the S&P 500 only after a strong January, you would have stayed out of the market entirely for 18 of the 52 years from 1950 to 2001. Of the 34 years you would have been invested in the market you would have gained an average of 9.6 percent, beating the average performance of the entire sample of 9.1 percent. The 9.6 percent return also takes into account the fact that market timers would not have been invested at all in January, which as we showed in the previous chapter has historically been the second best month of the year.

# The Twentieth Amendment to the Constitution

Prior to 1934, newly elected senators and representatives did not take office until December of the following year, or a full 13 months after they were elected, except when new presidents were inaugurated. Thus, the losing politician stayed in office for all of the following session, and became known as a "lame duck."

The Twentieth Amendment or the "lame duck" amendment changed that. According to this addition to the governing laws of the United States, congress will convene on January 3, including the newly elected representatives. The Twentieth Amendment also moved the presidential inauguration date from March 4 to January 20.

Thus, January has become an important month for Washington and the stock market. New representatives set laws and lobby for bills, and the president gives the all-important State of the Union Address. These factors set the political tone for the rest of the year, which affects the economy and the stock market. Thus, the January Barometer was born.

**Timing Tip**

Though as a standalone system the January Barometer has impressive results, the results get even better when you only include odd years, which is when a new congress convenes. Since 1950, the January Barometer has correctly assessed the direction of the S&P for the following 11 months every time in odd numbered years except in 2001. That's an amazing 96 percent accuracy rating for this little observation. For more information on the January Barometer, visit www.stocktradersalmanac.com.

# Numerology and the Market

Numerology is the study of the occult meanings of numbers and their supposed influence on human life. Though we are not going to even mention any broader significance to such matters, we are going to look at the years in a decade.

The years in a decade make sense as we as human beings tend to think in terms of decades and classify things in terms of decades. For example, the 1960s was the decade of the hippies, though their appearance wasn't prevalent until the latter half. The 1970s was the "me decade" or the disco era. The 1980s were typified by baby boomers, yuppies, and the pursuit of wealth.

Thus, the stage we are in within a decade may have some significance on the market. This idea was first presented by Edgar Lawrence Smith in *Common Stocks and Business Cycles* (William-Fredric Press, 1959). Smith observed that each decade tended to have three bull markets and three bear markets, which is fairly

**Trading Traps**

Much of the work done on the decennial cycle was based on the old business cycle. However, not since the mid-1960s has the business cycle of boom and bust been a regularly occurring event. In more recent years, expansions have been longer and contractions as well, with less regularity and pre-dictability. As such, numerology or counting the years of a market may be useless, due to this changing cycle.

close to the pattern we discussed in the first section of this book. He also observed that the strongest of these bull markets tended to occur around halfway through the decade.

Though other cycles seem to have dominated the market since Mr. Smith's publication of his wonderful work, the basic tendency for strength around the middle of the decade and weakness at the end of the decade is still prevalent.

The following table shows the performance of the Dow Jones Industrial Average year by year for each decade, showing that Mr. Smith's work may still be partially relevant.

## Annual % Change in the Dow Jones Industrial Average by Year of Decade from 1881 to 2000

|  | 1st | 2nd | 3rd | 4th | 5th | 6th | 7th | 8th | 9th | 10th |
|---|---|---|---|---|---|---|---|---|---|---|
| Total % Change | 7% | 40% | 41% | 89% | 369% | 72% | -38% | 222% | 111% | -87% |
| Up Years | 8 | 7 | 5 | 7 | 12 | 7 | 6 | 10 | 9 | 4 |
| Down Years | 4 | 5 | 7 | 5 | 0 | 5 | 6 | 2 | 3 | 8 |

As you can see, the midpoint of the decade, or years ending in five, have been extremely good for the market. In the last century and a quarter, the Dow Jones Industrial Average has never had a negative return in mid decade years. The five-year occurred in 1885, when the Dow Jones Industrials returned a paltry 2.3 percent.

Though not as bad as fives are good, the last year of a decade tends to be a big disappointment. Declining in 8 of the last 12 occurrences, 0's or 10's have had an average return of −7.25 percent. Also of note is the performance of 8's and 9's, in anticipation of the change of decade.

**Timing Tips**

As a standalone, you would be foolish to look to base your investment decisions on whether the year ends in an even or odd number. However, when combined with other effects and indicators, this little study, based on the U.S. political cycle, may give an added insight into the market to make sound market timing decisions.

# Even and Odd Years

No study of the decennial pattern, if there is such a thing, would be complete without looking at the performance of "even" and "odd" years.

We chose to follow Mr. Hirsch's observation that the ratification of the Twentieth Amendment to the Constitution may have changed the relation, and only examined "even" and "odd" ending years from 1933 forward, which made a much better bias as well, providing further evidence for the link between Washington and Wall Street discussed in the next section of this book.

From 1933 through 2001, we have had 34 even-numbered years and 35 odd-numbered years. The odd-numbered years, when a new congress is convening have solidly outperformed the even years by a factor of almost 150 percent.

The following table illustrates the point that odd years when a new congress is convening have outperformed even number years.

## Average % Change of the Dow Jones Industrials from 1933 to 2001 in Even and Odd Years

|                  | Even  | Odd   |
|------------------|-------|-------|
| Years            | 34    | 35    |
| Up Years         | 23    | 25    |
| Down Years       | 11    | 10    |
| Average % Change | 7.3%  | 10.9% |

The average return in even years was 7.3 percent during the sample period, with 23 out of the 34 years showing a market advance. Odd years however advanced in 25 of the last 35 occurrences, gaining an average of 10.9 percent.

## The Least You Need to Know

- ◆ Small capitalization stocks tend to outperform large capitalization stocks at the beginning of the year. This tendency, known as the January Effect, should encourage market timers to invest in smaller capitalization stocks at the beginning of the year, such as those represented by the Value Line Index or the NASDAQ.

- ◆ You can improve upon the Best Six Months strategy without excessively increasing risk by investing in the S&P 500 in November and December, and then switching to the NASDAQ index in January and February and back to the S&P 500 in March and April. If one would have followed this strategy since 1971, when the NASDAQ index began, they would have beat the total return of being in the S&P 500 for the entire time.

- ◆ The direction of January also tends to point the direction of the rest of the year. As the Hirsch Organization's *Stock Trader's Almanac* points out, "As goes January, so goes the year." Since the ratification of the Twentieth Amendment to the Constitution in 1933, this indicator has only incorrectly predicted the market two times, once in 1934 and in 2001.

◆ The stock market may follow a decennial cycle. The best years of the decade have historically been fifth, eighth, and ninth. The worst years of a decade have historically been first and last.

◆ When a new congress convenes every odd year, the market has tended to out-perform the even years, providing further proof of the connection between Washington and Wall Street.

# Chapter 12

# Shorter-Term Calendar Anomalies

## In This Chapter

◆ Paychecks make the best days

◆ Mid-month and end-of-month market behavior

◆ Days of the week and the market

◆ Holidays ... good or bad?

So far, in the calendar studies we have looked at, we have concentrated on longer-term biases in the market. In this chapter, we will look at shorter-term biases.

Knowing that this is not a book about day trading, we are looking at these anomalies not with the intention of jumping into and out of the market every couple of days or several times a day, but with the intention of fine-tuning our strategies. After all, every little bit helps.

Also, by understanding some the microstructures of the marketplace, you can make more informed longer-term decisions. After all, the longer term is just a collection of shorter periods of time.

# Paychecks and Market Performance

Anyone who really sits down and thinks about what drives stock prices higher or lower can come up with a one-word answer to explain the reason. Not the "Fed," nor "inflation," the "economy," "earnings," or even "expectations." The real answer is *money!*

More money flowing into a stock or into a collection of stocks than being taken out means that prices will rise. When buyers are more aggressive than sellers, stock prices rise. When sellers are more aggressive than buyers, stock prices fall. Levels of aggression are measured by how freely the buyers and sellers use their money. The markets are a money game, money moving in and money moving out.

People's expectations of the future are reflected in the movement of their money, buying and selling. The market is the tallying machine of all the opinions of everyone about the future. If they have a rosy view of the future, they buy. If they fear weaker earnings, a recession, or have a negative outlook about the future they sell. The result of these opinions, when acted out in the marketplace en masse, is money moving into or out of stocks.

**Timing Tips**

There is an old saying that "Wall Street is the only place on earth where everyone can think the world is currently going to end, but in six months it will get better." This type of mentality can be seen in analysts who think the short-term picture is good, but the long-term picture is poor, or vice versa. Obviously, these short-term swings in emotion can move the markets, making returns from short-term systems extremely erratic.

Therefore it makes sense that the stock market is shaped partially, at least in the short-term, by when people get money! Most people in the United States, myself included, are paid either monthly or bi-monthly. Monthly paychecks are usually received around either the last business day of the month, or the first, give or take a few days.

Most people who are paid every two weeks are generally paid around the middle of the month, and around the end of the month or first of the month.

Thus, with automatic deposits and contributions to 401k's and/or IRA's, lots of money is funneled into Wall Street around this time. Hence, when we get paid, Wall Street gets paid, too. This money all seems to go into the stock market around the same times each month, and should be reflected within a couple of days by higher prices.

## Last Plus First Four Days

This idea has been tested by many, as it makes sense. Many different variations exist on the short-term cycles of the market, but they all seem to show the same basic bias.

The stock market tends to go up around the end of the month and around mid-month when we get paychecks.

Thus, looking at the performance of the Dow Jones Industrial Average from the last day of the preceding month to the fourth day of the new month, from 1997 to 2002, we can show the paycheck relationship to be true:

| | Study Days | Rest of Month | Study Days | Rest of Month | Study Days | Rest of Month |
|---|---|---|---|---|---|---|
| | **1997** | | **1998** | | **1999** | |
| Jan | 0.11 | 274.38 | -113.35 | 170.1 | 368.68 | -361.99 |
| Feb | 31.94 | 69.27 | 216.47 | 301.18 | 22.91 | 62.1 |
| Mar | 75.82 | -260.3 | 78.72 | 212.73 | 369.74 | 177.18 |
| Apr | -184.68 | 406.12 | 174.38 | -4.98 | 284.44 | 680.68 |
| May | 123.62 | 244.53 | 25.16 | -6.48 | 153.21 | -564.66 |
| Jun | 105.6 | 251.94 | 67.51 | -40.35 | 442.45 | -94.03 |
| Jul | 274.59 | 292.58 | 177.61 | -148.02 | 311.54 | -335.6 |
| Aug | -66.89 | -493.57 | -428.93 | -546.34 | -77.26 | 200.1 |
| Sep | 140.75 | 156.25 | -30.9 | 59.74 | 122.21 | -822.86 |
| Oct | 186.88 | -796.64 | -338.83 | 753.34 | 323.57 | 85.48 |
| Nov | 199.65 | 213.46 | 480.43 | 357.62 | 81.95 | 243.44 |
| Dec | 354.35 | -233.16 | -262.61 | 204.17 | 158.73 | 346.21 |
| **Totals** | **1241.74** | **124.86** | **45.66** | **1313.01** | **2562.17** | **-383.95** |
| **Average** | **103.48** | **10.4** | **3.8** | **54.71** | **213.51** | **-10.67** |
| | **2000** | | **2001** | | **2002** | |
| Jan | 69.7 | -783.69 | -247.41 | 259.85 | 13.56 | -387.69 |
| Feb | 166.92 | -867.14 | 65.52 | -309.84 | -137.42 | 502.14 |
| Mar | -242.62 | 1184.22 | 92.72 | -930.54 | 397.79 | -98.46 |
| Apr | 131.23 | -223.38 | -7.97 | 1018.96 | -155.27 | -451.77 |
| May | -310.24 | -50.73 | 125.12 | -62.53 | 16.68 | 75.14 |
| Jun | 285.73 | -414.82 | 218.1 | -524.53 | -322.02 | -319.75 |
| Jul | 248.54 | -135.41 | -266.81 | 102.32 | | |

*continues*

*continued*

| | Study Days | Rest of Month | Study Days | Rest of Month | Study Days | Rest of Month |
|---|---|---|---|---|---|---|
| | **1997** | | **1998** | | **1999** | |
| Aug | 355.84 | 236 | 57.02 | -539.16 | | |
| Sep | 117.64 | -396.59 | -314.07 | -924.09 | | |
| Oct | -227.52 | 239.23 | 438.35 | 2.21 | | |
| Nov | 116.41 | -323.07 | 432.39 | 275.05 | | |
| Dec | -11.75 | 251.4 | 220.04 | 87.53 | | |
| **Totals** | **699.88** | **-1283.98** | **813** | **-1544.77** | **-186.68** | **-680.39** |
| **Average** | **58.32** | **-26.75** | **67.75** | **-25.75** | **-31.11** | **-10.31** |

Following this simple strategy over the last five years, you would have gained a total of +415.75 points on the Dow Jones Industrial Average, having been invested only on the five-day period ranging from the last day of the month through the first four days of the following month.

If you had been invested in all the other days, except the study days (last + first four) over the five-year period from 1997 through June of 2002, then you would have lost a total of –2,455.22 points on the Dow Jones Industrials.

**Trading Traps**

Many people have written about the end-of-month effect in stocks. At one time, the best combination was trading the last day of the month and the first four. At another time the best combination was the last two and first four, while other times it has been the last four and first two. All of these methods have shown good results short term, ignoring transaction costs (like commissions and fees). However, there has been a lot of variability in them and the days. They shift! They shift, because when a short-term method like this gets popular, others start going in ahead of the crowd, driving prices up in advance and selling to the crowd when they come in. In the first chapter on calendar anomalies, we warned people about the risk of ever-changing cycles, and how things can change. This is just another example. Just like a contrarian, when things seem to work too well, and everyone is following something, it stops working!

## Mid-Month and the Markets

Some people also tend to get paid at mid-month. The following graphics show the percentage of times the Dow Jones Industrial Averages have rallied or broken in a typical month on a particular day.

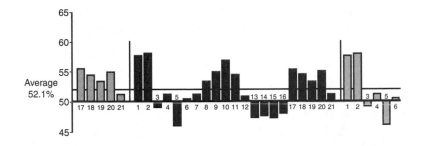

*Typical month for the Dow Jones Industrial Average Percentage of Higher Close based on Trading Day Number.*

*(Source: 2001* Stock Trader's Almanac *www.stocktradersalmanac.com).*

This figure covers the Dow Jones Industrials from 1982 to 2001, or the last major bull market. Notice how the bars point higher at the end of the month and in the middle.

Again, this is proof positive that the market is affected by the inflows of money around paydays.

However, these shorter-term anomalies are very hard to make sense of. In fact, much of this short-term seasonality has shifted in the last several years because so many people were switching from equity funds after the prime five, or super six days into money market funds, every month that many mutual fund companies and brokerages started restricting the number of times you can switch in a year, or imposing fees for frequent switching.

Then people started investing their mid-month checks into mutual funds and the strength mid-month took off. For example, from 1997 through June of 2002, if you were to invest in the Dow Jones Industrial Average only on the eighth to the eleventh business days of the month, you would have reaped a total return of 2,637.39 points. Investing in the rest of the month, which includes the end-of-month bullishness, you would have gained only 223.67 points on the Dow Jones Industrials. In other words, mid-month price increases would have produced over 10 times the return in a four-day period than the rest of the month, which is roughly 17 days. In both 2001 and through June 2002, you would have made money investing only around mid-month strength, while the rest of the month suffered bad losses.

Of course, as we have tried to point out before, this strategy could fall apart at any time, as this bias becomes more well-known and more people start trading it in anticipation of the event.

# Days of the Week Examined

Several expressions and much market lore surround the days of the week. Traders have nicknamed periods as Black Friday and Blue Monday.

This short-term bias seems to be more related to the general trend of the market than the calendar. From 1991 through 2001, Mondays and Tuesdays have historically—more often than any other day of the week—been the worst performing days.

*The performance of the market from 1991 through 2001 by day of the week.*

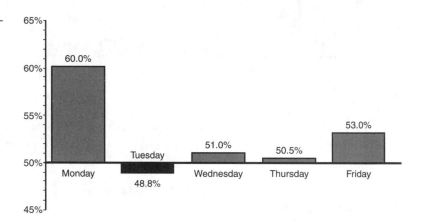

However, the period from 1991 through 2001 also marked an incredible bull market for stocks. If you examine a bearish market environment, such as from 2000 through 2002, then the results look different.

*Daily performance by weekday in a bearish period to highlight the differences in daily movements based on the general direction of the market.*

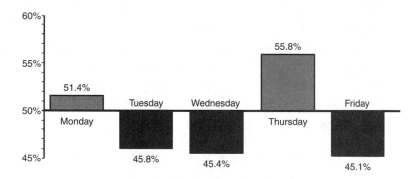

The strongest day of the week is Thursday and the weakest day of the week is Friday. Monday now reverts to the second strongest day of the week.

This type of thing has led to many different sayings and such, probably the most well known is "Turn Around Tuesday."

**Timing Tips**

Mondays have gotten a bad wrap! Monday Massacre, Black Monday, Blue Monday, and many other euphemisms have been coined about Mondays. However, as we have shown in this chapter, Mondays have been one of the better performing days of the week—especially in bear markets. Whenever possible, try to time investment purchases for Friday's and exits on Monday's close. History shows the results are worth it.

# Don't Sell Stocks on Monday, Unless They're Up

Turn Around Tuesday is an anomaly in many markets, from stocks to bonds, to soybeans and silver. Basically, what this effect is, as the name implies, is that markets have a tendency to go in the opposite direction Tuesday that they do on Monday.

This makes pretty good sense if you think about the psychology of the marketplace. Over the weekend, people often look at their portfolios and examine their financial situations. They are also subjected to news, and can catch up on their reading, as well as watching Louis Rukyser, or *Wall $treet Week*.

Over the weekend investors have two days to make decisions, which are implemented on Monday. Mass feelings of euphoria result in buying, while bad news or mass hysteria can result in strong selling. However, once this buying or selling has run its course, stock prices often bounce back.

Thus the "Turn Around Tuesday" phenomena is born!

So, if you're looking to sell your stocks on Monday after horrible news, you may wish to wait until Tuesday, as history shows that you may stand a good chance of getting better prices.

**Timing Tip**

"Turn Around Tuesday" is not limited to the stock market. This phenomena can be seen in most speculative markets. There is a strong tendency for grain and livestock futures to follow this same pattern of Tuesday going in the opposite direction as Monday. It can also be seen in the currency markets, as well.

# Holiday Cheer

Holidays are a cultural phenomena which bring mass moods to the populace. For example, isn't everyone a little more romantic around Valentine's Day? Or in a slightly better mood around Christmas, or at least more tolerant of others? How about the propensity for people to wear red, white or blue—or all three—around the fourth of July?

Well, the stock market is simply the reflection of all of its participants. Therefore it makes sense—at least to me—that the market should have a general bias surrounding the holidays. After all, if holidays can affect our moods and dressing patterns, can they not affect our money?

There are eight major holidays for the stock exchange: New Year's Day, President's Day, Good Friday (Easter), Memorial Day, Independence Day, Labor Day, Thanksgiving, and Christmas.

**Timing Tips**

Though not an official exchange holiday, St. Patrick's Day market behavior shows that we all have a wee bit of the blarney in us. The day before St. Patrick's Day has a stellar market history. On average it has gained 0.32 percent based on the average daily performance of the Dow Jones Industrial Average. The day prior to St. Patrick's Day is second to only the day before Christmas. With the huge parades in New York and the dying green of the Chicago River, is it any wonder that moods escalate as well as stock prices.

In the past, the markets tended to go up leading into holidays and down the day after. Perhaps this was due to enthusiasm or good feelings going into a holiday, and profit-taking afterward. However, as this holiday pattern—which goes against the conventional explanation offered whenever the market sells off ahead of holiday, which is "profit-taking by traders ahead of the holiday"—shows, the profit taking explanation for pre-holiday breaks is not necessarily based in fact and may be more market rumor or the media attempting to find a cause.

The following table shows the behavior of the Dow Jones Industrial Average and the S&P 500 three days on either side of the holiday, with average percentage returns for each day.

## Dow Jones Industrials Holiday Behavior Three Days Pre- and Post-Holiday Average Daily Performance (in Average Daily % Change)

| 3 Days Before | 2 Days Before | 1 Day Before | | 1 Day After | 2 Days After | 3 Days After |
|---|---|---|---|---|---|---|
| -0.03 | 0.31 | -0.19 | New Year's | 0.11 | 0.45 | 0.10 |
| 0.23 | 0.04 | -0.37 | President's Day | -0.11 | -0.24 | 0.02 |

| 3 Days Before | 2 Days Before | 1 Day Before | | 1 Day After | 2 Days After | 3 Days After |
|---|---|---|---|---|---|---|
| 0.15 | -0.03 | 0.22 | Good Friday | -0.35 | 0.60 | 0.13 |
| 0.12 | -0.22 | 0.02 | Memorial Day | 0.49 | 0.22 | 0.22 |
| 0.05 | 0.14 | 0.10 | Independence Day | -0.34 | 0.17 | 0.23 |
| 0.06 | -0.46 | 0.23 | Labor Day | 0.21 | 0.03 | -0.04 |
| -0.05 | 0.15 | 0.24 | Thanksgiving | 0.15 | -0.30 | 0.40 |
| 0.22 | 0.27 | 0.39 | Christmas | 0.27 | 0.04 | 0.33 |

The strongest pre-holiday bias appears historically to be before Christmas. On average, from 1980 through 2001, the Dow Jones Industrial Average has gained 0.88 percent in the three days preceding Christmas.

The strongest post-holiday bias has historically been after Memorial Day. In the three days following Memorial Day, the Dow Jones Industrial has gained an average of 0.93 percent. It is interesting to note, as well, that leading up to Memorial Day the market generally has sold off, dropping an average of –0.08 percent in the three preceding days.

> **Trading Traps**
>
> Behavior around the holidays can be extremely quiet or extremely volatile. This is because many exchange-based traders take long weekends around the holidays, thus causing less liquidity in the markets. During periods of lower liquidity, bid/offer spreads increase, making the cost of trading higher. Remember the bid is the price you sell your stocks at, while the ask (or offer) is the price you buy at. The bigger the difference or spread, the greater the stock must move in order to make a profit. Many refer to this as vigourish.

The worst holiday behavior, and the only holiday in which performance for the six days surrounding the holiday are negative has historically been President's Day. Though no formal explanation can be given for this, it does make sense if looked at from the slightly politically jaded point of view of this author ... who can get excited and filled with hope and optimism for a holiday celebrating politicians?

The back-to-back holidays of Christmas and New Year's support another bias we have discussed. The idea that "If Santa Claus should fail to call, bears may come to Broad and Wall", expressed by Yale Hirsch in the *Stock Trader's Almanac*. This idea makes a bit of sense, in that if people can't get excited about the future at Christmas—celebrating the birth of Jesus and the feeling of "Peace on earth and goodwill toward mankind" nor about the prospects of new hope surrounding the celebration of the New Year, then the coming months may be pretty meek.

> **Timing Tips**
>
> There is an old adage that you should buy Rosh Hashanah and sell Yom Kippur. It is interesting because both of these holidays occur in September, which is historically the worst month of the year. It is also interesting that Rosh Hashanah occurs early in the month, which usually sees strength, while Yom Kippur occurs near mid-month, which usually starts a September slide. With the large number of members of the Jewish faith in New York and on the exchanges, this adage may be worth listening to, or have at least as much relevance as the other religious and non-secular holidays.

Thus, in general, holidays tend to see market rises. The old adage of traders lightening their loads, or position squaring ahead of the holiday seems to be more myth than reality.

# Times Change but a Few Extra Points Always Help

In this chapter, we have stressed two major points, which are especially true about short-term market anomalies. First and foremost, is that they can change. As they become more and more popular, especially with the growth of day traders, these market biases will most likely shift. Traders will buy ahead of the event, and sell earlier, hoping to catch the wave of public orders to trade against.

The second major point is that these are very short-term and thus very small. Gains are measured in a few percentage points or less. This makes them impractical for most investors to use. However, they are not useless. Market timers can use these shorter-term anomalies to fine-tune purchases and withdrawals of their funds from the market, and as such, hopefully gain a few extra points.

Review the miracle of compounding in the first section of this book. Look how adding even a half of a percentage to your gain over the course of a decade can greatly increase the amount of wealth you amass. Perhaps, some of these short-term market biases will help you do this.

## The Least You Need to Know

♦ Most people invest in the stock market either at the end of the month or mid-month, periods that coincide with paychecks. As such, these periods tend to be the strongest.

♦ The last plus first four days of the month have tended to see the lion's share of gains, as measured by the Dow Jones or S&P 500. Including the middle three days gives a shorter-term trader the ability to catch most of the markets gains historically, and yet only be invested in the market about a third of the time. However, be warned that this cycle shifts as it becomes more well-known.

♦ During periods of rising prices, the best days for the stock market have historically been Mondays and Fridays. During sharp bear markets, Mondays have been pretty good, but Thursdays have been the best. Thus, periods of rising prices are usually typified by beginning- and end-of-week strength, while bear markets are typified by end-of-week weakness, and midweek strength.

♦ Often times, sharply lower Mondays or week beginnings are reversed—at least partially—on the following trading day. Referred to as "Turn Around Tuesday," this phenomenon is market lore that may well be respected by market timers looking for an extra edge.

♦ Markets tend toward strength during the periods surrounding holidays, such as New Year's, Christmas, and Memorial Day. However, be warned that the market takes a dim view of celebrating politicians, which is evident by the fact that the weakest of the eight holiday periods is President's Day.

♦ Though short-term biases are beyond the reach of most investors and much too labor intensive to be of use by themselves, market timers may find them of use in fine-tuning entry and exits from the market, hopefully adding over the years. A few extra percentage points can make a big difference over an extended period of time, thanks to the miracle of compound interest.

# Part **5**

# Washington and Wall Street

By understanding the political process and its influences on the economy, you can get a leg up on performance. Inside this part, we examine the influences that politicians have on the economy and ultimately the stock market.

Special emphasis is provided on the performance of the market historically under different divisions of power in the government, and several myths regarding the tie between Washington and Wall Street are shattered.

At the core of this part, you will see how the electoral process is used to manipulate the economy, providing investors with great opportunities for low risk investments in the stock market, and the best times to avoid the market because the risk is the greatest.

# Presidents and Portfolios

## In This Chapter

- ◆ Understanding the presidential cycle
- ◆ Pre-election and election years and markets
- ◆ Midterm market malaise
- ◆ New presidents and new trends
- ◆ Incumbents and market trends

The relationship between Wall Street and Washington should be taken very seriously. Washington and our elected officials have a great deal of power and set the environment through legislation and their governing in which companies do business.

As President Clinton remarked in the 1996 campaign, "It's the economy, stupid," Washington can have a large effect on the economy. The economy as we have shown in subsequent chapters has a large effect on the stock market; therefore, it is only logical to assume a relationship between Washington and the markets of Wall Street.

Inside this chapter, we will examine the presidential cycle and how this political cycle influences the stock market.

# The Presidential Cycle and the Markets

The price of individual firms are in part determined by the past and prospective indicators of their corporate performance. Share prices are also in part determined by the nature of the markets and industries in which they compete. But the last and often most significant determinant of share values are overall movements of the stock markets on which they are listed. Thus, the general tide of the market, or the secular bull and bear markets, tend to lift and decrease all share prices.

Secular or primary bull and bear markets are influenced by three factors:

◆ Major financial events or notable changes in the level of interest rates;

◆ Major fiscal events or essentially the shifting patterns of revenues, spending and borrowing reflected in government budgets;

◆ Major political events that could have dramatic effects on both financial and fiscal matters and through them on the future course of the national economy.

For the stock markets of the industrialized and democratic world, often the key political issue is the electoral cycle and how this might affect the business cycle. It would not be much of a stretch of the imagination for incumbent governments to engineer a boom just prior to an election, and such expansionary policies, aimed at reducing unemployment and taxes, may boost equity markets. After an election, though, as their inflationary consequences kick in and growth turns into recession, they are likely to be followed by contractionary policies, which will generally dampen market enthusiasm.

**Timing Tips**

Though I could not find the original finder of the presidential cycle, most of the works I found made reference to the Hirsch Organization's *Stock Trader's Almanac* and Yale Hirsch's comments on the phenomena. Anyone interested in this subject will be well-served by visiting www.stocktradersalmanac.com and ordering a copy of this wonderful book.

There is a well-documented "presidential cycle" in U.S. equity markets, which highlights favorable market forces in the fourth year of a presidential term. The suggestion is that political powers favor expansionary policies to attract voters. This makes sense, as all presidents want to be reelected to a second term, or if they are not able to run again, they want to do everything possible to ensure that their party, be it Democrat or Republican, retain control of the White House. People tend to vote their pocketbooks, and a strong economy with good employment prospects makes for contented voters, who then tend to vote for the incumbent or his party.

After the election, however, regardless of the outcome, markets tend to retrench to compensate for the politically induced pre-election policy.

These political business cycle effects may be tempered by the political color and commitments of incumbent or incoming governments. For example, governing parties of the left have traditionally been regarded as less fiscally responsible than those of the right, and hence less positive for the markets—a subject we will cover in the next chapter. It is also influenced by the control of the House and Congress.

Another politically determined influence on a country's economic prospects, which appears to be increasingly important and may counter the electoral cycle, is the degree of independence of the central bank or Federal Reserve. Remember, though we are talking about the political cycle in this section, do not ignore the job of the Federal Reserve, for the Federal Reserve controls (or at least attempts to control) the major fiscal events and interest rates, which greatly shape the economy and the markets.

# Presidential Cycle Defined

According to Presidential Market Cycle Theory, the economy fluctuates in fairly regular patterns over the course of each presidential term: The first two years after a presidential election tend to be weak, while years three (the pre-election year) and four (the election year) offer strong returns for the stock market.

The reason: Politics, of course!

The party in power, Democrat or Republican, wants to remain in power. So, during pre-election and election years, the incumbent government increases the money supply and popular government programs, while reducing taxes—whatever it takes to keep business and the market moving up. Prosperous businesspeople, employed workers and moderately contented taxpayers add up to reelection.

In the lackluster part of the cycle, the years just following the election year, the president makes the difficult decisions, hoping they will be forgotten by the time reelection comes around. These decisions, usually involving more taxes, spending and regulation, eat into business profits. Because stock prices follow corporate earnings to an extent, these decisions have a negative impact on the stock market.

> **Timing Tips**
>
> Never in the last half-century has a president passed a tax hike in the third or fourth year in office. If this is not proof that presidents cater to the politics of money near election time, I'm not sure what is. Also, though not a political institution, the Federal Reserve has been very reluctant to raise interest rates during an election year.

In the past fifty years, stock market movements from high to low to high again have run almost uniformly in four-year patterns. In fact, there have been 13 identifiable complete stock market cycles showing a high and a low since the end of World War II. Of these 13 periods, 92 percent of the cycle "lows" occurred in the first and second years of the presidential term. Similarly, the "highs" should occur in the third and fourth years (the election year) of a presidential cycle. In approximately 85 percent of the four-year cycles, the high point was reached in the third or fourth year.

# Election Years and New Beginnings

The American Heritage dictionary defines a cycle as "an interval of time during which a characteristic, often regularly repeated event or sequence of events occurs." Every four years, we have such a cycle as laid out by Article II of the Constitution of the United States—we start a presidential cycle.

Incumbent presidents have a vested interest in either being reelected, or in seeing their party continue in power. Just like employees try not to get sick and are on their best behavior during review periods, presidents prime the economic pumps going into reelection. They avoid raising taxes and make decisions based not only on what is good for the country, but also what is good for reelection.

This priming of the pumps tends to be favored by the markets.

## Pre-Election Markets

Presidential campaigns are well-thought-out and well-organized affairs. Candidates do not start campaigning in the months prior to the general election; they begin campaigning effectively before the primaries. Incumbent presidents usually start priming the pumps for reelection the year before the election.

For example, President Clinton may have helped foster an environment in 1999 for Al Gore's unsuccessful presidential campaign in 2000. Thus, against this background we will classify pre-election years as the third year of a president's four-year administration.

This has historically been the strongest period for stocks in the presidential cycle. Since the election of 1948 through the 2000 election, the Dow Jones Industrial Average has never declined in a pre-election year.

The worst pre-election years occurred in 1987—that crash sure helped trounce that year. In 1979, raging inflation and U.S. hostages being taken in Iran put a damper on the markets as well. The Vietnam War coupled with Nixon's wage/price controls put a damper on 1971. But even in these years in which major economic events put pressure on prices, the market still managed to gain.

**Trading Traps** _____

Problems with a presidency can also have a dramatic effect. Nixon, who was plagued by problems, stemming from inflation to the war in Vietnam to Watergate, saw three of the five worst market years in the last half-century. The problems don't have to be as severe. Anyone watching the Clinton impeachment hearings could see the market drop almost point for point with damaging testimony. The contested election between George W. Bush and Al Gore also caused a great deal of market volatility. The presidency is closely tied to the markets, so pay attention to any turmoil surrounding it.

On average, in pre-election years, the Dow Jones Industrial Average has gained 18 percent. This is much better than the average yearly gain of 9.2 percent during the same period, including all years.

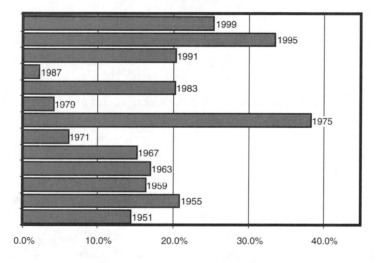

*The performance of the market in pre-election years using the Dow Jones Industrials as a proxy for the market*

*(Source: Data compliments of www.chartbook. com).*

# Election Markets

The actual election year does not fair as well as the year prior. Usually presidential political and economic maneuvering is done prior to the election, while the president focuses on getting himself, or his party's candidate elected during an election year.

Since 1948 through 2000, the Dow Jones Industrial Average has posted gains in 10 of the last 14 election years. On average the Dow Jones Industrial's have gained 7.0 percent. In no election year has the Dow Jones Industrials ever dropped more than –10 percent, but the 1960 election year decline of –9.3 percent was fairly close.

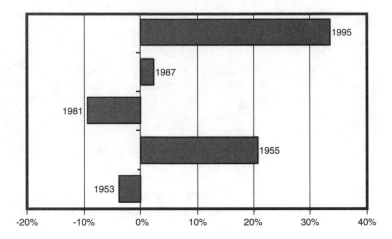

*Election year performance using the Dow Jones Industrial Average from 1948 to 2000.*

## Playing Election Tendencies

Mr. Dick A. Stoken, in his book *Strategic Investment Timing* states that, "The really juicy part of the election cycle is the fifteen-month period beginning in early October, two years before the election, and lasting until early January of the election year."

Testing this theory over the same data set as we did the election and pre-election year biases, we found that Mr. Stoken has indeed found a very useful bias. However, building upon the Best Six Months strategy, we found that the results can be improved slightly by taking the 18-month period beginning at the end of October, two years before the election and lasting through April of the election year.

### Timing Tips

Presidential election years tend to be more volatile than any other year on average. Most presidential elections are decided on the economy. Generally, Republicans tend to lose on domestic affairs, such as George H. Bush's loss to Bill Clinton, during a weak economy. Democrats tend to lose on foreign affairs. For example, President Carter was ahead in the polls until the failed Iranian hostage rescue attempt.

For example, given the 2000 election, you would have invested at the end of October 1998 and held the position until the end of April 2000. In this example, the market timer would have gained 24.9 percent. Buy and hold from December 1997 through 2000, would have returned 36.0 percent during the period, but would have had you invested 36 months, or twice as long, and the volatility would have been greater. Also, had you continued to hold through 2001, as buy and hold implies, you would have had a three-year return of only 27 percent, which is only slightly better than holding during the prime 18-month period of the presidential cycle—excluding any interest you could have earned in a money market fund, or other alternative investments.

| Election | Best 18 Months | Rest of Cycle |
|----------|----------------|---------------|
| 1948 | 6.7% | 24.7% |
| 1952 | 14.5% | 36.7% |
| 1956 | 46.6% | 5.3% |
| 1960 | 10.8% | -2.0% |
| 1964 | 37.5% | -0.5% |
| 1968 | 13.0% | -17.2% |
| 1972 | 26.3% | -30.3% |
| 1976 | 49.8% | -20.5% |
| 1980 | 3.1% | 21.4% |
| 1984 | 18.1% | 60.4% |
| 1988 | 8.2% | 20.2% |
| 1992 | 37.5% | 16.3% |
| 1996 | 42.5% | 54.3% |
| 2000 | 24.9% | -6.6% |

On average, from the election of 1948 through the end of 2001, the best 18 months surrounding an election has returned 24.2 percent, and never experienced a losing period. The other 30 months combined have returned an average of 13.0 percent, with eight profitable periods and six losing periods. Though the best period has only returned a higher amount than the other period 8 of the last 14 election cycles, the volatility has been significantly less, making for better sleep at night and less worry.

By simply studying the election cycle, you can make informed investment decisions, showing that politics pays—and not only for the politicians.

**Timing Tips**

Notice how you can build upon the lessons learned in this book. By combining the Best Six Months strategy explained earlier with the tendency for pre-election years to be strong, you can get above average returns with conceivably lower risk. Though we can't cover all the tricks of market timers in this book, be sure to remember many of the tricks presented, as they can be combined to help you weather stormy markets, or hopefully avoid them all together.

# Presidents and the Markets

The president is the head of our country, the commander-in-chief. Though not all presidents have been extremely effectual or influential in the long run, all have exacted their influence on the political climate of the country, which in turn influences the markets.

Presidencies can influence entire generations or decades. Anyone alive in the 1960's was influenced by Kennedy. Eisenhower and Nixon also influenced their generation greatly, for it was Ike and Dick Nixon that halted the Korean War, and Nixon ran on the same peace platform in 1968.

The 1980's were typified by Reagan, and his "Reagannomics" as well as the pursuit of wealth and power. No self-respecting investment advisor during the time was without a "power tie."

The president's influence goes beyond cultural. Kennedy's involvement in Vietnam lasted much longer than his tragic presidency. Reagan's influence and involvement in the Cold War changed the world and ended the Eastern Bloc. In these two cases, it is easy to see the major influences they had on the economy and the markets.

On average, from 1950 through 2000, the third year and fourth years in office have been the strongest, and the first two years have been the weakest. As we attempted to show and explain in the presidential cycle section preceding this, this is most likely due to pumping the economy prior to elections. The dismal first-year performance may be due to making of the hard decisions and cleaning up the mess caused by the election.

## Dow Jones Industrial Average Return per Year in Office (1952 to 2000)

|     | 1st year | 2nd Year | 3rd Year | 4th Year |
| --- | --- | --- | --- | --- |
| All | 4% | 7% | 18% | 8% |

## Changing of the Guard—New Presidents

From 1952 to 2001, we have had nine different presidents, including the father and son Bush duo.

## Dow Jones Performance by Year in Office for New Presidents

|      | 1st Yr | 2nd Yr | 3rd Yr | 4th Yr |
|------|--------|--------|--------|--------|
| 1952 | -3.8%  | 44.0%  | 20.8%  | 2.3%   |
| 1960 | 18.7%  | -10.8% | 17.0%  | 14.6%  |
| 1964 | 10.9%  | -18.9% | 15.2%  | 4.3%   |
| 1968 | -15.2% | 4.8%   | 6.1%   | 14.6%  |
| 1976 | -17.3% | -3.1%  | 4.2%   | 14.9%  |
| 1980 | -9.2%  | 19.6%  | 20.3%  | -3.7%  |
| 1988 | 27%    | -4%    | 20%    | 4%     |
| 1992 | 14%    | 2%     | 33%    | 26%    |
| 2000 | -7%    |        |        |        |

*Source: Data provided by www.chartbook.com*

This changing of the guard has seen the market follow the same basic pattern. The first year in office has seen the worst performance. When Nixon beat Johnson in 1968, the Dow Jones Industrial Average got killed in 1969, Nixon's first year in office after the election. A worse decline was seen following Watergate, when Jimmy Carter became President, and the country was mired in stagflation.

Kennedy's second year in office, 1962, saw a –10.8 percent decline, while LBJ's second year in office saw the worst yearly decline for a new president since 1950 of –18.9 percent.

### Trading Traps

In the unlikely event of a presidential assassination, watch out. History shows that assassination attempts and other disasters can have a negative effect on the market. The September 11 terrorist attacks, the Kennedy assassination, Pearl Harbor, the Oklahoma bombing, and the first World Trade Center attack all saw the stock market break very quickly. However, market timers should not panic. Usually following such events, the market comes back and fills in the ground lost. Though it may go back to lower lows, usually a better time to react to the event is in the month following instead of at the time of the event.

The third year in office is typically the strongest period in a president's term. The actual year of the election has been impressive, but usually not as good as the year prior.

## New Parties Are a Party for Wall Street

One of the interesting tenets about politics and investing is that Wall Street in conservative. Though in the next chapter, we will show that this axiom is not true on some levels, it is when you take the literal definition of a conservative.

A conservative is one who favors traditional views and values; tending to oppose change. Wall Street may be home to many Republicans and may be considered the bastion of the right wing, but it also tends to frown upon change. When the White House changes hands, the markets tend to underperform.

## Dow Jones Industrial Behavior by Year in Office
## Same Party vs. New Party

| Party Change | | | | | Party Same | | | | |
|---|---|---|---|---|---|---|---|---|---|
| Election | 1 Yr | 2 Yr | 3 Yr | 4 Yr | Election | 1 Yr | 2 Yr | 3 Yr | 4 Yr |
| 1952 | -3.8% | 44.0% | 20.8% | 2.3% | 1956 | -12.8% | 34.0% | 16.4% | -9.3% |
| 1960 | 18.7% | -10.8% | 17.0% | 14.6% | 1964 | 10.9% | -18.9% | 15.2% | 4.3% |
| 1968 | -15.2% | 4.8% | 6.1% | 14.6% | 1972 | -16.6% | -27.6% | 38.3% | 17.9% |
| 1976 | -17.3% | -3.1% | 4.2% | 14.9% | 1984 | 27.7% | 22.6% | 2.3% | 11.8% |
| 1980 | -9.2% | 19.6% | 20.3% | -3.7% | 1996 | 22.6% | 16.1% | 25.2% | -6.2% |
| 1992 | 13.7% | 2.1% | 33.5% | 26.0% | | | | | |

*Source: Data compliments of www.chartbook.com*

After a party change, the first year of a new presidency has been mired by bear markets on four of six occasion, causing an average change of –2.2 percent in the Dow Jones Industrials for the new president's first year in office. However, when the party remains the same in the White House, the average first-year performance has been 6.4 percent. The new party seems to come into its own by the second year, returning an average of 9.4 percent versus 5.2 percent for incumbent-party presidents. However, the strongest year, the pre-election year, underperforms with new-party presidents.

However, maybe new-party presidents try harder in election years to secure a second term. New-party returns in the following election year have outpaced incumbent returns in most years, racking up an impressive 11.4 percent return in the election year on average, versus an average of only 3.7 percent for incumbent-party administrations in election years.

Thus, over all, Wall Street may not be as conservative as many think, in that Wall Street has tended to favor new administrations and parties over incumbents over the entire four-year cycle by a slight advantage. Though Wall Street may be resistant to change, as is evidenced by the poor first-year performances, in the second half of the term, the street may fear change more than the new guy.

This little tidbit may speak well for G. W. Bush's final two years in office, especially the election year of 2004.

## Incumbents, Presidential Politics, and Market Observations

One can sum up the presidential cycle by saying that the strength tends to be in the last two years of the term in office, while the first two years tend to be weaker. Generally, the less the change the less the risk in the first two years of a new presidency. Change tends to create more risk and worse market performance. However, incumbents tend to spend early and have better returns in the third year, and less than stellar performance in the election year, than first-term candidates or parties.

> **Timing Tips** _____
>
> The best first and second years market-wise have occurred when a president is elected to a second term. On average second-term presidents have enjoyed a yearly return of 8.3 percent as measured by the Dow Jones Industrials since 1952. Though this has been true for Reagan and Clinton, the previous two two-term presidents, Nixon and Eisenhower, saw very bad market breaks in the first two years of office. Of course, both of these can be blamed on wars—Vietnam and Korea. Watch out in the first two years of a second term during times of conflict.

This cycle played out almost perfectly in 2000; 1999 saw stellar market gains, as the incumbent Clinton administration greased the wheels in an attempt to have Al Gore continue the eight years of democratic rule of the White House. However, when the election finally went to G. W. Bush, the bear market began to take hold, which saw prices break during his first year in office, 2001.

By 2004, this may spell good things for the market, as G. W., being a first-term president in a first-term party, may see oversized gains in 2003, his third year in office and the year before the 2004 elections.

## The Least You Need to Know

◆ The president of the United States of America is elected every four years. This cycle has a dramatic effect on the stock market, which has coined the term "the presidential cycle" to describe the phenomenon.

◆ The president's first year in office tends to be the worst, especially for new presidents, and especially when the White House changes parties, like it did in 2000 for President G. W. Bush. The president's second year in office is usually a bit better, but still tends toward weakness.

◆ The year prior to an election, the third year of a presidential term, appears to be the best year of the cycle. From 1952 through 2000, the third year of a presidency has never seen a market decline on a year-over-year basis, as measured by the Dow Jones Industrial Average.

◆ Usually the best time to take advantage of the third year of a presidency is to buy in October of the second year and hold until April of the election year.

◆ New presidents and party changes tend to make for a poor investment climate in the first two years in office. These breaks tend to be milder during second-term presidencies, or when the same party retains control.

◆ Politics cannot be divorced from investing, as they are intertwined. Whether you are a Republican, Democrat, or have another party affiliation, the presidential cycle will most likely continue to have a dramatic effect on your savings.

# Chapter 14

# Republicans and Democrats and Stock Market Returns

## In This Chapter

- ◆ Other branches of government—do they matter?
- ◆ Party control in Congress and the markets
- ◆ Politics may affect the markets, but markets love lack of politics.
- ◆ Effects of Congress on the presidential cycle

The legislative branch of the United States government is made up of two houses of Congress: the House of Representatives and the Senate.

The House of Representatives is the majority house of Congress, meaning that states are represented in Congress based on their population. States with higher populations have more congressional representatives. The Senate, on the other hand, is represented simply by state, with each state electing only two senators.

The House of Representatives is charged with originating bills. Bills are written in the House and then must be passed by the Senate.

Every bill that is approved by both the House and the Senate must then be approved by the president of the United States. So even though the president of the United States has the authority to command the army and set policy, he does not have the ability to write laws, only approve them.

In the event that the president does not approve a bill, it does not become a law under Presidential Veto, unless a two-thirds majority of the Senate votes to overrule the veto.

Inside this chapter, we will examine and discuss the effects the other branches of government have on the stock market and the best total political environment in which to invest in equities.

# Control of the Houses of Congress and the Markets

Under the checks and balances system, the president can't pass or veto laws without the help of both houses of Congress. Thus, though the president has enormous power, his power is somewhat limited by Congress. As such, it is only logical that if the party of the presidency and changing of parties in the presidency affect the markets, then party politics and changes in the legislative branch of government should affect the markets as well.

# House of Representatives

The House of Representatives is the most populated branch of the government. Congressmen are elected for two-year terms, and the number of congressmen elected per state is determined by population. Thus, every two years a new Congress is convened.

The majority party in power at the start of every new Congress gets to elect the Speaker of the House. As such, we will look at the party of the House Speaker to determine the majority party of the House of Representatives.

Since 1953 we have had nine unique Speakers of the House, as it is common for a party to reelect House Speakers. Of these nine Speakers, six have been Democrats and three have been Republicans.

Following the last nine changes in the Speaker of the House, the market has rallied six times and broken three times, with the Dow Jones Industrials scoring an average increase of 9.2 percent. When the party in power was ousted and a new Speaker from a different party was elected, which has only happened twice in this time frame—in 1953 and 1995—the market broke once and rallied very strongly once. In fact, when the Speaker was Republican the market has rallied twice and broken once, while when the Speaker has been a Democrat it has rallied four times and broken twice. Though the sample size is very small, and thus the conclusions are probably not worth noting, we will mention that the market appears to have done much better under Republican Congresses than Democratic, by a wide margin (18.3 percent average gain in the first year vs. 4.7 percent gain—as measured by the Dow Jones Industrial Average).

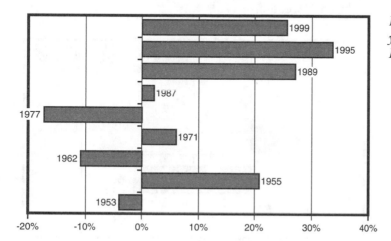

*Dow Jones performance in years when Speaker of the House changed.*

### Timing Tips

Unlike the presidency, in which the market has preferred Democrats, the market appears to have no preference for either party in Congress. However, if one is a staunch Republican he can retort back to those who say the market prefers Democrats with the fact that the market rewards Republican congresses by a very large margin over Democrats. Of course, what the market prefers most of all is split party control and true representation where our politicians actually have to work to seek common ground and not blindly push forward party politics.

## The Senate

Senators are elected by state, with each state sending two and only two representatives to Washington, no matter their population. Senators are elected to six-year terms, and tend to stay in office much longer than congressmen.

The majority party in the Senate elects the Senate majority leader. Though upon occasion a senator comes from a different party than either of the two majority parties, the Senate majority leader is a good representation of the party affiliation of the Senate.

Because senators have longer terms, and party control has not shifted very much, new Senate majority leaders are a fairly rare event. Since 1951, we have had only five different Senate majority leaders. Of these five different Senate majority leaders, three have been Republicans and two have been Democrats.

Following changes in the Senate majority leader, the Dow Jones Industrials has rallied three times and broken twice, posting an average gain of 8.7 percent as measured by the Dow Jones Industrial Average.

*Dow Jones performance in years when Senate Majority Leader changed.*

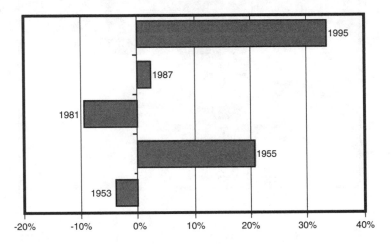

## Party Control of Legislature and the Presidency

As we eluded to in the previous chapters on the presidency, politics are such that the party of the president may not be the guiding force behind the market. It is our opinion that if this is true, then the presidency's effect on the markets maybe overshadowed by the president's relationship with the legislative branch.

Remember, in our system of checks and balances, bills are started in the legislative branch of the government, and after being approved by both the Congress and the Senate, they are then submitted for approval by the president. In order to get anything done, all three must generally agree on a course of action.

**Timing Tips**

The system of checks and balances between the White House and the legislative branch of government seems to be favored by the markets. When one party controls both the White House and the two houses of Congress, the market has put in an average return of +0.9 percent in the first year. However, when Congress and the White House are split amongst the parties, the average return in the first year has been 7.5 percent—as measured by the Dow Jones Industrials for a calendar year.

# Split Parties Between Legislative and Executive Branches

It has often been joked that an honest politician is one who stays bought and the best politician is one who does nothing. Though this view may be a bit extreme, a market place guided by Adam Smith's invisible hand doctrine—which states that the market will reward those enterprises that make above average profits and will punish those which do not—appears to support this concept.

In times when the legislative branch and the executive branch have been ruled by different parties, the market has done better than in times when both are controlled by one party.

For example, from 1995 to 2000, we had a Republican acting as both the Speaker of the House (Mr. Gingrich and Mr. Hastert) and as Republican Senate majority leader (Mr. Dole and Mr. Lott). This was countered by the Clinton presidency, which forced both parties to work in harmony—at least partially—for a tremendous bull market. However, when President George W. Bush came into office, the House and Senate were both Republicans, a combination that has not favored excess returns.

## Split Power Between Legislator and Executive Branch Is Better

From 1953 through to 2001, we have had 17 years where one party had control over both houses of Congress and the presidency. During these 17 years, the average annual return for stocks, as measured by the yearly price change in the Dow Jones industrial Average has been 5.8 percent.

During the same period, we have had 32 years where neither party controlled both houses of Congress and the presidency. During these 32 years, the Dow Jones Industrial average has enjoyed an average increase of 10.3 percent.

### Dow Jones Industrial vs. Control of Executive and Legislative Branches

|                   | Same   | Spilt   |
| ----------------- | ------ | ------- |
| # of Years        | 17     | 32      |
| # Up              | 11     | 23      |
| # Down            | 6      | 9       |
| Total % Change    | 98.6%  | 329.2%  |
| Average % Change  | 5.8%   | 10.3%   |

Simply looking at yearly advances and declines, a one-party system is roughly 25 percent more likely to see a decline than a split party executive and legislative branch. The average gain under joint control of the governmental branches versus one party domination is 30 percent greater, while the average break is only 15 percent greater.

---

**Trading Traps** _____

Many a bad market break has occurred when one party has lost control of either the White House or one of the houses of Congress. Though the market appears to prefer a split between the executive and legislative branches, following the split—especially after a long period of consolidation in the political power structure—the market has often broken hard. Just look at 1969, 1981, and 2001, as examples. All saw splits in control for the first time in years and all saw market breaks, at least in the short-term.

---

Thus, it is plain to see that the marketplace seems to favor a divided Washington as opposed to a single party domination of the government.

The worst period in this study was the early 1970s, when the House and Senate were under democratic control and the Nixon White House was wrangling with the possibility of impeachment hearings and the Watergate scandal. With the power of the presidency effectively dwarfed by the scandal, is it any wonder that the market suffered its worst yearly decline during the study period in 1974, when President Nixon resigned and Gerald Ford was appointed as the thirty-eighth President of the United States?

The best periods have come when either we have had a very strong executive branch and a strong congress controlled by the opposite party, as we have seen in recent years, or when Congress is mixed. In other words, the best political situation for Wall Street is one in which the politicians are forced to work collectively together for the greater good, as opposed to pushing forth party lines.

## Congress and the Presidential Cycle

Throughout this section, the dominant theme has been the presidential cycle and the tendency for the stock market to perform well in the second half of a president's administration and lag in the first half.

This cycle is purported to be true because presidents tend to make all of the hard and painful decisions—such as raising taxes or major economic decisions—at the beginning of their administrations and avoid these decisions in the later half on the hopes of either getting reelected or seeing that their party retains control over the presidency.

Obviously, if the executive branch has to work with the legislative branch to make any changes, the political make-up of the legislative branch of the government should have an effect on this cycle, which it does.

# Bears Are Milder Under Split Control

The first tenet of the presidential cycle is that the first two years of an administration more often than not tend to see a break in stock prices.

This tends to be especially true when the party in the White House also controls both houses of Congress. Since 1953, this situation has occurred six times, and has seen the market score losses in the first year of the president's term half of the time. The average gain in the first year of a president's administration when joint control occurs has been 2.5 percent, versus an average of 3.4 percent when control is split—as measured by the average yearly percentage change in the Dow Jones Industrials.

The second year of an administration follows a similar pattern. Of the five declines in the second year of a presidency—which have occurred since 1953 through 2001—three have been when one party control both houses of Congress and the White House. On average in this situation during the aforementioned time period, the average yearly return on the Dow Jones Industrial Average has been 2.6 percent, versus an average return of 9.3 percent when control of the Congress and White House are split.

Thus, as can clearly be seen, when party control is split, declines in the first two years of a presidential cycle tend to be much more mild, while declines when one party has control tend to be much more severe.

## Timing Tips

Many claim the persistence of the presidential cycle due to the fact that presidents do all they can to ensure reelection or continuation of their party control over the White House by pumping up the economy before an election. When the president doesn't have a strong control or power base in the legislative branch, this is more difficult, as can be seen by the fact that election years tend to underperform election year averages when one party has control. But, on the bright side, the economic binges necessary to the scales are less, so the resulting breaks are less, too. When Congress is split from the president, bear markets have historically been milder.

*Presidential cycle first two years—same party control versus split control.*

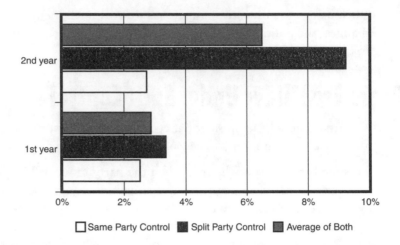

Same Party Control    Split Party Control    Average of Both

# Bull Markets Prefer Unison

The second tenet of the presidential cycle as applied to market timing is that the stock market tends toward strength in the second half of a president's term, as he strokes the economy and polishes it to ensure either reelection or continuation of control by his party. This is based on the fact that since 1953, the last two years of an administration has outperformed the first two years by a factor of greater than 2.5 to 1.

Again, since the president's power is in part granted to him by the houses of Congress under the checks and balances system, this too should be affected by the make-up of Congress.

Though in general the stock market has tended toward higher performance when one party does not control both the legislative and executive branches, that has been because breaks in the first two years of the presidential cycle have been milder, not because the second two years have outperformed under split control versus unanimous control.

The fact is that the third year—or the year prior to the election year—has generally been pretty much equal under all scenarios at slightly better than +18.0 percent average yearly gain in the Dow Jones Industrial Average. The big difference comes in the election year itself, and provides further anecdotal evidence for the presidential cycle.

In years when one party controls both the White House and Congress, the stock market has tended much more toward strength. In these cases, since 1953, the Dow Jones Industrial Average has gained an average of 12.4 percent, while when control is split it has gained a paltry 4.2 percent on average. The worst declines in election years have occurred when deep divisions in philosophy are present, or the election is extremely close, as was the case in 2000, and 1984, both of which saw nasty declines.

This makes sense—at least to this author—as it is easier to manipulate the process when you have control over both branches than when you don't. Thus, as a president is attempting to grease the wheels of the economy, an opposing Congress can thwart the effort, as they, too, view this as essential in their own reelection campaigns. When politics is viewed not as a process of passing laws and protecting the people, but as a process of protecting party lines and individual power, the effects on the market sadly become much more apparent.

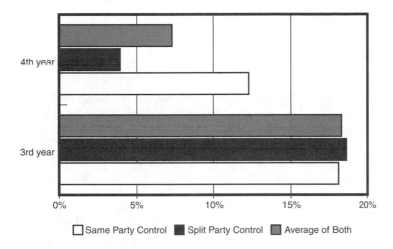

*Presidential cycle last two years—same party control versus split control.*

# Legislative Branch and the Presidential Cycle

The basic structure of the presidential cycle is amplified depending upon the balance of power between the legislative and executive branches of our government.

When a majority controls both house of Congress as well as the White House, expect the market to enter into more severe bear markets in the first two years of a presidency. In the second two years, expect the market to tend more toward strength, especially in the third year.

**Timing Tips** _____

Volatility in market returns appears to be greater when power is consolidated with one party as opposed to split between two parties. In the first two years of a president's administration, bear markets are more severe when one party has power. But, the second two years tend toward more strength. When no party has power over both houses of Congress and the executive branch, both bull and bear markets appear to be more controlled.

When power is split between the parties in the House and the executive branch, expect the bear markets of the first two years to be much more mild, but also expect the strength of the second half—especially election years—to be much more subdued.

## The Least You Need to Know

◆ The presidential cycle is strongly affected by the split of power in the executive and legislative branches of government. The best market performance has come when no party controls the entire bailiwick, but instead power is spread out between parties, forcing them to put aside partisan politics.

◆ The first two years in office tend to be the worst, despite party affiliation. However, when a single party has control over the executive and legislative branches of government, bear markets during this time period have historically been much more severe.

◆ When the system of checks and balances is in full swing, and control over the executive and legislative branches of government are split, bear markets in the first two years of a presidential administration appear to be less severe—unless strong outside forces dictate otherwise.

◆ When one party has strong political control, the year before a presidential election tends to be extremely strong. This strength usually continues into the election year as well, which is not the case when power is split in an election year.

# Part 6

# Beating the Dow from the Inside and Outside

Inside this part, we examine diversification and specific tricks for picking small baskets of stocks that can outperform the stock market. A very popular method for "beating the Dow" is examined closely and an old trusted service is highlighted.

This part also highlights how one well-respected analyst and institutional money manager has beaten the performance of the stock market in the 1990s by avoiding the stock market altogether, and how he judges the relationship between bonds and stocks and picks which is the better future investment.

No discussion of diversification would be complete without discussing how you can expand beyond stocks and bonds into the world of put and call options to smooth out the risks of investing.

# Chapter 15

# Beating the Market from the Inside Out

## In This Chapter

- ◆ Don't put all your eggs in one basket
- ◆ Putting all your eggs in one basket and watching it closely
- ◆ Thinking against the crowd ... the dogs of the dow
- ◆ Following a proven leader, the Value Line index

In this chapter, we will go beyond the study of market indexes and look at some variations on passive investing, and look at constructing portfolios that may help you beat the market. Two basic approaches are outlined, with both of them historically beating the market.

## Diversification

One of the most accepted aspects of investing is the concept of diversification. In a nutshell, diversification means you spread your risks out across a whole series of investments, so that no one investment, if it goes sour, can affect your portfolio too greatly.

For example, when you invest in an index fund, you are buying a proxy of 500 stocks, if it is an S&P 500 index fund. These 500 stocks are spread across several different industries and represent a good cross-section of the stock market itself.

The basic premise behind this approach is that you achieve diversification because of the risk spread out across a number of different stocks in different industry groups. Therefore if one or two stocks fail to meet earnings, get sued, or other devastating things happen, the entire market will not collapse.

However, this approach misses on a few basic premises as well. Though the few company-specific items that can dramatically affect an investment may be spread out across a wide range of stocks, the investor also doesn't benefit from the exceptional stocks much, either. Thus the major benefit of diversification, that of spreading out risk, also is a major weakness of diversification, as well.

## Benefits of Diversification

Index investing is much better suited for many people than individual stock picking. First, you have the benefit of a broad range of stocks that covers 10 basic industry groups (see the following table). Thus, if one sector is doing very poorly, then hopefully the other nine industry groups will do better, and even out the performance.

## S&P 500 Industry Group Weightings

| Sector | Weight in S&P 500 (%) | Change in Sector Index (%) | Sector Contribution to S&P 500 Change (%) |
|---|---|---|---|
| Telecommunications Services | 3.8 | (0.88) | (0.03) |
| Industrials | 11.9 | (1.26) | (0.15) |
| Consumer Discretionary | 14.0 | (1.46) | (0.20) |
| Information Technology | 13.4 | (1.56) | (0.21) |
| Materials | 2.7 | (1.92) | (0.05) |
| Financials | 20.5 | (2.10) | (0.43) |
| Health Care | 14.8 | (2.17) | (0.32) |
| Consumer Staples | 10.2 | (2.58) | (0.26) |
| Energy | 6.0 | (3.54) | (0.21) |
| Utilities | 2.8 | (3.67) | (0.10) |

This is a key feature of diversification. For example, assume that interest rates are extremely volatile, which tends to have a negative effect on financial stocks. Though this may tend to put downward pressure on financial stocks, because they make up only 20 percent of the total index, other sectors can even out their performance.

---

**Trading Traps**

Many people consider diversification as owning several different mutual funds. However, many of these funds may have the same basic core holdings in them, so the only thing you are diversifying is the place they send your statements from. When investing in mutual funds, be sure to compare the current holdings of all the funds to make sure you are not just investing in the same half dozen or so companies through different funds.

---

Diversification can also help out with company-specific problems. Take, for example, Enron, the Texas-based energy company that went bankrupt in 2002 amid accounting scandals and such. This stock went from a valuable company to a worthless company in a matter of months as the accounting scandal became known. This company-specific item dragged down several other energy and utility companies with it, causing the entire sector to plummet.

Though this scandal did drag the entire market down with it, the broad market did not become worthless. Thus, diversification made the extreme losses in Enron a small part of the entire portfolio.

Diversification also ensures that one will always have a position or investment in the hot sector of the time. As money flows from one part of the stock market to the next, being diversified assures the investor that he/she will have a position in the companies that are going up.

The basic premise of diversification is very similar to that of not putting all your eggs in one basket. Through diversification, you are exposed to the general economy, and not specific companies. With investments spread out across 500 companies, in 10 different industry groups, the entire portfolio will not be dramatically over-affected by any one company.

## Problems with Diversification

One of the major problems with diversification is that the general stock market tends to move as a whole. This is the basic premise behind market timing—that the stock market moves in broad, secular bull and bear markets.

For many investors, it is of little comfort that their entire portfolio is down. Though they may have avoided a total loss of capital, by avoiding or having a very small position in a company that fails, they have still lost money.

**Timing Tips**

When a company is added to the S&P 500, it has historically outperformed the market shortly before being added and shortly afterward. This index effect is caused by the fact that a lot of money is invested by mutual funds in tracking indexes, and when a new company is added these companies have to buy it, which usually pushes the price up. Consider this for short-term trades only.

Though a good diversified portfolio does prevent some of the excess volatility and movement that may happen when picking individual stocks, it is still subject to the broad movements of the market.

Diversified portfolios, such as the S&P 500, are designed to mimic the general market. In fact, when most people think about the market, they think not in terms of every stock listed, but instead in terms of indexes, like the Dow Jones Industrial Average and S&P 500 indexes.

## Diversified Is Not Always Diversified

Another problem with diversification is that when stocks are added to indexes or removed from indexes it changes the nature of the index itself.

For example, at the end of 1999, Standard and Poor's changed the make-up of the S&P 500, giving it a more heavy weighting in technology stocks. S&P justified this change because the S&P 500 is supposed to be a general gauge of the stock market and the American economy. Both of these needed to be reflected in the make-up of the S&P 500 index, thus the change.

However, this change in the make-up of the index magnified the break in stock prices, as measured by the S&P 500 in 2000 and 2001. The technology sector received a higher weighting, just as those stocks were about to be the hardest hit. Thus, changes by the S&P 500 index committee in the relative weighting of this one sector, caused losses in the following year to be magnified.

As such, when one is investing in an index, one needs to remember that the particular weighting of that index can be changed. However, even though this happens quite infrequently, one should be aware of it and the cost it could have on one's investments.

# A Nondiversified Approach

There is an old comeback to the comment about the risk of putting all your eggs one basket, which is usually that it is okay to do this if one watches the basket very closely.

This is the argument used by many professional mutual fund managers, who use their expertise in picking stocks to hopefully outperform the general stock market, as measured by the indexes.

They scour over annual reports, and look for patterns in trading, that hopefully will allow them to beat the market through their own personal stock-picking prowess.

Though the idea of having a professional manager looking after your money sounds appealing, and a logical way to proceed, the results are often less than stellar.

Several studies have shown that 80 percent of all professionally managed mutual funds underperform the broad stock market or industry sector they are designed to beat. Thus, if these high priced stock pickers, with access to loads of the latest information can't beat the market, what hope do we have as average investors?

The answer to that is much more than one would think.

## Benefits of the Small Portfolio Approach

Many investors discount their own personal expertise, instead leaning toward ideas put forth by Wall Street because they sound very good. This is a big mistake!

Peter Lynch, the former head of one of the best performing mutual funds in history, the Fidelity Magellan Fund, said that his stock-picking prowess had more to do with common sense than anything else.

He tells a great story in his book, *One Up On Wall Street*, about buying into a small company. His wife had returned from the grocery store with a bunch of strange shaped plastic eggs. He asked her what they were, and she replied they were "panty hose," or a disposable type of stocking, that she could buy at the grocery store instead of in the women's department of a clothing store. She went on and on, about how they were inexpensive, and sold more conveniently than stockings.

Mr. Lynch went to the grocery store and saw hordes of ladies picking over the display, which was already half empty by that time.

By using a little common sense, he bought shares in the company (LEGGS), which produced these new "panty hose" and gleefully watched as the stock quadrupled. He scored a home run, not by the conventional Wall Street way, but by seeing a product that he saw firsthand was selling well.

**Timing Tips**

Think of buying a stock like buying a home. Most of us, when we purchase our homes, don't think about resale value, but instead find a home that we can both afford and fulfills our needs. Choose a stock the same way. Would you be comfortable owning this stock at a lower price? Does it have good long-term prospects, and is it in good shape currently. Buy companies where you might know more than most people. Invest in the industry you work in, or the products you buy. It worked for Peter Lynch, and it could work for you.

Panty hose was not the only investment that Mr. Lynch made based on common sense. He bought Dunkin Donuts and scored big there, not because of fancy analysis on income statements, but because he liked their doughnuts and coffee.

My father bought shares of a small computer company many years ago. They made the first portable computer. He was an engineer, not a computer scientist, so he did not really understand what differentiated this computer from all the rest. The only thing he knew was he could take this computer home with him from work and plug it in and get caught up on some work in the evening and on weekends because it was designed to be portable. Thus, back in the late 1970s or early 1980s, my father purchased several hundred shares of COMPAQ computer, who made the first portable computer—which was about the size of a small suitcase.

Like Peter Lynch and my father, many of us are very capable of knowing what will sell to the general public and what will not. We, as consumers, in fact are probably more adept at this than many of the Wall Street analysts. We can spot new trends and new products quicker than the large institutions can. As such, we have an advantage.

That advantage can also spell trouble. If we put all of our investment into one stock, and it is not the next panty hose or portable computer it could go down and down sharply. However, with prudent money management and cutting these losses at acceptable levels, we may be able to use our common sense to build better portfolios than those constructed by Wall Street.

## Problems with the Small Portfolio Approach

The major problem of this is the risk. On Wall Street, as in much of life, risk is commensurate with reward. By placing all your money into relatively few stocks, one is making a very large bet. If the bet pays off, then we are happy. However, it may also go the way of many companies, especially small growth companies, and be worthless in a few years. The risk, and rewards are both great to this approach.

Another major problem with this approach, is that it lacks a definite criteria for getting into and out of the market. If the stock declines 5 percent do you sell or do you continue to hold? How about 10 percent declines, or 25 percent or 50 percent declines. At what point does one say that the stock play may not work out.

> **Trading Traps** _____
>
> Common sense is a big part of investing and market timing as well. However, one needs to practice discipline as well in investing. Before anyone invests in a stock, mutual fund, or other speculative arena, they should make a list of the reasons why they are investing, what their goals are, and what risk they are comfortable with. The investment should be reviewed against this list and adjusted accordingly. Most people fail in the stock market because they fail to plan, and act emotionally not rationally, when faced with losses.

You will notice that with all of the market approaches we have presented in this book, we have given a basic criteria for the position. For example, using Dow's Theory gives the investor a definite signal for entering and exiting the market, as does the presidential cycle, moving averages, or even the calendar-based systems.

Along these lines we are going to present two very basic approaches to establishing a stock portfolio, one based on a small number of stocks with a complete set of rules for picking them and how long to hold them, and a diversified approach based on the analytical work of an established company that has managed to outperform the broad stock market for the last 50 years.

# The Dogs of the Dow

There are 30 stocks in the Dow Jones Average, representing the 30 biggest and best companies in the world. These titans have established products and services, the best management money can buy and are internationally diversified. The Dow Thirty Industrial Stocks represent the corporate elite of America.

Michael O'Higgins, author of *Beating the Dow*, noted that these bellwethers of industry had a particular pattern. These were major companies, which probably will not fold up shop. In fact, most of them pay dividends every year and have long histories. As such, he hypothesizes that if a company's stock is not doing well, its management and board of directors will do everything in their power to turn the performance around. Thus, he developed a strategy for beating the Dow by concentrating on the worst performing stocks within that index … the *dogs!*

## Constructing a Doggy Portfolio

Many companies on the Dow pay a dividend. This dividend remains fairly stable throughout the year, while the average price of a stock fluctuates more than 50 percent.

When the stock price goes down and the dividend remains unchanged, the dividend yield goes up. The key to the Dogs of the Dow strategy is to buy the 10 stocks with the highest dividend yield that year, hold them for a year and sell them. O'Higgins later changed the holding period to 18 months because when you sell your investment after 18 months, any gains will be treated as long-term (rather than short-term) capital gains.

**Timing Tips**

For a current list of the Dogs of the Dow and several of the variations of this style visit www. dogsofthedow.com.

This approach is very simple. The only tools you need are the price of all 30 Dow Jones Industrial Stocks, and their dividend yields.

A dividend is a payment many companies make to shareholders out of their excess earnings. It's usually expressed as a per-share amount. When you compare companies' dividends, however, you talk about the "dividend yield," or simply the "yield." That's the dividend amount divided by the stock price. It tells you what percentage of your purchase price the company will return to you in dividends. For example, if a stock pays an annual dividend of $2 and is trading at $50 a share, it would have a yield of 4 percent.

Here is a sample of a Dogs of the Dow Portfolio for 2001. Remember, this is constructed by simply buying the 10 highest yield Dow stocks on the last trading day of the year.

| Symbol | Company | Price | Yield |
|--------|---------|-------|-------|
| *(NYSE/NASDAQ)* | *(The Dow stocks ranked by yield on 12/29/00)* | | |
| MO | Philip Morris | 44 | 4.82% |
| EK | Eastman Kodak | 39 ⅜ | 4.47% |
| GM | General Motors | 50 ¹⁵/₁₆ | 3.93% |
| DD | DuPont | 48 ⁵/₁₆ | 2.90% |
| CAT | Caterpillar | 47 ⁵/₁₆ | 2.87% |
| JPM | JP Morgan Chase | 45 ⁷/₁₆ | 2.82% |

| Symbol | Company | Price | Yield |
|--------|---------|-------|-------|
| *(NYSE/NASDAQ) (The Dow stocks ranked by yield on 12/29/00)* | | | |
| IP | International Paper | 40 $^{13}/_{16}$ | 2.45% |
| SBC | SBC Communications | 47 ¾ | 2.12% |
| XOM | ExxonMobil | 86 $^{15}/_{16}$ | 2.02% |
| MMM | Minnesota Mining & Manufacturing | 120 ½ | 1.93% |

## Dogs of the Dow Returns

The Dogs of the Dow had a very impressive track record going into the mid-1990s. If you invested $10,000 in the S&P 500, the Dow Jones Industrial Average and the Dogs of the Dow in 1973—and held continuously for 25 years in each investment—your returns would be as follows:

## Comparison of Return

| | Return on $10,000 from 1973 to 1998 |
|--|-------------------------------------|
| DJIA | $211,375 |
| S&P 500 | $214,148 |
| Dogs of the Dow | $665,843 |

*Assuming no commissions and all dividends re-invested*

As you can see, the Dogs of the Dow return more than tripled that of the Dow Jones Industrials and the S&P 500 during this period.

It may be its own success that has caused its downfall. As the Dogs of the Dow became more and more well-known, the returns of the Dogs of Dow has deteriorated.

This method, though originally discovered by O'Higgins, was popularized in recent years by the Motley Fools. These English majors, turned stock market gurus, showed investors that a simple little system like the Dogs of the Dow could outperform the market. They further went on to show people how to manage their debts, and gave practical investment advice in an entertaining fashion. However, as their own popularity and that of the Dogs of the Dow increased, the Dog strategy has suffered.

From 1997 through 1999, the Dogs of the Dow underperformed the Dow Jones Industrials:

|  | Dogs of the Dow | DJIA | S&P 500 |
| --- | --- | --- | --- |
| 1997 | 22.20 | 24.80 | 33.30 |
| 1998 | 10.70 | 18.10 | 28.60 |
| 1999 | 4.00 | 27.20 | 21.10 |
| 2000 | 6.40 | -4.70 | -9.20 |
| 2001 | -4.90 | -5.40 | -11.90 |
| 1 Year | -4.90 | -5.40 | -11.90 |
| 3 Year | 1.80 | 5.70 | 0.00 |
| 5 Year | 7.70 | 12.00 | 12.4 |
| 10 Year | 15.00 | 15.50 | 14.1 |

In 1997, the Dogs of the Dow returned an impressive 22.2 percent return for the year. However, the Dow Jones Industrials surpassed that by posting a 24.8 percent return. In 1998, the Dow Jones Industrials returned 18.1 percent while the Dogs returned a paltry 18.1 percent.

In 2000, the Dog strategy did return 6.4 percent to the Dow's loss of –4.7 percent, and in 2001 the Dogs of the Dow had a loss of –4.9 percent versus the Dow's loss of –5.4 percent.

Thus, as the Dogs of the Dow became more popular, its performance has suffered. The Dogs of the Dow has underperformed the Dow Jones Industrial in total return for both the last 5 years as well as the last 10 years.

The sheer popularity of this simple strategy has led its founder, to note that it may "have become too popular and the market has become too high" for the gambit to keep working.

**Timing Tips**

If you want to invest in a Dogs of the Dow portfolio, but do not wish to buy all 10 stocks individually, consider investing in a unit investment trust. Unit investment trusts are similar to mutual funds, in that one can invest in them for a small amount and receive the benefits of diversification. There are multiple unit trusts established to track the Dogs of the Dow strategy. Most brokers can assist you with this.

## Dogs of the Dow Variations

The Dogs of the Dow propelled O'Higgins from a relatively unknown money manager to the limelight. However, he is passing his discovery by as noted by the comment above, but his own comment may have been taken out of context, as he qualified the statement with the "market has become too high" expressing his displeasure with the valuation of the stock market.

Several different variations of the original Dogs of the Dow are now extremely popular, such as the Flying Five and Foolish Four which concentrate on buying the lowest priced members of the Dogs.

However, our own research shows that investors may be better off timing the Dogs of the Dow with the best months of the year, establishing a Dogs portfolio at the end of October and holding the portfolio until the end of the best six months, or April of the following year. This variation has outperformed the Dow Jones Industrials more often than the original strategy has in recent years, and also benefits from those still looking at year-end investments.

The Dogs of the Dow theory is still most likely a very valid approach to picking blue chip stocks and most likely will continue to be an excellent way for many individual investors to play the stock market. However, we seriously doubt given its popularity it will enjoy the same large advantage it did when it was an undiscovered phenomenon. The markets usually have a way of changing these cycles.

# Value in Value Line

Not all stock-picking services or strategies are doomed to failure once they become successful. One service, which has been a staple for investors for more than a half of a century and has consistently beaten the major stock market indexes, is Value Line.

Value Line is probably the most trusted and prestigious name in the investment field. For more than a half-century Value Line has published more than a dozen print and electronic products utilized by more than half a million investors for timely information on stocks, mutual funds, special situations, options, and convertibles.

The company is best known for the Value Line Investment Survey, the most widely used independent investment service in the world.

The Value Line Investment Survey is a comprehensive source of information and advice on approximately 1,700 stocks, more than 90 industries, the stock market, and the economy. It is made up of three main parts:

◆ The Ratings & Reports section contains one-page reports on approximately 1,700 companies and more than 90 industries. Each company report contains, among other things, Value Line's Timeliness, Safety, and Technical ranks, financial and stock price forecasts for the coming three to five years, an analyst's written commentary, and much more.

◆ The Summary & Index contains an index of all stocks in the publication as well as many up-to-date statistics to keep investors informed about the latest company results.

◆ The Selection & Opinion section contains Value Line's latest economic and stock market forecasts, one-page write-ups of interesting and attractive stocks, model portfolios, and financial and stock market statistics.

One of the key features of the Value Line Service is their proprietary system for stock ranking (see www.valueline.com). This timeliness ranking has a proven record for forecasting the next 6 to 12 months of relative price performance for the stocks featured in the Value Line Investment Survey.

## Timely Stocks Are Just That!

Over a 35-year period Value Line's Timeliness Ranking System has accurately anticipated stocks' subsequent relative price performance. An investor who purchased all stocks rated number one by Value Line at the start of each year since 1965 and sold them at the end of each year would have seen her investments appreciate more than 18,000 percent through the end of 1999!

*Value groups versus major stock market indexes.*

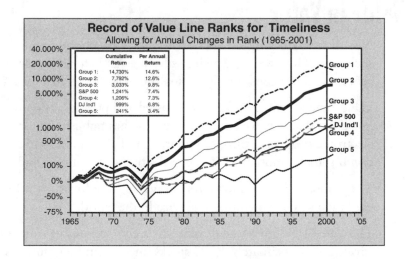

A stock portfolio of number one ranked stocks for timeliness from the Value Line Investment Survey, beginning in 1965 and updated at the beginning of each year, would have shown a gain of 14,703 percent through December 31, 2001. This compares with a gain of 999 percent in the Dow Jones Industrial Average over the same period. In other words, Value Line number one ranked stocks outperformed the Dow by over 14 to 1. The Value Line number one ranked stocks have beaten the S&P 500 by 11 to 1 for the same time span.

## Will This Cycle End Up Doggy, Too?

One of the fears one should have in the marketplace and relying upon historical observation is the fact that these cycles can and do sometimes change.

This changing cycle feature is evident in the fact that the Dogs of the Dow systems performance has decreased substantially as its popularity has increased. However, one does not need to fear this happening to the Value Line Service, though another variant could change its performance in the future, as no investment is a guaranteed winner, free of all risk.

Value Line is already and has been extremely popular for decades, and why not? It is a wonderful product, with a great track record for sound investment advice.

> **Timing Tips**
>
> The money management end of the Value Line Company is Value Line Securities. They can be found on the Web at www.vlfunds.com. You can contact them for information about their funds at Value Line Securities, Inc., 220 East 42nd Street, New York, NY 10017. For more complete information, including management fees and expenses, call for a free prospectus today: 1-800-223-0818, 24 hours a day; 7 days a week.

With over a half million subscribers, Value Line need not worry about its discovery driving down its performance. Value Line has already been discovered by most Wall Streeters, and investors.

They are also an expensive service, with a yearly subscription costing almost $700 per year. Of course, with the valuable insights they provide, it may be money well spent for most serious investors.

Value Line is and has been available for many decades in most public libraries. Simply ask your local librarian where the Value Line Investment Surveys are, and you, too, can take advantage of this wonderful investment product.

Investors can invest with Value Line Mutual Funds, which is the money management arm of the venerable Value Line Research Company. Established in 1950, The Value Line Fund is the oldest in the Value Line family of funds. The Value Line Fund managers make investment decisions using data from the same Value Line analysts widely acclaimed for their quality research and the same proprietary computer models, including the Value Line Timeliness Ranking System.

The fund invests in a well-diversified portfolio of common stocks or securities convertible into common stock and, will usually invest in those securities ranked one or two by the Value Line Ranking System for earnings and price momentum. For added income and diversification, the Fund may also invest up to 15 percent of assets in stocks ranked three. Overall, the fund maintains a growth-stock approach and focuses on the managers' key strength, i.e. individual stock-picking.

## The Least You Need to Know

- Diversification, or spreading your investments over a wide variety of stocks in different industry groups, is a good idea because it prevents the performance of any one holding from too badly affecting your entire portfolio. This is why, for most investors, investing in mutual funds primarily is a good idea.

- The diversification that a mutual fund offers comes at a price. Studies have shown that 80 percent of all mutual funds, despite their staff of analysts and diligent research, have tended to underperform the broad-based stock market indexes. As such, investors may be better off buying index funds, and investing a portion of their portfolios in individual stocks themselves.

- The average investor is much smarter than he/she thinks. One of the most successful fund managers in history, Peter Lynch, guided the successful Magellan fund with the principle of buying companies whose products he would personally use. Since we are all consumers, we may be able to find the next big, great stock, by simply paying attention and using our own common sense.

- Several theories for selecting a few stocks with certain characteristics have been purported to allow investors a simple and easy way to beat the market. The most popular of which has been the Dogs of Dow, which entails buying the 10 highest dividend yielding stocks of the Dow Jones Industrial Average. However, due to its popularity, this strategy has underperformed the market in recent years, though it may be rebounding.

- Value Line Investment Services, an independent research firm, has a proprietary method for picking stocks that has outperformed the market substantially for the last 50 years. Investors can access these reports and research services, or invest in funds run by the Value Line Investment Company. This may be a way of outperforming the market and achieving the benefits of diversification.

# Chapter 16

# Beating the Market with Bonds

## In This Chapter

- ◆ Understanding bonds
- ◆ Coupon, yields, and bond prices
- ◆ Inflation and bond returns
- ◆ Bonds and stocks … use 'em both and beat the market

In the last chapter, we presented an idea originated by Michael B. O'Higgins, the Dogs of the Dow concept. As we stated in the last chapter, this idea did wonderfully for several years, before it became immensely popular. As the popularity of the Dogs of the Dow increased, the returns associated with it decreased.

In fact, several years ago, O'Higgins stated publicly that this strategy (Dogs of the Dow) may "have become too popular and the market has become too high" for the gambit to keep working.

Inside this chapter, we will look at his latest discovery, as outlined in his book *Beating the Dow With Bonds: A High-Return, Low-Risk Strategy for Outperforming the Pros Even When Stocks Go South.*

# What Are Bonds?

A bond is a *debt security*, similar to an I.O.U. When you purchase a bond, you are lending money to a government, municipality, corporation, federal agency or other entity known as the issuer. In return for the loan, the issuer promises to pay you a specified rate of interest during the life of the bond and to repay the face value of the bond (the principal) when it "matures," or comes due.

**Wall Street Words**

A bond is a debt instrument (**debt security**) issued for a period of more than one year with the purpose of raising capital by borrowing. The federal government, states, cities, corporations, and many other types of institutions sell bonds. A bond is generally a promise to repay the principal along with interest on a specified date (maturity).

Among the types of bonds you can choose from are: U.S. government securities, municipal bonds, corporate bonds, mortgage and asset-backed securities, federal agency securities, and foreign government bonds.

All bonds have three basic components:

◆ Maturity date: the length of time until the principle is repaid, for example 10 years from issuance date.

◆ Principle: (or face value) of the bond is the amount to be prepaid. This is usually in $1,000 increments and $5,000 increments thereafter, such as $1,000, $5,000, $10,000, etc.

◆ Coupon: the amount of interest to be paid annually, expressed as a percentage of the principle amount.

When a bond is issued, the price you pay is known as its "face value." Once you buy it, the issuer promises to pay you back on a particular day—the maturity date—at a predetermined rate of interest—the coupon. Say, for instance, you buy a bond with a $1,000 face value, a 5 percent coupon, and a 10-year maturity. You would collect interest payments totaling $50 in each of those 10 years. When the decade was up, you'd get back your $1,000 and walk away.

A key difference between stocks and bonds is that stocks make no promises about dividends or returns. General Electric's dividend may be as regular as a heartbeat, but the company is under no obligation to pay it. And while GE stock spends most of its time moving upward, it has been known to spend months—even years—going the other way.

When GE issues a bond, however, the company guarantees to pay back your principal (the face value) plus interest. If you buy the bond and hold it to maturity, you know exactly how much you're going to get back (in most cases, anyway; I'll discuss some exceptions later). That's why bonds are also known as "fixed-income" investments—they assure you a steady payout or yearly income. And although they can carry plenty of risk, this regular income is what makes them inherently less volatile than stocks.

# Coupons, Yields, and Bond Prices

Just because bonds have a reputation as conservative investments doesn't mean they're always safe. Any time you lend money, after all, you run the risk it won't be paid back. Companies, cities and counties occasionally do go bankrupt or default on their debts for extended periods. U.S. Treasury bonds alone are considered rock-solid. In fact, economists label the yield of the shortest-term U.S. bonds, or Treasury Bills, "the risk-free rate of return."

The coupon on a bond is a function of the current interest rate environment as well as the creditworthiness of the borrower. The more the risk of non-payment on the bond, the higher the coupon.

### Trading Traps

Generally the less creditworthy a borrower is, the higher the coupon payment will be, because bond holders want to receive their principle back as well. When a company's credit rating is downgraded, usually the price of their bonds goes down dramatically as well. Credit risk is serious business and as such, most retail investors should look at bond funds as an alternative to corporate bonds for diversification, just like they do in the stock market.

## Credit Ratings

Several agencies keep track of credit ratings on companies and issuers of debt. The two most popular are Standard and Poor's (S&P) and Moody's. They both use a basic alphabetical rating system which goes AAA to C or D, as follows:

| Rating Service | | |
|---|---|---|
| Moody's | S&P's | Explanation of Rating in English |
| Aaa | AAA | The highest quality, lowest risk bonds |
| Aa | AA | High quality debt obligations with minimal repayment risk |
| A | A | Quality bonds with a strong capacity to repay principle and interest but are somewhat susceptible to adverse economic conditions |

*continues*

*continued*

| Rating Service | | |
| Moody's | S&P's | Explanation of Rating in English |
| --- | --- | --- |
| Baa | BBB | Quality bonds with adequate capacity to pay back principle and interest but are somewhat more susceptible to adverse economic conditions |
| Ba | BB | Medium grade bonds with few desirable characteristics |
| B | B | Speculative bonds with a major degree of risk in adverse economic conditions |
| Caa | CCC | Issuers in poor standing |
| Ca | CC | Issuer may be in default |
| C | C | Income bonds which no interest is being paid |
| - | D | Bonds in default |

The rating system is used to classify a company's debt issuance. Generally, the lower the rating, the higher the coupon because the higher the likelihood that the issuer of the debt will not repay the principle amount of the bond.

The lower-rated bonds, those below Baa/BBB, are commonly referred to as "junk bonds" because many feel the debt is very likely to not be repaid, hence the paper they are printed on is "junk."

Generally, the only bonds without some credit risk are those issued by the U.S. government, or Treasury Securities. Because these bonds carry no credit risk, their return is wholly a function of interest rates.

## Bond Yields and Bond Prices

The return on a bond is a function of the face value of the bond as well as the coupon. When a bond is issued, they are usually issued in increments of $1,000 and $5,000 there after. In other words, when you buy a 10-year bond with a 12 percent coupon, you pay $1,000 and get $120 a year for the next 10 years and then receive your $1,000 back.

**Timing Tips**

The longer a bond has to maturity, generally the larger the coupon. This makes sense, as inflation risk as well as defaulture risk increases with time. See ... time really is money.

However, what happens if you want to sell your bond before 10 years is up? There is a very active market made for bonds after issuance. People buy bonds all the time, not from the original issuer, in a secondary market much like we buy stocks not when they are issued but from previous holders.

Bonds are known as fixed income securities because if they are held to maturity, then they do offer a fixed return. However, if you do not hold the bond to maturity, then you do have risk based on what interest rates have done.

## Bond Pricing

A bond's price moves in the opposite direction of interest rates. For example, let's assume that we buy a $1,000 bond with a coupon of 12 percent, when interest rates are at 12 percent. Now at the end of a year, interest rates have dropped to 10 percent and we want to sell that bond. What will it be worth?

With interest rates at 10 percent, our 12 percent coupon bond should be selling for roughly $1,100. In other words, if we went to sell that bond today we should receive about $1,100 for it.

It is worth more today, because our bond pays $120 a year while similar bonds pay only $100 a year. But, if we pay an extra $180 for a bond today, and only get back $1,000 in 10 years, do we not lose $180?

No you don't, because every year, you get an extra $20 because the coupon is higher. Thus over the next nine years, a 10 percent coupon bond would pay you a total of $900, while the 12 percent coupon would pay you a total of $1,080. The extra $180 is paid back to you over the course of the next nine years, thus the 12 percent coupon bond is worth the extra $180 today, roughly.

> **Timing Tips**
>
> A bond's price is a function of the coupon rate and the current interest rates. If interest rates go up, a bond holder will lose money if they sell their bonds before maturity. However, if interest rates drop, the bond holder can reap a major capital gain for selling the bond prior to maturity. The effect of interest rate changes on bond prices is magnified the longer the time to maturity.

So, if you are holding a bond and interest rates drop, you can reap an extra windfall by selling early. In our example, the investor in the 12 percent coupon bond after one year would have had a return of $120 in coupon payments, plus an extra $180 in appreciation of the principle of the bond for a 30 percent return in one year … not bad for a slow-moving investment.

However, interest rates can go up. If instead of buying a 12 percent coupon bond and interest rates dropping to 10 percent, let's assume that we purchased a 10 percent coupon bond and interest rates increased to 12 percent. At the end of one year, our bond holder would have to sell his bond for a loss, and a substantial one at that. Assuming interest rates are at 12 percent, our bond holder only receives $100 in coupon on a 10 percent bond, while the holder of a newly issued 12 percent coupon bond would receive $120, thus the buyer of the 10 percent coupon bond would buy it for less than $1,000 to recoup the loss of $20 per year on the investment. The buyer of the 10 percent coupon bond would probably pay roughly $820 to buy this bond, as it would generate $900 in coupons over the next nine years, and he would get paid back $1,000 or $180 more than he paid for it, for a total gain of $1,080, while the holder of the 12 percent coupon bond would get the same $1,080 in coupon payments. Thus, the holder of our bond lost $60 by investing in this fixed income security when he sold, or –6 percent.

Thus, the holder of a bond has interest rate risk. If interest rates go up, he will suffer a capital loss because the bond will be sold at less than face value, if he/she sells the bond before maturity. However, if interest rates go down, the bond holder can reap a capital gain by selling he bond before maturity because the bond will be worth more than face value.

Obviously, bonds can be fixed income, but only if they are held to maturity. With most bonds issued in 10- and 20-year maturities, holding until maturity is a very long term investment. Now if you look at current interest rates, and see them near 4 percent, you have to ask yourself if you are happy only getting 4 percent on your money for the next 10 or 20 years.

> **Timing Tip**
>
> As long as the bond is not "callable," any bond can be held all the way to maturity. However, most bonds are not held to maturity, but sold earlier and capital gains and/or losses are made.

Thus, for most people, the choice to go into bonds is not a decision to hold until maturity but really a bet that interest rates will decline in the coming months or years, so they can benefit from the increase in price of the bond.

# Inflation and Bond Risks

As we have said in previous chapters, interest rates are a function of the supply and demand of money. When the demand for money (the need for borrowing) exceeds the supply of money available to lend, the lenders demand a higher rate of interest. Thus, if the borrower really wishes to borrow, then she must pay the rate being asked. However, when the supply of money exceeds the demand for it, interest rates tend to decline as borrowers may opt not to borrow money if the rate being charged is too high.

Interest rates are definitely tied to the economy and the supply and demand for money. But they are also tied to inflation and the future purchasing power of a dollar. Inflation is simply the rate of degradation of the purchasing power of a dollar. We have all heard the stories from our parents or grandparents about when you used to be able to buy a soda for a nickel. Now a soda costs about 50 cents, thus the price of a soda has increased 1,000 percent. That's inflation.

> **Timing Tips**
>
> Generally, interest rates move in the same direction as the economy. When the economy is strong, the demand for money is high and interest rates increase. When the economy is weak, the demand for money is low, and interest rates decline. Bond prices move in the opposite direction as interest rates. Thus, the best time to buy bonds is when the economy is peaking and turning toward recession. The worst time to buy bonds is during a recession or just as the economy is entering into growth.

Inflation is of major concern to the bond market. After all, if you are going to get repaid in 10 years, you hope that in a decade the $1,000 of principle that is returned will be worth something. Hence, to a bond holder, inflation is about his worst enemy.

## Causes of Inflation

Inflation is really more than rising prices; it is the degradation of the purchasing power of a currency. The two main causes of inflation are the supply of money and the demand for goods and services.

Generally, inflation tends to be at its lowest when the economy is weak. In a weak economy the government may be printing more money, increasing the supply of money, but the demand for goods and services is less.

To simplify this, think about yourself for a moment. If you have $50,000 in a savings account what will you do with it? That depends on your current situation. If you are in a job that you feel is safe and are due for a raise next month, you may take that $50,000 and buy a new car, fix up your house, or at least take the family on a trip to Disneyland. However, if you just lost your job, or are fearful that you may, you will save that money for a "rainy day" that may be just around the corner.

The general economy behaves in the same way. As economic prospects increase, people are more likely to spend their money on goods and services. The more money they have, the more they will spend. This is very similar to young people and new families who usually buy more home than they need, because they will grow into it and as they advance in their careers, they will be able to better afford it. It is in these economic environments that when the government increases the supply of money that inflation can increase.

People will spend more. If the rate of money growth outstrips the growth in the supply of money, then the prices of goods and services will rise at an increasing rate as money chases these goods and services. It will build upon itself, as companies expand their production and give raises to workers, who, in turn, buy more things.

> **Trading Traps**
>
> Inflation is the long-term bond holder's worst enemy! Inflation not only lessens the real rate of return of the coupon payment, but also lessens the purchasing power of the principle when it is repaid. Think of it this way: If inflation rises at 5 percent a year for the next 30 years, your $1,000 prepaid will have the purchasing power of only $250 today. Get the picture?

The increasing money chases the production and moves ahead of it, causing prices to rise rapidly and inflation is present.

In a weak economy, however the opposite is true. The consumer retrenches and spends less. Companies are cutting back on production of goods and services, but a slower rate than that at which sales are declining. People are laid off and spend less, and though the supply of money available may have increased, the demand for it is decreasing. Prices will remain static or fall in this environment, and thus, inflation is minimal or nonexistent.

Thus, the bond market, which does not like inflation, tends to react positively to a slowing economy and is fearful of a strengthening economy that may bring inflation.

Another benefit of a slowing economy to bond investors is the fact that the Federal Reserve tends to lower interest rates to stimulate economic growth. Thus, they can sell their bonds early and receive the excess returns generated by lower interest rates due to appreciation in the price of the bond above the principle amount.

However, in a strong economy, bond holders are fearful of inflation as well as rising interest rates. The Federal Reserve will raise interest rates when they see inflation or fear it, slowing down the economy. But the rising interest rates would have a holder of bonds having to sell their bonds at a price below the face value and see capital losses.

As you can see from the above, the bond market moves in the opposite direction of perceived changes in interest rates and inflation.

## Inflation Measures

Typically, when you think of inflation or the rate of inflation you think of the consumer price index (CPI). This is a government measure of the change in price of a basket of goods and services, and is reported monthly.

Another measure of the rate of inflation is the price of gold, according to O'Higgins. Gold is considered a hedge against inflation, because in times of crisis or inflation gold tends to increase in value, thus counteracting the effects of inflation because gold is considered a store of value.

Gold is used because it has a long history as being a median of exchange. Ancient Romans used gold coins, and up until 1973, the U.S. dollar was convertible into gold. Thus, gold has a long history as a medium of exchange and a store of value and so rising gold prices are seen as inflationary.

> **Timing Tip**
>
> Gold is considered a hedge against inflation, because during times of inflation many investors flock to gold as a sorce of value. Thus, rising gold prices are considered as a leading indicator for inflation. This theory is purported not only by O'Higgins, but it is also said that Federal Reserve Chairman Greenspan watches gold prices for the same reason.

# Beating the Dow with Bonds

In his groundbreaking book, *Beating the Dow with Bonds*, O'Higgins recommends that investors should switch assets in their investment portfolios based upon risks and rewards. The basic premise behind this is that investors should only invest in riskier asset classes, like stocks or long-term bonds, when they are compensated for that risk.

Like his Dogs of the Dow theory, this one is very easy to implement and has historically done very well for timing the market.

The basic tenet of it is that investors should only invest in the stock market when earnings justify it. If earnings justify investing in stocks, then they should invest in the Dogs of the Dow. However, should the stock market be priced in such a way that earnings do not justify holding stocks, then they should consider

> **Timing Tips**
>
> As can clearly be seen in O'Higgins second book, *Beating the Dow with Bonds* his comments about the Dogs of the Dow stock selection system usefulness is not being questioned. The fact that he hasn't invested in it has more to do with market valuations than with the merits of this strategy.

long-term bonds, as long as inflation is not rising. If inflation is heating up, then investors should invest heavily in short-term interest rate vehicles, like T-Bills.

## Earnings Justification

The measure of earnings justification that O'Higgins recommends is the earnings yield on the S&P 500. This measure is simply the earnings per share for the most recent 12 months divided by current price per share, or the reciprocal of the price earnings ratio. For example, if a company has a current stock price of $40 per share and has yearly earnings $2 per share, then the earnings yield would be 5 percent, or $2 in earnings divided by $40 per share.

> **Timing Tips**
>
> Stock valuations are definitely tied to earnings expectations for the future. Thus, the higher earnings are as a percentage of price, the cheaper the market is valued. Since stocks and bonds are usually thought of as competing investments, meaning we put our money in one asset class or the other, it makes logical sense to compare earnings yields to returns on treasuries. This brilliant observation is brought to you by Michael B. O'Higgins, author of *Beating the Dow with Bonds*.

O'Higgins feels that unless the earnings yield on the S&P 500 Index surpasses the current yield on a 10-year Treasury bond, then the risk in the stock market is too high.

In such a case, he recommends that investors look to investing in bonds. It is interesting to note that this measure has shown stocks overvalued for the last three years.

The information on the S&P 500 earnings and earnings yield can be found in many financial publications. O'Higgins recommends that readers of his book use *Barron's* magazine, published weekly by Dow Jones and Company, and readily available at a newspaper stand or bookstore near you.

## Long- or Short-Term Bonds

If stocks appear to be overvalued, then the investor is faced with the decision to go into long-term bonds, which O'Higgins recommends zero coupon 30-year Treasury bonds or Treasury bills (T-Bills) with a one-year maturity.

This decision is based on looking at the price of gold. Remember, many feel that gold is a proxy for inflation. Thus if gold prices are higher than they were a year ago, O'Higgins recommends that investors invest in one-year T-Bills.

However, when inflation is not present, as measured by gold price changes from one year ago, then investors should look at investing in 30-year zero coupon bonds.

> ## Timing Tips
>
> Bond returns are a function of interest rate changes, if the bond is not held to maturity. The amount of change in the bonds price corresponding to changes in interest rates is a function of the time to maturity. Since interest rates are a reflection of inflation expectations, in an inflationary environment, or one of rising interest rates, it is better to invest in short-term securities like T-Bills as opposed to longer-term interest rate vehicles like 20-year Treasury bonds.

A zero coupon bond is one in which the coupon payment has been separated and only the principle portion of the bond remains. These are extremely sensitive to changes in interest rates, and move very dramatically when rates change. Just like all other bonds, zero coupon bonds increase in price dramatically when interest rates fall, and they decrease in price dramatically when interest rates increase.

## O'Higgins Beats the Dow Again, Even in the 1990s

From 1980 to 2000, O'Higgins strategy would had you invested in the stock market only one year, 1980. However, buy using zero coupon Treasury bonds as well as T-Bills very aggressively, you would have still wracked up very impressive gains. Over this period the average annual return for implementing O'Higgins strategy on January 1 of each year, would have been 31 percent on average versus an investment in the 30 Dow stocks that would have returned only 17.2 percent on average each year, excluding dividends.

The following table is taken directly from his book, with the last two years interpreted by this author:

| Year | Strategy | % Return | Dow Return % |
| --- | --- | --- | --- |
| 1980 | STOCKS | 40.5 | 21.41 |
| 1981 | T-BILLS | 13.25 | -3.4 |
| 1982 | BONDS | 156.12 | 25.79 |
| 1983 | T-BILLS | 10.03 | 25.68 |
| 1984 | BONDS | 20.44 | 1.05 |
| 1985 | BONDS | 106.9 | 32.78 |

*continues*

*continued*

| Year | Strategy | % Return | Dow Return % |
|------|----------|----------|--------------|
| 1986 | T-BILLS | 5.92 | 26.92 |
| 1987 | T-BILLS | 5.21 | 6.02 |
| 1988 | T-BILLS | 8.99 | 15.95 |
| 1989 | BONDS | 45.25 | 31.71 |
| 1990 | BONDS | 0.33 | -0.58 |
| 1991 | BONDS | 35.79 | 23.93 |
| 1992 | BONDS | 7.82 | 7.35 |
| 1993 | BONDS | 39.47 | 16.74 |
| 1994 | T-BILLS | 7.15 | 4.98 |
| 1995 | BONDS | 85.11 | 36.49 |
| 1996 | T-BILLS | 5.49 | 28.61 |
| 1997 | BONDS | 29.22 | 24.74 |
| 1998 | BONDS | 24.39 | 16.1 |
| 1999 | T-BILLS | 5.10 | 25.2 |
| 2000 | T-BILLS | 6.10 | -6.17 |

*Source:* Beating the Dow, *pages 151 and 152*

Like his previous strategy, which he recommends using to pick your stock market investments, O'Higgins' current strategy is very simple to understand and to implement and has done extremely well historically.

**Timing Tips**

In many circles, O'Higgins has been criticized for missing one of the best stock markets in history, at least recent history. However, the trend for falling interest rates has been just as strong, if not stronger. Thus his strategy of investing in long-term zero coupon bonds, which appreciate substantially when interest rates fall, has paid off handsomely. It doesn't matter how a runner crosses home plate, just as long as he does, and O'Higgins definitely hit a home run with his strategy for beating the Dow with bonds in recent years.

Many financial professionals say the most important decision you make is not what stocks to buy, but what assets to invest in. O'Higgins gives very good guidance in this department as well in his latest book, which we strongly recommend that any serious student of the market purchases.

It is also interesting to note that currently in 2002, the Earnings Yield on the S&P 500 index is very close to the yield on 10-year Treasury Bonds, and as such it may flash a buy signal for stocks in 2003.

But, despite not having been invested in stocks at all for one of the greatest run-ups in history, his method for choosing investments has outperformed the stock market.

## The Least You Need to Know

♦ A bond is an I.O.U. to repay a specific amount of principle—known as the face value—in a specific number of years, and paying a particular amount of interest—known as the coupon.

♦ Bonds are known as fixed income securities because they pay interest on a regular basis. However, if you do not hold the bond until it comes due (maturity), it is possible to get a dramatically different rate of return, as it will no longer be fixed.

♦ The buyer of a bond benefits from lower interest rates because following lower interest rates, she can sell the bond for a greater amount than the face value. If interest rates increase, however, the holder of a bond will suffer a loss as she will have to sell the bond for less than face value. Thus, bond prices move in the opposite direction as do interest rates.

♦ Interest rates tend to move in the opposite direction as the economy. Generally a strong economy sees higher interest rates, and a weak economy sees lower interest rates. The enemy of a long-term bond holder is inflation.

♦ O'Higgins in his book *Beating the Dow with Bonds* states that the best time to buy stocks is when the earnings yield of the stock market is greater than the return on 10-year Treasury notes.

♦ O'Higgins also shows his readers how to switch from long-term bonds to short-term bills based on the inflation outlook. His method has outperformed the stock quite strongly in the last 20 years.

# Chapter 17

# You Have Options:
# Hedging the Market
# with Puts and Calls

## In This Chapter

- ◆ Understanding options
- ◆ Calling up the market
- ◆ Time, volatility, and options
- ◆ Putting down the market
- ◆ Options strategies for everyday use

In this chapter, we will briefly cover the subject of options, or puts and calls. These investment vehicles give the holder of the option the right to buy or sell stocks or market indexes at a predetermined price for a limited amount of time.

Options offer incredible leverage, and as such are a favorite vehicle among speculators for making large bets on the markets. However, options can also be used to reduce the risk of stock ownership as well.

In this chapter, we will highlight the options market and how a market timer can use options to either time the market with greater leverage or reduce their exposure to the risks of investing.

# What Is an Option?

An option provides a choice. The buyer of an option acquires the right—but not the obligation—to buy or sell an underlying instrument (stock or index) under specific conditions in exchange for payment for that right (premium). The buyer of an option has the right to exercise the option, converting it into the financial instrument if it is profitable for him/her to do so.

There are two basic types of options:

- ◆ Call option gives the buyer the right, but not the obligation, to purchase at a specific price anytime during the life of the option.

- ◆ Put option gives the buyer the right, but not the obligation, to sell at a specific price anytime during the life of the option.

The price at which the buyer of a call option has the right to purchase or the buyer of the put option has the right to sell is known as the strike price (or exercise price).

The amount of time the purchaser of the option has the right to purchase (call options) or sell (put options) is known as the expiration month.

Options contracts are standardized, so that if you buy an option, you can sell it on the exchange at a later time easily. Each option has predetermined strike prices, and expiration dates. Each options contract can only be offset before expiration by either selling a like option (same stock, commodity, or index, month, and strike price, call or put). The only variable in the equation is the price paid for this right, known as premium.

# Call Options and How They Work

A call option is an option to buy a stock at a specific price on or before a certain date. In this way, call options are like security deposits.

If, for example, you wanted to rent a certain property, and left a security deposit for it, the money would be used to ensure that you could, in fact, rent that property at the price agreed upon when you returned.

If you never returned, you would give up your security deposit, but you would have no other liability. Call options usually increase in value as the value of the underlying instrument increases.

When you buy a call option, the price you pay for it, called the option premium, secures your right to buy that certain stock at a specified price, called the strike price.

If you decide not to use the option to buy the stock, and you are not obligated to, your only cost is the option premium.

## Call Option Example

For example, let's assume that you expect the stock of a fictitious company, XYZ, looks attractive to the speculator. It is March and the investor thinks the stock will increase in the next several months.

Assume that XYZ stock is trading about $31 per share. He can buy a May 30 call option for $2 per share. As we mentioned earlier, options are standardized, meaning they represent a fixed amount of time, and a fixed number of shares. For example, XYZ stock options, like almost all standard stock options, represent the right to buy 100 shares.

| Call Quote | XYZ | Put Quote |
|---|---|---|
| * 6.50-7.00 * | * APR25 | * 0.15-0.25 * |
| * 1.55-1.90 * | * APR30 | * 0.15-0.25 * |
| * 0.15-0.25 * | * APR35 | * 3.10-3.50 * |
| * 6.50-7.00 * | * MAY25 | * 0.05-0.15 * |
| * 4.10-4.50 * | * MAY27½ | * 0.15-0.25 * |
| * 1.75-2.00 * | * MAY30 | * 0.20-0.45 * |
| * 0.45-0.70 * | * MAY32½ | * 1.15-1.40 * |
| * 0.15-0.25 * | * MAY35 | * 3.10-3.50 * |
| * 6.90-7.40 * | * AUG25 | * 0.15-0.25 * |
| * 2.75-3.10 * | * AUG30 | * 0.90-1.00 * |
| * 0.50-0.75 * | * AUG35 | * 3.40-3.80 * |

*A sample option quote screen.*

So our speculator, who thinks the stock will appreciate in price, can buy the stock at $31 per share, or spending $3,100 for the stock. Or she can purchase a May 30 call option, which gives her the right—but not the obligation—to buy the stock at $30 per share on the third Friday of May, for $2 per share, or $200.00.

Let's assume for a moment that the stock appreciates, and from the end of March when the option was purchased, until the third Friday in May, XYZ increase in value from $31 per share to $40 per share. If our speculator had purchased the stock, she would have made $9 per share (or $900 before commissions and fees), or a 29 percent rate of return.

**Timing Tips**

The best time to purchase a call option is when you not only expect the underlying market to increase, but you also expect the underlying market to become more volatile. As a general rule of thumb when purchasing options, look to buy options as far out as you possibly can. Nothing is more frustrating than buying a call, seeing the move you had anticipated, but having the move take place a few weeks after your option has expired.

If our speculator had purchased the May 30 call options, the options would have expired at a price of $10 per share. Because the stock is at $40 per share and the strike price is at $30 per share, the option at expiration will be worth exactly the difference between the strike price and the stock, if it is above the strike price, or $10 per share in this case. This represents a gain of $800, or ($10 per share—$2 per share cost of the option). But on a percentage basis, this option gave a 400 percent rate of return.

## Premiums, Strike Prices, and Options

The price of an option is a function of where the underlying market is in relation to the strike price, the amount of time left until expiration, and the volatility of the underlying instrument. Option prices are based on these factors, and are determined in trading pits in a fashion very similar to stocks.

The biggest factor in determining the price of an option is where the underlying market is in relation to the strike price. A call option with a strike price below the current price of the underlying market has intrinsic value. For example, a July 10,000 call option Dow Jones Industrial Average is worth at least 200 points (intrinsic value) if the Dow Jones is trading at 10,200. A put option with a strike price above the current price of the underlying market has intrinsic value as well. For example, if the Dow Jones was trading at 9,800, a July 10,000 put would be worth at least 200 points. Basically an option has intrinsic value when it can be exercised profitably. For example, the right to buy the Dow Jones at 10,000 is worth at least 200 points when the price of the Dow Jones is at 10,200. If the option traded for anything less, arbitragers would buy the call options and sell the underlying market, profiting from the differential until the two came back into line.

*Intrinsic value* is the difference, if any, between the market price of the underlying market and the strike price of the option. A call option has intrinsic value if its strike price is below the price of the underlying futures price. A put option has intrinsic value if the strike price is above the current underlying market price. Any option that has intrinsic value is said to be *in the money*. As a general rule, the larger the amount of intrinsic value of an option, the higher the premium paid for that option will be.

**Wall Street Words** _____

The **intrinsic value** of an option is the amount of money that option would be worth if it were exercised and turned into the underlying market today. For example, a 100 call option with the underlying market at 120 would have an intrinsic value of 20. A 100 put option with the underlying at 80 would also have an intrinsic value of 20. For call options, intrinsic value = underlying market − strike. For put options, intrinsic value = strike − underlying market.

If an option has no intrinsic value, it is said to be either *at the money* or *out of the money*. An "at the money" option is one where the underlying market price is equal to the strike price of the option. For example, with Dow Jones trading at 9,000, the 9,000 Calls and Puts are referred to as "at-the-money" options. If a call option has a strike price higher than the current underlying market price, the option is said to be "out of the money." If a put option has a strike price below the current underlying market price, the put option is said to be "out of the money." At the money and out of the money options have what is known as extrinsic value or "time value."

The second major component of an option price—or premium—is time value. Time value is the amount of money that option buyers are willing to pay for an option in the anticipation that over time the price of the underlying market will change in value causing the option to increase in value. Time value also reflects the amount of money that a seller of an option requires to relinquish the right to the purchaser.

**Wall Street Words** _____

A call option is considered **in the money** if the underlying market price is above the strike price. Put options are considered **out of the money** if the underlying market is trading below the strike price of the put. If the strike price of the option equals the futures price, the option is considered **at the money**.

| | Call | Put |
| --- | --- | --- |
| In the money | Underlying > Strike | Underlying < Strike |
| At the money | Underlying = Strike | Underlying = Strike |
| Out of the money | Underlying < Strike | Underlying > Strike |

Generally speaking, the longer the amount of time until an option's expiration, the greater the time value of the option will be. This is because the right to buy or sell something is more valuable to a market participant if he has several months to decide what to do, than if he only has several days. Conversely, the option seller has more risk over time that the option will go in the money (or stay in the money) and thus demands more premium in exchange for selling the right to buy or sell over a longer period of time.

Some parallels can be made between options and insurance policies in this case. The premium charged for term causality insurance increases the longer the policy period, because obviously the likelihood of a claim was being made increases with the length of the policy. The longer the time of the policy, the greater the likelihood that the policyholder will make a claim, hence the greater the risk to the policy writer (the insurance company), and thus, the higher the premium paid for the policy.

The same general principle applies to the options market—the longer the time to expiration the greater the likelihood that the option will be exercised, hence the greater the risk to the option writer, and thus the higher the premium charged for the option. In general, because of the risk and potential reward associated with time, the greater the amount of time to expiration of the option, the more expensive the premium of the option will be.

> **Wall Street Words**
>
> **Volatility** is the amount of movement in the underlying market over a period of time. Options tend to be more expensive when volatility is high and tend to be cheaper when volatility is low. Options buyers should look to buy quiet markets and sell their options when prices become volatile.

Another component of extrinsic value—or time value—is the *volatility* of the underlying futures contract. Volatility is the amount of movement in the underlying market over a period of time. Obviously, if prices are jumping up and down and changing by large amounts, obviously the risk and potential reward associated with this market is greater, and hence the price of the option will be greater.

For example, assume that XYZ prices have traded between $43.00 per share and $53.00 per share for the last year. The risk associated with writing a $55.00 call option may seem minute, as well as the profit potential of this option. Thus, in this case, the cost of this option would be relatively small, as the risk to the option should be perceived as minimal and the potential reward perceived by the buyer would be small. However, if XYZ prices were to rise from $43.00 to $53.00 in a single week, suddenly the risk associated with writing a $55.00 call option would seem large, as well the potential reward in purchasing such an option. Thus, the price commanded by sellers in return for the right would increase and buyers would be more willing to pay this price. So, generally speaking, the greater the volatility, the greater the price of the option.

Volatility and time to expiration have tremendous impact on the price of out-of-the-money and at-the-money options. These factors also affect the extrinsic value portion of an in-the-money option as well. Just because an option is in the money does not mean that it doesn't have any extrinsic value. But as an option gets deeper and deeper in the money, it loses time value as a component of its pricing.

Because options have extrinsic value, or time value, they are decaying assets. As time passes, the amount of time value decreases. The rate of decay of time value increases as you get closer to expiration, speeding way up close to six weeks until expiration. Hence, for the option purchaser, time is the enemy, slowly eroding the value of an option.

# Put Options and How They Work

Put options are options to sell a stock at a specific price on or before a certain date. In this way, put options are like insurance policies.

If you buy a new car, and then buy auto insurance on the car, you pay a premium and are, hence, protected if the asset is damaged in an accident. If this happens, you can use your policy to regain the insured value of the car. In this way, the put option gains in value as the value of the underlying instrument decreases. If all goes well and the insurance is not needed, the insurance company keeps your premium in return for taking on the risk.

With a put option, you can "insure" a stock by fixing a selling price. If something happens which causes the stock price to fall, and thus, "damages" your asset, you can exercise your option and sell it at its "insured" price level. If the price of your stock goes up, and there is no "damage," then you do not need to use the insurance, and, once again, your only cost is the premium. This is the primary function of listed options, to allow investors ways to manage risk.

**Timing Tips**

Put options are an excellent alternative to selling a stock short. When you sell a stock short, you have to borrow the shares, which has a cost associated with it. Usually you borrow stock at the broker call rate of interest. Stock short-sellers also have to pay out any dividends, which can also increase the cost of holding a short position. However, a put option purchaser doesn't have to worry about any of these things. Their risk is limited to the cost of the option (the premium), and they have no other costs except commissions and fees.

## Put Option Example

For example, let's assume that you expect the stock of a fictitious company, XYZ, will decrease in value to the speculator. It is March and you think the stock will decrease in the next several months.

Assume that XYZ Stock is trading about $31 per share. You can buy a May 30 put option for $1.40 per share. As we mentioned earlier, options are standardized, meaning the represent a fixed amount of time, and a fixed number of shares. For example, XYZ put options, like almost all standard stock options, represent the right to sell 100 shares.

*Another sample option quote screen.*

| Call Quote | XYZ | Put Quote |
|---|---|---|
| * 6.50-7.00 * | * APR25 * | * 0.15-0.25 * |
| * 1.55-1.90 * | * APR30 * | * 0.15-0.25 * |
| * 0.15-0.25 * | * APR35 * | * 3.10-3.50 * |
| * 6.50-7.00 * | * MAY25 * | * 0.05-0.15 * |
| * 4.10-4.50 * | * MAY27½ * | * 0.15-0.25 * |
| * 1.75-2.00 * | * MAY30 * | * 0.20-0.45 * |
| * 0.45-0.70 * | * MAY32½ * | * 1.15-(1.40)* |
| * 0.15-0.25 * | * MAY35 * | * 3.10-3.50 * |
| * 6.90-7.40 * | * APR25 * | * 0.15-0.25 * |
| * 2.75-3.10 * | * APR30 * | * 0.90-1.00 * |
| * 0.50-0.75 * | * APR35 * | * 3.40-3.80 * |

Thus, our speculator can sell XYZ stock short—meaning to borrow the stock and pay a charge for doing so and place a bet that the price will decrease—at $31 per share or he can purchase a May 32½ put option for $1.40 per share or $140 before commissions and fees.

### CAUTION

**Trading Traps** _____

Do not assume that all options are traded with a contract size of 100 shares. Following splits and reverse split, stock dividends, and other situations, options can represent more or less than 100 shares. Before purchasing or writing any options, be sure to understand the risks and rewards. As all brokers will warn you, options are not a suitable investment for everyone. Speculators and investors should be sure that option trading fits in with their overall goals and should understand the risks before buying and selling options.

Let's assume, like we did in the previous example, that XYZ stock rises to $40 a share by the third Friday of the month. The speculator who sold stock short would have had a loss of $900 before commissions and fees, plus an interest charge for borrowing the stock to sell short. However, the put option purchaser would lose only $140 before commissions and fees, as the option would have expired worthless. The buyer of the option has the right, not the obligation, to exercise the option into a stocks (or the underlying asset), so when it would result in a greater loss, they choose not to exercise their right.

However, had the stock declined, the option purchaser would have been happy with the put purchase. For example, assume that XYZ declined from $31 a share to $20 a share. The $32^1/_2$ put option would be $12^1/_2$ per share in-the-money, meaning it would be worth $1,250. With an initial cost of $140, the put option purchase would have yielded a profit of $1,110 before commissions and fees, or a return of 892 percent before commissions. The speculator who sold the stock short, would also be happy, getting a return of 32 percent or $1,100 before commissions, fees, and the cost of borrowing the stock.

Hence, as you can see, option offer tremendous leverage and you can bet on both sides of the market, up or down with very little effort. But options can also be used to hedge and lower the risk involved in the market place.

# Option Strategies for Everyday Use

Options are a risky investment. Literature shows that most people who trade options lose money. Remember, options are a decaying asset. Like holding credit card debt, holding options over a long period of time causes you to lose money, because as each day passes the option loses a little bit of time value.

This makes purchasing options extremely risky. However, for market participants who are looking at a hot stock or acting on a tip—not a recommended activity, but one most market participants partake in on occasion—option purchases offer an excellent limited risk, potentially unlimited reward way to trade the market.

But as market timers we can use options to lower our risk as well, using two simple strategies: protective puts and covered writes.

## Protective Puts

Today, investors are often concerned with the many uncertainties of the stock market. During bull markets, investors are worried about market corrections, and during bear markets, they are worried that their stocks could fall further. This uncertainty can lead to a reluctance to invest, and strong up moves might be missed. Buying puts against an existing stock position or simultaneously purchasing stock and puts can supply the insurance needed to overcome the uncertainty of the marketplace. People

**Wall Street Words**

Protective puts provide complete coverage for decreasing stock prices. These positions are established by either buying puts against an existing stock position or simultaneously purchasing stock and puts. However, even though the stock is hedged against downside deterioration below the strike price and the cost of the option, the upside is also diminished by the cost of the option.

insure their valuable assets, but most investors have not realized that many of their stock positions also can be insured. That is exactly what a *protective put* does. Typically, by paying a relatively small premium (compared to the market value of the stock), an investor knows that no matter how far the stock drops, it can be sold at the strike price of the put anytime up until the put expires.

Buying a protective put involves the purchase of one put contract for every 100 shares of stock already owned or purchased. A put gives the owner the right but not the obligation to sell the underlying security at a certain price (the strike or exercise price) up to the expiration date. Puts (and calls) are available with expirations of up to eight months on over 1700 stocks.

## Example of a Protective Put

First, let's look at buying a stock without owning a put for protection. If stock is bought at $50 per share, as soon as the stock drops below the purchase price the investor begins to lose money. The entire $50 purchase price is at risk. Correspondingly, if the price increases, the investor benefits from the entire increase without incurring the cost of the put premium or insurance.

When only the stock is bought, there is no protection or insurance. The investor is at risk of losing the total investment.

Let's now compare buying ZYX stock to buying ZYX with a protective put. In this example, ZYX is still at $50 per share. A six-month put with a strike price of 50 can be bought for 2$^1/_4$ or $225 per contract (2$^1/_4$ x $100). This put can be considered insurance "without a deductible," because the stock is purchased at $50 and an at-the-money put with the same strike price, 50, is purchased. If the stock drops below $50, the put or insurance will begin to offset any loss in ZYX (less the cost of the put).

|  | **Buy ZYX** | **Buy ZYX and Six-Month 50 Put** |
| --- | --- | --- |
| Stock Cost | $50 | $50 ---- |
| Put Cost | 0 | $ 2$^1/_4$ |
| Total Cost | $50 | $52$^1/_4$ |
| Risk | $50 | $ 2$^1/_4$ |

No matter how low ZYX falls, buying the six-month put with a 50 strike price gives the investor the right to sell ZYX at $50 up until expiration. The downside risk is only 2¼: the total cost for this position, $52¼, less 50 (strike price). This strategy gives an investor the advantage of having downside protection without limiting upside potential above the total cost of the position, or $52¼.

The only disadvantage is that the investor will not begin to profit until the stock rises above $52¼. If ZYX remains at $50 or above, the put will expire worthless and the premium would be lost. If just the stock had been bought, the investor would begin to profit as soon as the stock rose above $50. However, the investor would have no protection from the risk of the stock declining in value. Owning a put along with stock ensures limited risk, while increasing the breakeven on the stock by the cost of the put, but still allowing for unlimited profit potential above the breakeven.

Another way to get the benefits of protection, though limited, and to also get some of the benefit of appreciation is to do a covered write.

> **Trading Traps**
>
> Buying puts can get very expensive. Over the long haul, fully insuring your portfolio will most likely lead to losses. Just as the old saying goes, the best insurance is self-insurance; the disciplined trader should learn to cut losing positions from her portfolio. However, in times of great upheaval, traders may wish to purchase puts as they offer protection. However, protection comes at a price.

## Covered Call Writing

*Covered call writing* is either the simultaneous purchase of stock and the sale of a call option or the sale of a call option against a stock currently held by an investor. Generally, one call option is sold for every 100 shares of stock. The writer receives cash for selling the call but will be obligated to sell the stock at the strike price of the call if the call is assigned to his account. In other words, an investor is "paid" to agree to sell his holdings at a certain level (the strike price). In exchange for being paid, the investor gives up any increase in the stock above the strike price.

> **Wall Street Words**
>
> **Covered call writing** is either the simultaneous purchase of stock and the sale of a call option or the sale of a call option against a stock currently held by an investor. This strategy serves to limit the downside exposure of the stock by the premium received while at the same time limiting the potential gain to the difference between the underlying market and the strike price of the option, plus the premium received.

If an investor is neutral to moderately bullish on a stock currently owned, the covered call might be a strategy he would consider. Let's say that 100 shares are currently held in his account. If the investor was to sell one slightly out-of-the-money call, he would be paid a premium to be obligated to sell the stock at a predetermined price, the strike price. In addition to receiving the premium, the investor would also continue to receive the dividends (if any) as long as he still owns the stock.

The covered call can also be used if the investor is considering buying a stock on which he is moderately bullish for the near term. A call could be sold at the same time the stock is purchased. The premium collected reduces the effective cost of the stock and he will continue to collect dividends (if any) or as long as the stock is held.

In either case, the investor is at risk of losing the stock if it rises above the strike price. Remember, in exchange for receiving the premium for having sold the calls, the investor is obligated to sell the stock. However, as you will see in the following example, even though he has given up some upside potential there can still be a good return on the investment.

For example, let's assume that Stock ZYX currently is priced at $41^7/_8$, and the investor thinks this might be a good purchase. The three-month 45 calls can be sold for $1^1/_4$. Historically, ZYX has paid a quarterly dividend of 25 cents. By selling the three-month 45 call the investor is agreeing to sell ZYX at 45 should the owner of the call decide to exercise his right to buy the stock. Keep in mind that the call owner may exercise the option if the stock is above 45, because he or she will be able to buy the stock for less than it is currently trading for in the open market. But, as you will see, his return will be greater than if he had held the stock until it reached 45 and then sold it at that price.

> **Timing Tips**
>
> Covered call writing is a better strategy longer term than buying protective puts, as the premium received from writing the options serves to insulate the portfolio from declines. This strategy is best implemented when prices are going sideways to slightly up. The ideal situation is to write the option and have the stock move just up to the strike price, so you receive the option premium but don't have to forfeit your stock (have it called away).

Let's take a look at what happens to a covered call position as the underlying stock moves up or down. Commissions have not been taken into consideration in these examples; however, they can have a significant effect on your returns.

Now let's assume that ZYX remains below 45 between now and expiration, and therefore the call will not be assigned. The call option will expire worthless. The premium of $1^1/_4$ and the stock position will be retained. In effect you have paid $40^5/_8$ (which is also the breakeven price) for ZYX (41⅞ purchase cost—1¼ premium received for sale of call). This would be offset by any dividends that were received, which in this example would be 25¢.

When the ZYX call expires worthless, the covered call writer can sell another call going further out in time taking in additional premium. Once again, this produces an even lower purchase cost or breakeven.

If ZYX remains below 45 for an entire year, the investor can sell these calls four times. For this example we will make the hypothetical assumption that the price of the stock and option premiums remain constant throughout the year. 1¼ (Call Premium Received) x 4 = $5 in Premium + any dividends paid = Total Income.

As you can, though you can lose money on the purchase ZYX stock, some of those losses will be offset by the sale of the option. Now let's assume that ZYX stock rises above 45 between now and expiration and therefore the call assigned, and we will have to forfeit our stock.

**Timing Tips**

Several mutual funds have covered call writing programs. These funds specialize in searching out situations where a covered call would be a good strategy. With over 1,700 stocks with listed options on them, they can trade a very diversified portfolio, and get the benefit of receiving premiums. These funds tend to be the strongest performers when the stock market in general is slowly appreciating.

The call buyer can exercise his right to buy the stock and the call seller will have to sell ZYX at 45, even though ZYX has risen above 45. But remember the call seller has taken in the premium of the call and has been earning dividends (if any) on the stock.

If ZYX stock is called away at expiration:

| | | |
|---|---|---|
| Receive | 45 for stock | $4,500.00 |
| | 1¼ for premium | $125.00 |
| Less | 41 7/8 stock cost | $4,625.00 |
| | | ($4,187.50) |
| Return | 10.40% | $437.50* |

*In three months plus dividends (if any) received.*

As you can see, the covered call write is a strategy that has the ability to meet the needs of a wide range of investors. It can be used in your Keogh, margin, cash account or IRA against stock you already own or are planning on buying. Though it limits the upside rewards, it also insulates portfolios of stocks to the downside. This is an excellent way for investors to reap some of the benefit in a slowly upward grinning market.

## The Least You Need to Know

◆ A call option represents the *right* to buy at a predetermined price during a specific time period.

◆ A put option represents the *right* to sell at a predetermined price during a specific time period.

◆ The buyer of an option (long position) has risk limited to the amount paid for the option, and potentially unlimited profit potential.

◆ The seller of an option (short position) has potentially unlimited risk potential, and profit potential limited to the amount someone paid for the option. However, most options expire worthless and options are a decaying asset, so either strategy can be profitable if proper risk management is used.

◆ By purchasing a put option as insurance against stocks or indexes you already own, you can limit or insure your portfolio against losses. However, this insurance has a cost associated with it, and your returns will be diminished by the cost of the option. This is usually a good situation to be in when you are projecting the end of a bear market, but not sure on the exact timing of the end of the secular down move.

◆ Another way to use options in your portfolio is to write call options against your holdings. This gives limited downside protection, as you collect the option premium, effectively lowering your cost of buying the stock. However, writing calls also limits your upside gain. Therefore this type of strategy is good where one expects slow appreciation within a bull market.

# Part  Putting It All Together

Inside this part, specific advice is offered about mutual funds and how to pick ones that will offer good performance. Though the benefits of mutual fund investing are widely known, the first chapter in this part presents an unprecedented look at some of the hidden costs and the effects these seemingly minor costs can have on your longer-term performance.

Asset allocation is also discussed as a means of diversifying your portfolio for a more constant and less volatile way to achieve performance.

The concepts of trends following political cycles and asset allocation are then applied together, forming the basis of a well-thought-out approach to timing the market.

# Chapter 18

# Picking Funds

## In This Chapter

- ◆ What exactly are mutual funds
- ◆ Open and closed, load and no-load funds
- ◆ Fees and other forms of vigorish
- ◆ Passive versus active funds

The first bona fide mutual fund came onto the scene in 1868 in England in the form of Colonial Government Trust, which was formed to provide the investor of moderate means "the same advantages as large capitalists, in diminishing the risks of investing in Foreign and Colonial Government stocks, by spreading the investment over a number of different stocks."

The early 1920s saw the mutual fund move across the Atlantic and take its modern form that we know of today. Massachusetts Investors Trust, the first of the modern genre, was introduced in March 1924. Shortly following it came State Street Investment Corporation. These were followed in 1925 by Incorporated Investors, which are now a part of the Putnam Family of Funds. From these modest beginnings the number of mutual funds has flourished, with the total number of mutual funds in existence today surpassing the total number of stocks listed on the New York Stock Exchange.

# What Mutual Funds Are and Aren't

Legally speaking, there is no such thing as a *mutual fund*. That's merely a name coined to embrace a variety of investment corporations and investment trusts created for the mutual investment under professional management of assets contributed by several individuals.

**Wall Street Words**

A collective investment funds or portfolios registered with the Securities and Exchange Commission (SEC) under the Investment Advisors Act of 1940 is commonly referred to as a **mutual fund**. Each investors interest in the fund is represented by shares of ownership the same way a share of stock represents ownership in a corporation.

Mutual funds of all types are collective investment funds or portfolios registered with the Securities and Exchange Commission (SEC) under the Investment Advisors Act of 1940, known in the industry as the "40 Act." Individual investors' interests are represented by shares of stock, as is the case with many corporations.

The shares of stock in a mutual fund are kind of like pro forma shares in the stocks they hold. Suppose, for a moment, that 1,000 people each put $50 into a mutual fund. The fund then goes out and buys $50,000 worth of stock. No one investor could possibly buy as diversified a portfolio as the fund can, but each is given a 1/1,000 interest in the fund as a whole. Thus, mutual funds allow investors to pool their investments.

# Pooling and Net Asset Value

Shares in mutual funds can either be traded in a fashion very similarly to those of stock, or are done on an end-of-day basis, depending upon the type of fund it is—closed or open-ended, respectively.

The value of a mutual fund is a reflection of its current holdings. For example, in our case above, where we had 1,000 investors each investing $50 into a mutual fund, the value of the fund at end-of-day you would be $50,000 or $50 a share.

Each share may represent partial ownership of a whole list of stocks, in varying quantities. For example, let's assume that our $50,000 mutual fund buys the following stocks:

| Company Name | Stock Price | Number of Shares |
|---|---|---|
| Eastman Kodak | 28.21 | 355 |
| JP Morgan | 21.71 | 461 |
| Phillip Morris | 47.41 | 210 |

| Company Name | Stock Price | Number of Shares |
|---|---|---|
| General Motors | 44.61 | 225 |
| Microsoft | 47.48 | 210 |

So each of the 1,000 shares in our mutual fund would represent roughly .35 of a share of Eastman Kodak, .46 shares of JP Morgan, .21 shares of Phillip Morris, .22 shares of General Motors, and .21 shares of Microsoft. But, the value of each share is simply a reflection of the value of the entire fund—less management fees, expenses, and other fees—divided by the number of shares outstanding.

This is referred to as net asset value. *Net asset value*, or *NAV* in shorthand, is the dollar value of all marketable securities (stocks, bonds, etc.) owned by a mutual fund, less expenses, and divided by the total number of shares outstanding.

**Wall Street Words**

Net Asset Value (NAV) is the dollar amount of all marketable securities (stocks, bonds, etc.) owned by a particular mutual fund, less expenses, divided by the number of shares outstanding.

Some mutual funds trade at net asset value, while others trade at a premium or discount to net asset value. Those funds that commonly trade above or below net asset value are known as closed end funds, while typically open-ended funds trade at net asset value.

## Open and Closed Funds

Most mutual funds fall into the open-ended category, meaning that they can issue shares whenever they are needed. Purchasing an *open-ended fund* is usually done by contacting your broker or the fund company directly. You simply state the dollar amount of the fund you wish to buy and they will sell the nearest whole number of shares. They then take your money and add it to the existing fund and create more shares in the fund.

The price you pay for an open-ended fund is based on the net asset value (NAV) of the fund at the end of the day. Thus, usually if you wish to buy a fund on a specific day, you need to have your order in by 4:00 P.M. Eastern Time, as usually orders received after 4:00 P.M. Eastern Time are priced at the following day's net asset value.

The first mutual funds were *closed-end funds*. Closed-end funds differ from open-ended funds in that the number of shares to be offered in a closed-ended fund is fixed at the outset of the fund. The fund operator may not create new shares on demand, unlike the open-ended fund.

### Wall Street Words

**Open-ended funds** have an unlimited number of shares available and new shares can be issued at any time. Open-ended funds can be redeemed from the mutual fund company at net asset value. **Closed-end funds** have a limited number of shares outstanding, set at issuance. No new shares can be issued. These funds trade on stock exchange floors and in the over-the-counter market. Their price is set by market forces and can trade above (premium to) or below (discount to) net asset value.

Closed-end funds also differ in the fact that they are traded on an exchange floor, or electronically. In an open-ended fund, the fund management will buy back an investor's shares at net asset value, called a redemption. Closed-end funds make no such guarantee as toward redemption. Instead the value of the fund is determined on the floor of a stock exchange, or in the over-the-counter market, just like the value of a stock is determined. Thus, closed-ended funds do not always trade at net asset value (NAV).

## Closed-Ended Funds, Discounts, and Premiums

When the shares of a closed-ended fund are trading at a price above the net asset value (NAV) of the fund, it is said to be trading at a premium. When the shares are trading below the net asset value of the fund, they are trading at a discount.

### Timing Tips

Just because a fund is trading at a discount to net asset value, does not mean that it has to ever close this discount. Many closed-end mutual funds have traded for decades at a discount to net asset value. Usually, there is a very good reason why a closed-ended fund trades at a discount to net asset value. Don't be lulled in by a deep discount to net asset value, as Wall Street very rarely gives money away free!

Discounts and premiums are set by the marketplace for closed-end funds. Remember, closed-end funds are priced like that of a stock. Since net asset value is a function not only of the value of the holdings of the fund, but also includes management fees and costs for running the funds, most closed-end funds trade at a discount to net asset value.

Closed-end funds discount or premium to net asset value is generally a perception about future performance. If investors feel that this fund will do extremely well in the future, they will pay a premium for the fund. For example, closed-end funds are usually designed for a very specific market — niches—as we will explain later. Thus, when that particular niche becomes popular and the demand from investors for this fund outstrips the limited number of shares outstanding, new investors who want in have to pay a premium to entice existing shareholders to part with their shares.

The exact opposite causes a fund to trade at a discount. In fact, most closed-ended mutual funds trade at a discount to net asset value, as the risk is greater in these types of funds because they are not redeemable. Thus, for new investors to be enticed into buying shares, they have to get a discount.

Remember, though some closed-end funds do trade at significant discounts to their net asset value, there is usually a reason. It is not uncommon for some funds to trade at a discount as much as 20 percent to their net asset value. In fact, some closed-end funds have traded at discounts to their net asset values for decades. But upon occasion, especially in wild bull markets, some closed-end funds can close the discount on top of the strong market performance, giving investors a double boost on their performance.

## Why Be Closed?

At first glance, the decision to run a closed-ended mutual fund does not seem very bright. Remember, mutual funds are businesses just like any other, with the goal of making money. They make money by managing funds. Thus by running a closed-ended fund, they are restricting the amount of money they can manage, as the number of shares, and thus some of the potential money under management is limited. However, in certain cases, running a closed-end fund makes perfect sense.

Most closed-end funds today are set up to trade specific market niches, such as emerging overseas investments, state and municipal bond funds, etc. Basically, most of these types of investments are in markets that are illiquid, meaning they do not have a large volume. Thus, the risk of mass-redemption of a mutual fund could ruin the long-term performance of the fund.

For example, assume a closed-end fund is set up to invest strictly in Bangladesh stocks. If civil unrest were to sweep the country, then the holders of the fund may en mass wish to redeem their shares at net asset value. The fund would have to sell its holdings, and the mass selling by the fund would further drive prices. Thus, as shareholders sold (redeemed) their mutual funds, due to the bad news, then the mutual fund manager would be forced to sell its underlying holdings, even if he felt the price being received wasn't in the best interest of the remaining investors.

To avoid this, especially in highly specialized investment portfolios that cannot absorb large orders, the management issued the fund as a closed-ended fund. Thus, when investors wished to liquidate (sell) their holdings in the fund, they could do so, but instead of shares being redeemed, causing the management company to sell assets to raise the money necessary to redeem, the shares are absorbed on the open market, in the same way a stock is traded.

> ### Timing Tips
>
> Never, ever pay a premium for a closed-ended fund, especially if it has previous a history of trading at net asset value or below. Because closed-end funds typically represent small niches, sometimes when that niche becomes extremely popular, the fund can trade at a significant premium to net asset value. This is usually indicative of a market top. As an investor it pays to go against the crowd, and closed-end funds only trade at a premium when the crowd loves them. Remember being a contrarian pays!

These situations can cause some funds to trade at very large discounts to net asset value. But, before buying a closed-end fund just because it is at a large discount to net asset value, be aware that there may be a very legitimate reason for the discount. Also, some funds have a long history of trading at a discount, and in fact, a discount may be there normal pricing situation. Be sure to consult the funds prospectus and/or mutual fund research firms, such as Morningstar, to see the history of the closed-end fund and its relationship to net asset value.

# Load and No Load Mutual Funds

Wall Street has a language all its own. This is true of any industry, especially those in which large sums of money are involved.

For example, when searching for a house, if a listing exclaims the wonders of the "fruit trees" in the garden, that is real estate code for "this house is in real need of repairs and the best feature we can highlight are some trees." "Located conveniently" means that the house is located on a major road and traffic may be a problem. An up and coming neighborhood means that the house is located one step above a war zone. Code words for desirability are not just restricted to real estate. The computer industry uses all sorts of acronyms to confuse us and make the computer people seem smarter.

Wall Street has its own little code words for things as well. Very rarely is the term "sales charge" or "commission" used when explaining mutual funds. Instead, the word of choice when investing in mutual funds is "*load.*"

## What a Load of ...

Open-ended mutual funds fall into two major categories: load and no-load funds. They resemble each other in every way but one. Load funds are sold with a sales commission—the "load." Typically, these fees run from 5 to 10 percent of the dollar amount invested in the fund. The load is usually expressed as a percentage of the purchase price, or net asset value less the sales charge.

The way loads are calculated is very sneaky, as they are calculated off of the total investment amount, not the number of transactions. For example, if you were to buy 100 shares of XYZ stock, you may pay a commission of $80. This doesn't matter if XYZ is trading at $50 per share or $5 per share. Thus if you buy 100 shares of XYZ at $50, you pay $5,000 for the stock and an additional $80 for the execution of the trade by your stock brokerage firm. The total cost of $5,080 and you get 100 shares of stock.

The way loads are calculated is a bit deceptive, in that it is based on the dollar amount of the transaction. For example, let's assume you buy QRS mutual fund. This fund carries an 8.5 percent sales load to it and you wish to purchase $1,000 of the fund, which has a net asset value of $10. You pay a sales charge of $85, and you get $915, or 91 shares of QRS mutual fund.

> **Timing Tips**
>
> Historically, there is no big difference in the performance between load and no-load funds. Hence, investors are better off buying no-load funds and using the cost of the load to either invest more heavily, or perhaps to enjoy a good night on the town. Why pay an extra cost if you don't have to?

The sales load percentage is 8.5 percent, right? Nope, this is the sneaky part. By charging the load up front, you only get 91 shares or $910 worth of the mutual fund and have a $5 credit. Thus, instead of paying 8.5 percent of the purchase price, you are paying a true commission of 9.3 percent, as $85 divided by the amount purchased is 9.3 percent.

> **Timing Tips**
>
> There are two basic types of loads. Front loads, or sales commissions, are charged upon entering the fund. These type of funds and their corresponding loads, serve to lower the amount of your investment and understate the charge. Backend loads are charged only upon selling of the fund. The load is charged when you sell the fund. Though this type of load doesn't serve to misrepresent the fee being charged, it is still a fee, which may be unnecessary.

Looking at it another way, if you want a full $1,000 in securities by purchasing the mutual fund, you must spend $1,093.00 to achieve that.

Now, if you remember back to previous chapters, the average return on stocks is in the 11 to 15 percent range. By paying a 9.3 percent commission rate, or load, you are sacrificing almost an average year's worth of performance.

## Arguments in Favor of the Load

One of the most common misunderstandings on load vs. no-load is that though load funds charge an upfront sales fee, their performance is often better.

Studies by several academics over the years show that on average, this particular argument holds very little water. Some load funds have strongly outperformed the pack, while others have not. But, on average, for most investors, the load is a cost that should be avoided in most cases.

Thus, with respect to performance there is no appreciable difference between load and no-load mutual funds. Thus, why should an investor pay the load?

Mutual fund salespersons will proffer any number of arguments to justify the load. Probably the most common is that since you are investing over the long haul, the growth of the fund will reduce the effective cost of the load over time due to the funds great performance.

In rebuttal, as any investor who has been invested in 2000 and 2001 knows, you can't always count on asset appreciation. So, even if you amortize the load over a long period, such as nine years, your performance is still suffering by 1 percent, on a 9 percent load fund. Thus, if comparable no-load funds are posting the same performance, it is hard to justify this penalty, even if it is just 1 percent.

Another argument put forth in defense of the load is that it carries an element of service for the investor. The salesperson or broker to whom the load is paid stands ready to give advice, answer questions, and help iron out any kinks that might develop with regard to your fund account.

The question then becomes whether the service they are giving justifies this. For some, the answer may be a resounding yes. In fact, we strongly recommend that most investors have a trained and licensed broker help them with their financial planning and investment decisions. Usually, these professionals will charge a fee, which is based in part on performance. Many brokerages are now moving away from transaction-based services, and moving into fee-based services, based on the assets under management.

Unlike the old days when a broker got paid on the size of the load he sold, many of today's investment advisors are operating as assets under management. Instead of pushing the latest hot stock to write an order ticket and get a commission, under this new model the broker's pay increases as you make money. Since this fee is roughly equivalent to about 1 percent a year, the bigger your account balance, the more money the broker makes. However, when you suffer, so does the broker.

Thus, it is possible to get many of the same benefits as a mutual fund, or what one would get from paying a load, and still get professional help without investing in mutual funds. In fact, through many of these types of accounts, you can invest in in-house mutual funds, and avoid many of the hidden charges that go with no-load mutual funds.

## Hidden Charges in No-Loads

You can avoid a lot of the fees by only investing in no-load mutual funds, right?

Wrong! Though most people should avoid load mutual funds, the expenses associated with many no-load funds are difficult to track. It is almost as if the mutual fund industry, which was one of the hottest growth industries of the 1980s and 1990s, tries very hard to hide these fees.

Mutual funds are a lot more expensive than you think. It's like buying a Honda Accord and paying the upkeep of a Lexus. Funds have expenses that are passed along to the investor, even no-load funds. Most funds have yearly fees in the 2 to 3 percent range. In general, specialty funds that invest in niche sectors such as technology, small caps, or international equities will charge more. Also, load funds tend to have a higher expense ratio on average, according to Morningstar—an independent mutual fund rating service.

Mutual fund fees fall into several categories, the largest of which are management fees, trading fees, and *12b-1 fees*.

One of the benefits of a mutual fund is professional management. Of course, this management comes at a cost. Management fees can range anywhere from 0.10 percent to 3 percent or more. Usually, the larger the fund, the smaller this fee is, as it is a bit of a fixed cost, which can be spread out across more and more people, lowering the cost per investor.

**Timing Tips**

There are multiple firms that deliver plain English reports on mutual fund perform ance and fees charged by the funds. The most popular and probably the best of these services are Value Line and Morningstar. Morningstar concentrates almost exclusively on Mutual Funds and can be reached on the Internet at www.morningstar.com.

Probably the biggest fee is the trading fee. Every time a fund buys or sells a stock, it is charged a transaction fee. These fees are then passed along to the fund investors. The vast majority of U.S. diversified stock funds are in the middle-double digit range, with a turnover of 46 percent, meaning on average 46 percent of the stocks and bonds held in any one year will be sold, and new ones bought. Basically, this professional management rebalances their portfolio, and each rebalance causes more expenses. These trading costs are not included in the expense ratio, adding anywhere from 0.5 percent to 1.5 percent a year, according to Fund Democracy, a group that fights for shareholder rights. It's not uncommon to see transaction fees of as much as 3 percent a year, according to Fund Democracy.

Part of the problem is that the SEC doesn't require funds to tell you what they spend on trading costs. In some cases, you can dig it out of a fund's annual financial statement. But don't try looking in the prospectus or the semiannual report. Many funds will flat out say it's none of your business.

Another fee, which is restricted to no more than 1 percent—with a maximum of 0.25 percent going to the broker—is the 12b-1 fee. This fee is used as an inducement to brokers who have helped or may help sell shares of the fund load, but slightly different. These fees can also go towards advertising of the fund and are paid for by investors.

### Wall Street Words

The **12b-1 fee** was born in 1980 under the authorization of the Securities Exchange Commission (SEC). Its name is derived from the section in the Investment Company Act of 1940 that allows a mutual fund to pay distribution and marketing expenses out of the fund's assets. In theory, the 12b-1 fee was supposed to help investors. By marketing a mutual fund, the funds assets should increase and an increase in assets should provide better economies of scale providing investors with lower annual operational expenses. This has yet to be seen; 12b-1 fees have been used as a hidden way to pay brokers for using the fund. The SEC has limited the 12b-1 fee to 1 percent annually with maximum of 0.25 percent going to brokers. These fees serve only to hinder fund performance.

Thus, even no-load mutual funds have fees involved with them, which may degrade your performance. A fund that actively trades the market can incur higher costs. Add in expensive management, and 12b-1 fees, plus potential tax consequences, and it is possible that all of these fees even for a no-load fund can range as high as 5 or 7.5 percent a year.

With these kind hurdles to overcome, it is no wonder that 80 percent of all mutual funds have generally underperformed the market as measured by bench marks like the S&P 500 stock index.

# Passive Investing in the Market

One percent here, one percent there. Might not seem like a lot. But even one percentage point takes its toll over time. Consider this example from Vanguard Group. Let's say you invest $25,000 in Fund A, which has an expense ratio of 1.3 percent, and $25,000 in Fund B, which costs just 0.3 percent. Assume an 8 percent return, and in 20 years Fund A has earned $89,997 while Fund B has netted $109,740. The difference? Twenty years of higher expense has cost you nearly $20,000 in Fund A.

**Timing Tips**

Index investing is known as passive investing. It is termed passive because instead of trying to actively outperform the stock market, the index fund only tries to match the performance of the index, by passively following it. Passive investing has several advantages, such as broad diversification, as well substantially lower fees. Remember the old adage, a penny saved is a penny earned. Besides, with roughly 80 percent of all actively managed mutual funds underperforming the stock market, passive investing can lead to better results.

Imagine how much more it would cost you if you were paying an extra 2 or 3 percentage points more. Now add insult to injury and imagine that stocks are in a secular bear market.

Much of the extra expenses can be avoided by buying an index fund.

## Index Funds

Index investing is a strategy that many smart money managers have used for years. By using the benefits of pooling of capital, these funds are designed to mimic a stock index, such as the Dow Jones Industrial Average, S&P 500 index, or other indexes such as the NASDAQ 100, or Russell 2000.

Index funds maintain stock positions that are chosen to mirror the index, which they track. Thus, when you buy an index fund, you are buying the market, as represented by these indexes.

Index funds have several benefits over regular funds. First, expense rations are very low. Computer programs are set up to mimic the trading in the index. Therefore there are no expensive management and scores of research analysts to pay to pick stocks. The stock picking is done by the index committee, which sets up the index.

Second, because indexes are not changed very often, the trading fees, which can account for 2 or 3 percent a year, are virtually unheard of.

The cheapest option from an expense ratio standpoint is an index fund, such as Vanguard 500 index at a bargain price of 0.18 percent, or Schwab Total Stock Market Index, at 0.4 percent. Most major brokerage houses have an in-house index fund, which can be used to time your stock market commitments. Through index funds, you achieve the diversification of a mutual fund, and yet you pay a much smaller price.

Remember, 1 percent here and 1 percent there can really add up over time!

## The Least You Need to Know

- Mutual funds are collective investments where funds are pooled and the investor is able to achieve diversification by collective investing. The percent of participation is based on the amount invested, as participation is divided by shares issues—representing ownership.

- There are two basic structures to mutual funds: open-ended and closed-end. Open-ended funds can issue an unlimited number of shares while closed-end funds are restricted to a specific number of shares.

- There are two basic fee types associated with mutual funds: load and no-load. Load is Wall Street's word for a sales commission charged on entering the fund (front end load) or on exiting the fund (back end load). No-load funds charge no sales fee for the fund, or load, but these funds can have many hidden charges that can degrade performance over the long term.

- All mutual funds—including no-load funds—have a lot more expenses associated with them than many believe. Trading fees, management fees, advertising fees, and such tend to hurt performance as the costs are absorbed by the investors. One way to avoid these fees is through the managed accounts offered by most major brokerage houses, where a fixed percentage of the money is charged— such as 2 percent per year—and all other fees and costs are disregarded on participating products.

- The lowest fee funds are typically index funds, because they have low portfolio turnover and management fees.

# Chapter 19

# Asset Allocation

## In This Chapter

- ◆ What is asset allocation?
- ◆ Reviewing the risks of stocks and bonds
- ◆ Finding the right mix
- ◆ Nontraditional assets

So far we have only talked about two basic types of portfolios: those fully invested in stocks, or those fully invested in interest rate vehicles (bonds, Treasury securities, etc.).

But, part of diversification is being diversified across asset classes. A well-balanced portfolio will consist of being invested in many different asset classes. After all, there is more to investing than jumping into and out of the stock market.

The concept of portfolio balancing and asset allocation is extremely complex. Though it is not the general topic of this book, we felt it was important enough to include at least one chapter. It is important because a well-balanced portfolio can decrease risk and actually maximize returns.

# What Is Asset Allocation?

Generally, from the 1980s through the 1990s the place to be has been the stock market. A well-balanced portfolio during this period consisted of owning not only blue chip stocks, but also a smattering on high tech firms as well. In fact, by 1999 asset allocation meant owning the hottest dot.com stocks and a few chip manufacturers.

But, as we all learned, this was not really asset allocation. The good, the bad, and the pipedreams disappeared quickly as we entered into the major secular bear market.

> **Timing Tips**
>
> Asset allocation serves to diversify an investor's holdings across the spectrum of investment types. Hopefully through this diversification, the effects on any market will be offset by gains in another segment and the returns achieved will be more steady and predictable.

In 2000 and 2001, the top performing asset classes have been real estate investments as well as bonds.

Though anyone who had invested in these assets early would have underperformed the stellar gains of the markets in the later years of the 1990s bull market, by the time of the writing of this book, they would have caught up.

It is similar to the story of the tortoise and the hare. The rabbit can run extremely fast, but as he gets a comfortable lead, the rabbit will often take a breather. However, the turtle just slowly plods along, and eventually wins the race.

Asset allocation is the same principle. In asset allocation, the investor is diversifying his holdings across a spectrum of different markets, hoping to see not explosive gains, but a slow and steady growth in his/her investments with minimal risk. Just as a diversified stock portfolio lessens the risk that surprises in any one stock will totally wipe out your investment accounts, diversification across asset classes lessens the risk of a surprise in any one asset class.

# Event Risk and Diversification

One of the general themes of this book is not to teach people the magic formula for buying and selling the exact highs and lows of the stock market, because let's face it … if I had figured that out, I wouldn't be writing books, I would own a small island, like Manhattan!

The purpose of this book and of market timing is to help investors add discipline to their investing. To understand the risks and potential rewards, and to make decisions regarding your money that are not based on the emotions of the marketplace—fear and greed.

Wall Street for years has understood that fear and greed are the driving forces behind markets. This is why they recommend a diversified portfolio. Because, though a selection of just a few stocks can easily outperform the broad market, the risk of an event wiping out your account, or a substantial part of it, can be great.

For example, if you buy three stocks, and one of them happens to have "cooked the books" or the CEO of the firm is brought up on insider trading charges, then that stock's price could plummet. For example, let's say you own three stocks. XYZ makes electronic components. UVW is an Internet stock, which has promising new software, and ABC manufactures consumer staples. Let's assume that during the year, two of the stocks increase by 10 percent and 30 percent, respectively. However, one of the stocks plummets by 50 percent. Overall, the portfolio will decline by roughly 4 percent, given an equal investment in all three.

However, if you had just invested in the two stocks that moved the most—the 30 percent winner and the –50 percent loser—the value of your account would have dropped by –10 percent. However, if you had had 500 stocks and 499 of them went up by an average of 20 percent and only 1 dropped by 50 percent, you still would have had a 19.8 percent return. The one core meltdown position in your portfolio would have decreased your returns by only –0.4 percent. Thus, by diversifying across a broad spectrum of stocks, your exposure to the risks of any one stock is much smaller, and thus your returns over time will be more steady.

> **Timing Tips**
>
> Diversification is very similar to not putting all your eggs in one basket. By combining asset allocation with market timing, you are effectively trying to put all of your eggs in several different baskets and watching all of those baskets very closely. The goal of diversification is slow and steady growth with lower risk. This is the same as asset allocation.

The same principle can be said for asset classes. For example, during a stock market crash, like 1987, most stocks will decline. Seeing your portfolio drop by –22.6%—as did the Dow Jones Industrial on October 19, 1987—would definitely cause some worry. Do you buy more? Sell before the next day and see prices crash another –22.6 percent? Or do you weather the storm and hold pat?

Well the decision to buy more, or hold pat, which were the right decisions to make, can be made much easier if your portfolio is diversified. Instead of seeing your portfolio decline by –22 percent, like it would have during the crash, had you simply spread your risk across different asset classes (like bonds), and invested half of your portfolio in bonds, you would have seen your portfolio decline by only –8.5 percent.

Of course, being half in bonds and half in stocks would have had you miss out on a lot of the upside, as well. But, just like the main purpose of market timing is to instill some discipline into your market decisions, the main purpose of asset allocation is to give the investor some time to react to things.

Take a moment and really think about this. If you saw the value of your retirement come crashing down in one day by -22.0 percent, would you not panic. Remember, lots of people did. It was the selling of stocks, the mass panic, which drove prices down that day.

There are basic laws that govern the markets, in the same ways that the natural world is governed by laws, like gravity. In the markets, the basic tenet, which can very rarely be overcome, is the fact that risk and reward are commensurate.

# Stocks and Bonds and Risks and Rewards

Generally, an investment in common stocks has outperformed most other investments over the long haul. Many financial experts can show how a diversified investment in common stocks over the long haul has returned roughly 11.0 percent a year, while an investment in long-term Treasury bonds has had a long-term return of 5.3 percent, and investing in a money market account has returned only 3.1 percent.

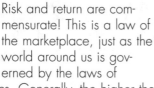

**Timing Tips**

Risk and return are commensurate! This is a law of the marketplace, just as the world around us is governed by the laws of physics. Generally, the higher the return, the higher the risk. Thus, on the spectrum of asset allocation, stocks have the highest risks and rewards, followed then by bonds, and the minimal returns of money market funds.

We can also see that an investment in common stocks has more risk. Very rarely do you see a bond investment drop by almost a quarter of its value in one day, especially not Treasury bonds. But, Treasury bonds do move, and as we know from our chapter on bond investing, if you sell a bond early before maturity, you can sell it at a loss. Thus, unless you wish to hold bonds until they mature, which can be more than a decade, you have risk as well. It is this duration risk that makes longer-term bonds usually return a higher amount than short-term interest rate vehicles like money markets.

As such, let's take a moment and review what each of these vehicles are and what risks are associated with them.

## Risks of Common Stocks

A stock is simply a share of ownership in a corporation. As a stockholder, you are a partial owner of that corporation. When you buy shares of Exxon-Mobil, you are one of literally thousands of owners.

Owners of a company make money when the company makes money. The profits of the corporation are distributed among its owners. Thus the value of a stock, or share of ownership, is a reflection of how much profit the company will make in the future. If the market perceives that earnings will increase over time, then the value associated with a share of those profits—the stock price—should increase. If the market place feels that the value of future earnings will decrease, or not grow at the same rate as it had been—then the value of those earnings will be discounted and the stock price will decrease.

> **Timing Tips**
>
> As we have said many times throughout this book, the stock market generally is anticipatory in nature. It does not react to the news today, but the perception of the future. Thus, when things look the brightest currently, stock prices usually top out, and when things look the darkest, prices usually bottom out. As such, it usually pays to buy when prices are depressed and stocks are shunned, and to lighten the load in your portfolio when everyone claims stocks are the place to be.

The stock is simply this same example extrapolated over every company. Basically, in an environment where people en masse feel that earnings are likely to increase, stock prices generally rise—not all, but most stocks. In an environment where people feel that corporations are likely to earn less money in the future—then stock prices tend to fall—not all, but most stocks. Thus, rising stock prices are a reflection of the environment in which they operate—the economy.

Thus, when the present is dim, but the future looks bright, stock prices stop falling and start to go higher. As long as the general perception is that the economy will continue to grow and corporations will make money, then stock prices rise. However, when the general perception is that the economy will slow and thus the growth in earnings will slow as well, then stock prices fall. Stock prices will continue to fall, until the perception changes to one of expanding earnings, and the cycle begins fresh again.

## Risks of Bonds

Interest rates are a function of the supply and demand of money. When the demand for money (the need for borrowing) exceeds the supply of money available to lend, the lenders demand a higher rate of interest. Thus, if the borrower really wishes to borrow, then she must pay the rate being asked. However, when the supply of money exceeds the demand for it, interest rates tend to decline as borrowers may opt not to borrow money if the rate being charged is too high.

When interest rates are put into economic perspective, they tend to reflect the general level of economic activity, as borrowers tend to drive the interest rate market.

During periods of economic distress, interest rates tend to be lower, as the demand for money is less. Thus, during recessions and such, the supply of money tends to outstrip the demand for money, and interest rates decline.

During periods of economic growth, interest rates tend to rise, as the demand for money outstrips the demand for it.

> **Timing Tips**
>
> Bonds move in the opposite direction of interest rates. Generally, interest rates move in the opposite direction of future economic activity. Therefore, generally the best time to be invested in bonds is when it is a poor environment for being invested in stocks.

Bond prices move in the opposite direction as interest rates. When interest rates fall, bond prices go up. When interest rates rise, bond prices go down. Interest rates tend to move in tandem with the economy. When the demand for money increases, such as during a strong economic environment, interest rates tend to rise as the demand for money outstrips the supply. However, when the economy tends to slow, so does the demand for money, causing interest rates to fall. Thus, bond prices move in the opposite general direction of the economy.

The risks associated with bond ownership are more closely tied to economic strength than weakness, the exact opposite of the stock market. This is because, though bonds pay a coupon, a drop in interest rates makes the coupon payments more valuable.

## Bond Coupons and Interest Rates

Bonds have two main components—the coupon and the principle. Bonds are usually sold in $1,000 increments, or $1,000 of coupon. For example, a 6 percent 10-year bond would represent quarterly payments of 1.5 percent each ($15 per quarter or $60.00 per year) for 10 years, and the repayment of $1,000 at the end of 10 years. Thus, the coupon represents the amount of interest earned on the money, 6 percent in this example, and the face value of the bond is the amount lent and received back at maturity.

Now if interest rates were to fall from 6 percent to 5 percent, how much would you be willing to pay to receive an extra $10 a year? Obviously, if the best you can get on your money with equivalent risk is 5 percent currently, you would be willing to pay more than the face value of the bond for the right to get an extra $10 per year. Thus, instead of paying $1,000 for the bond, a person may be willing to pay $1,080 for the bond today, to get $60 a year and be repaid $1,000 in 10 years.

Thus, the investor who had bought the 6 percent coupon bond and held it for one year as interest rates declined to 5 percent, may sell her bond a year later, and get to collect the $60 in coupon payments and sell the bond for $1,080. Thus, they made $140, or an $80 gain on the bond and collected $60 in interest. This equates to a return of 14 percent, which is much better than the return on the bond to begin with.

**Trading Traps**

Bond prices may offer a fixed and guaranteed rate of return when held until maturity; the return on bonds can be negative if they are not held until maturity. Bond prices move in the opposite direction of interest rates. Though bonds are often thought of as a safe investment for widows and orphans, the bond market and interest rates can be extremely volatile, as can bond fund returns. The closest you can come to risk-free investing is a money market account. However, the returns on such investments barely manage to keep up with inflation.

However, if interest rates were to increase, from 6 percent to 7 percent over the course of the year, the investor would not be able sell her bond at the end of one year for $1,000. After all, who would pay face value for a bond that pays $60 a year when other bonds of the risk and length of time pay $70 per year? In this case, if the bond holder were to sell the bond after one year, she may only get $920 for it. If you include the $60 in coupon payments received, the investor in the bond lost -$20 for holding bonds during the year.

Thus, as you can see by this very rough example, the holder of a bond is subject to interest rate risk, unless they are willing to hold the bond until maturity. Of course, even holding to maturity is a risk as well, as they may miss opportunities to get even more money.

## Money Market Accounts

At the lowest end of the risk spectrum is a money market account. These accounts pay interest daily, and the return is based on current interest rates. Each day, a money market account is marked to pay an interest rate and all interest is used to buy additional shares, with the value of shares always staying at $1. Thus, if you invest in a money market with $1,000 you can always be sure to get $1,000 back when you sell the shares, as they are always valued $1 per share. However, the return for that investment is very low.

They are not risk free, in that a money market account must beat inflation. Inflation is the rising prices of the goods and services we use. For example, I can remember when a movie cost $2, versus now when the cost at my local theatre is $7.50 for an adult. Thus, for $10 I could go see five movies. Today, for $10 I will be lucky to get to see one movie and get a small soda to enjoy. The rising costs of goods and services erodes the purchasing power of the dollar.

When we are investing, generally inflation is of a major concern. If we are investing for retirement, we not only have to have enough money salted away to provide for ourselves in the future when our income drops precipitously, but we also have to count on the fact that a dollar will not go as far.

> **Timing Tips**
>
> Indicators such as the consumer price index are designed to measure inflation. The rate of inflation is similar to the cost of living increases many people receive in their jobs. Money market returns closely match the rate of inflation, thus the real return on money in such investments is relatively nil after inflation is taken into account. Generally, inflation is bad news for bond and interest rate markets, as well as equity markets.

This is similar to the joke about a guy who falls asleep for 100 years, like Rip Van Winkle. When he awakes, he calls his broker and is ecstatic to find out that he has $3 million in his brokerage account. Wow, I'm rich, he thinks. He then walks down the street and buys a Coke, and the cashier says, "That will be $3 million, please."

Though the sum of money he had amassed was considerable, inflation made the purchasing power of the funds less than stellar. Thus, even in an almost risk-free investment like a money market account, there is risk.

What's an investor to do?

# Finding the Right Mix

As we have tried to show, each investment type has a risk associated with it. Generally speaking, the greater the long-term return, the higher the risk of that investment is in the short run.

Generally, few market timers fail to beat the long-term return of stocks in general because they are not always in stocks. However, very few long-term investors manage to get the long-term return on stocks because they tend to buy and sell stocks at the wrong time. When prices are high, they tend to buy aggressively, and when prices are crashing they tend to panic and sell.

However, by diversifying their holdings, they are able to avoid some of this. But what is the right way to manage this.

## Defining Your Risk Tolerance

The very first thing you should do is understand your own risk tolerance. Most brokerage houses or financial planners can help you with this. They have questionnaires that are designed to figure out not only your goals, but also your tolerance for risk.

Basically, the more risk adverse you are, the more you should lean towards investing in bonds. Generally, the more risk tolerant you are, the more heavily you should lean toward investing in stocks.

> **Trading Traps**
>
> For decades, investors have generally made the wrong decisions at the wrong time. They tend to buy near price peaks when greed takes over, and to sell near market lows when fear reigns their decisions. A way to avoid this trap is through asset allocation, or diversifying your portfolio across stocks and bonds, hopefully avoiding the excesses of emotions in your decision process. However, be sure to rebalance your asset allocation periodically—every couple of years—or you may find that a portfolio that was once balanced no longer is, and you are taking more risk than you are comfortable with.

It is our belief that stocks will continue to have a higher return on investment than either the bond or money markets over the next several decades. However, not everyone is capable of sitting through stock market crashes and the unavoidable ups and downs of the market. As such, they should define a core holding percentage of stocks and bonds. This core holding, or portfolio structuring to achieve diversification across the business cycle, is key toward long-term financial survival, and it is based not only on your risk tolerance but also how long-term oriented you can be.

> **Timing Tips**
>
> Generally the longer term your investment horizon, the more you should invest in stocks and the less in bonds. However, the shorter your investment horizon, the more you should invest in bonds over stocks, as the general volatility of the stock market can make very poor financial decisions when your money is on the line, and you don't have time to recover it.

## Defining Your Time Horizon

Before we enter into time horizons, I wish to bring up one more point on risk tolerances. I am self-employed, and in my mid-30s. Both of these factors make me extremely tolerant of risk, as by being self-employed I am a risk-taker by nature—as are all entrepreneurs—and because

I am relatively young, I can afford to take bigger risks as I have time to make up for my mistakes. However, your own situation may be different, thus I implore you to take the time to meet with a financial consultant and set up a plan that meets with your own personal risk tolerances, as my guidance may be a little more aggressive than what suits your situation.

According to financial experts, the best game in town this last century has been common stocks. Thus for long-term growth, people with a longer amount of time should concentrate on this for investing. However, as we get older and closer to retirement, we have less time to make up for investment mistakes or to recover losses in the market. Thus, even though the return on stocks has far outperformed the return on other assets, at some point the risks associated with such investments outweigh the returns.

Thus, a good rule of thumb to follow is the rule of two.

## The Right Mix and the Rule of Two

This simple rule of thumb multiplies the number of years until you need the money by two to find the percentage to invest in common stocks.

For example, I am 35, and I figure on retiring at the age of 65. Thus I have 30 years until retirement, so I should be 60 percent invested in stocks and 40 percent in bonds. Here is a simple table for you to get the idea:

| Age | Years to Retire | % in Stocks | % in Bonds |
| --- | --- | --- | --- |
| to 25 | 40 | $40 \times 2 = 80\%$ | 20% |
| 30 | 35 | $35 \times 2 = 70\%$ | 30% |
| 35 | 30 | $30 \times 2 = 60\%$ | 40% |
| 40 | 25 | $25 \times 2 = 50\%$ | 50% |
| 45 | 20 | $20 \times 2 = 40\%$ | 60% |
| 50 | 15 | $15 \times 2 = 30\%$ | 70% |
| 55 | 10 | $10 \times 2 = 20\%$ | 80% |

This general rule of thumb is just that. It is not suitable for everyone, but should give you a basic idea of how to achieve portfolio diversification. When investing for retirement, the younger you are, the more aggressive you should be. However, as you approach retirement, your concerns are more toward preserving your wealth and beating inflation, so you should be less aggressive.

Notice, that in this mix, we left off money market funds. This is because the average money market return barely keeps pace with inflation, thus it is our opinion that these should only be used for very short periods of time when you are planning your next purchase in either the stock or bond markets.

We also broke this down into five-year increments, because we are not professionals. You should adjust your holding percentages about every five years, and usually I would recommend that with active management of the stock side you should round down. For example, if you are 34 years old, and the market looks good, then invest like a 30-year-old ... but remember, I am a risk-taker.

**Timing Tips**

A simple rule of thumb for allocating assets between stocks and bonds is to take the number of years until you need the money and multiply that by two to find the percentage to invest in common stocks. For example, if you are 40 years old and have 25 years until retirement, you invest 50 percent in stocks and 50 percent in bonds as 25 x 2 = 50 percent, or your weighting between stocks and bonds.

We stopped at age 55, because if your holding period is less than 10 years, then you should consider 10 percent to 20 percent in stocks and the rest in bonds or short-term paper (notes, T-Bills, etc.) At this point in the game, with less than a decade, the wild swings of the stock market can severely damage your retirement nest egg, and as such you should concentrate more on saving and less on appreciation of capital.

## Using the Rule of Two and Stock Market Timing

Though the rule of two is just a rule of thumb, it does provide a basic framework for a partially balanced portfolio. As we know stocks tend to well when the economy is perceived to be improving and bonds tend to well when the economy is perceived to be slowing or entering recession. Thus, one segment of your portfolio will offset some of the losses in the other section of your portfolio.

**Timing Tips**

A simple rule of thumb for allocating assets between stocks and bonds is to take the number of years until you need the money and multiply that by two to find the percentage to invest in common stocks. When you are extremely bullish on the stock market, you may consider moving half the bond investment into stocks, and you may consider moving half the stock investment into bonds when bearish. This keeps a somewhat diversified portfolio, and yet still allows you to benefit from market timing.

However, one of the purposes of stock market timing is to be out of stocks when times are bad, and in only when times are good. Though this is our goal, it is an impossible task to accomplish. As such we play with the general mixes.

As another rule of thumb, building upon the models we have already demonstrated in previous chapters, you could take the half the position in bonds and invest it in stocks when they are bullish and half the investment in stocks and invest it in bonds when they are bearish. Here is an expanded asset allocation, based on three different market outlooks: neutral, bullish, and bearish.

| Age | Years to Retire | Neutral Mix | | Bullish Mix | | Bearish Mix | |
|---|---|---|---|---|---|---|---|
| | | % Stocks | % Bonds | % Stocks | % Bonds | % Stocks | % Bonds |
| to 25 | 40 | 80% | 20% | 90% | 10% | 10% | 90% |
| 30 | 35 | 70% | 30% | 85% | 15% | 15% | 85% |
| 35 | 30 | 60% | 40% | 80% | 20% | 20% | 80% |
| 40 | 25 | 50% | 50% | 75% | 25% | 25% | 75% |
| 45 | 20 | 40% | 60% | 70% | 30% | 30% | 70% |
| 50 | 15 | 30% | 70% | 65% | 35% | 35% | 65% |
| 55 | 10 | 20% | 80% | 60% | 40% | 40% | 60% |

Thus, by following this scenario, a speculator does have a bit of diversification, and you are heavily weighted toward stocks when you are bullish and lighten up when you are bearish.

**Timing Tips**

The fastest growing asset class in the last five years has been managed futures. The term managed futures describes the industry made up of professional money managers known as commodity trading advisors (CTAs). These professionals trade client accounts on a discretionary basis using global futures and cash currency markets as an investment medium.

# Alternative Investments

There is another asset class that is gaining favor amongst professional asset allocators and that is commodities and managed futures.

Generally as an asset class, the commodities futures market has no basic correlation to the stock market. They tend to do well in environments when both stocks and bonds do not do well, especially inflationary environments.

If you are interested in furthering your asset allocation, you may consider learning about this field, either to participate by trading futures and options contracts, or by passively investing in managed futures. To learn more about these, I would strongly recommend *The Complete Idiot's Guide to Options and Futures*, which is wonderfully written and explains in great detail how this alternative asset class behaves. Note: In case you haven't figured it out yet, I also wrote this book.

The best way for most people to participate in the futures markets is through a managed futures program, which is similar to a mutual fund, but instead of investing in stocks and/or bonds, it invests in futures contracts and options.

## Managed Futures

The term managed futures describes the industry made up of professional money managers known as commodity trading advisors (CTAs). These professionals trade client accounts on a discretionary basis using global futures and cash currency markets as an investment medium.

Managed futures programs offer a lot of different benefits, just like mutual funds can offer allot of different benefits for those interested in the stock market.

Managed futures, like mutual funds, are known as passive investments, meaning that the investor is not involved in the day-to-day trading of the program. One of the key benefits is that the person (or persons) who does make the day-to-day trading decisions is a professional! Another major benefit is that these programs are diversified across markets, allowing the program to participate in a variety of markets. In other words, managed futures programs tend to be more widely diversified than is possible for most individual traders.

The Chicago Board of Trade, in their booklet, "Portfolio Diversification Opportunities," shows that a portfolio with the *greatest risk* and *least amount of returns* was comprised 55 percent stocks, 45 percent bonds, and 0 percent managed futures. But, a portfolio comprised of 45 percent stocks,

**Timing Tips**

The returns of managed futures programs are generally not correlated with those of the stock or bond markets. Basically what this means is that these returns are independent and should not be affected by the same things. This makes this asset class an excellent way to achieve even more portfolio diversification.

**Timing Tips**

For those of you who are interested in a managed futures program, you may wish to take a look at the CTA Index Newsletter, available at www.cta-index.com. For investment information on managed futures, contact Wheatland Financial Services at 1-800-811-0156. They handle several different proprietaries, for which the author of this book consults on, as well as can help people find non-inhouse funds.

35 percent bonds, and 20 percent in managed futures yielded up to 50 percent more returns with less risk.

Several large pension funds, such as the California Public Teachers Retirement Fund have caught on to this, and have allocated 10 percent of their portfolio to managed futures. Diversification across asset classes can truly help increase your returns and minimize your risks.

## The Least You Need to Know

♦ Asset allocation is the diversifying of holdings across a spectrum of different markets, hoping to see not explosive gains, but a slow and steady growth in investments with reduced risk.

♦ Generally, when perceptions are for increasing economic growth and thus increasing earnings, stocks tend to be the favored asset class and have the highest returns, while the bond market suffers.

♦ Generally, when perceptions are for decreasing economic growth and thus decreasing earnings, stocks tend to be the worst asset class and have the lowest returns, while the bond market benefits.

♦ Historically, the return on stocks has surpassed that of bonds and money markets. But, the risk associated with stocks is also greater. By dividing assets across the spectrum, the investor is less likely to panic due to the ups and downs of the business cycle.

♦ The closer you are to needing the money you are investing, such as the closer you are to retirement, the less you should invest in riskier assets and the more you should invest in safer assets. The longer it is until they need their funds, the more aggressive you should be.

♦ Investors should consider alternative investments, such as managed futures, for a small portion of their investment portfolio. Though the risks in such programs are high, the diversification can really add to its bottom line.

# Chapter 20

# Combining Indicators

## In This Chapter

- ◆ The presidential cycle and asset allocation
- ◆ Moving averages and the best months
- ◆ Using the January barometer
- ◆ When things don't agree

In this chapter, we will concentrate on putting some of the things we have learned together. We are going to concentrate on three main studies we have presented: the presidential cycle, the best months, and the January barometer.

Hopefully, we will be able to illustrate how you can use these tools, along with a well-balanced portfolio, to show everyone how they can practically time the stock market in their own investment accounts.

## Election Cycles and Stock Investing

One of the most powerful stock market timing tools, in the longer term, is the presidential cycle. Remember back from a previous chapter, where we showed how stock returns tend to be strongest in the last two years of a presidency and weakest in the first two years of a presidency?

*Dow Jones Industrial yearly performance versus presidential cycle.*

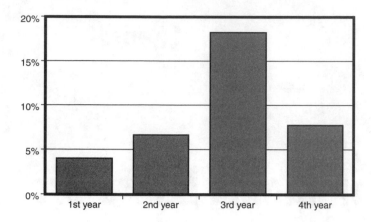

In the last 12 presidential cycles since 1954, the first year in office of a new president has seen the Dow Jones Industrials return a paltry 3.0 percent on average. The second year of the presidential term has seen better returns, of 6.5 percent on average. However, the third year, or the year preceding the election, has seen the Dow Jones post an impressive 18.3 percent return, and has never seen a market decline. The last year of a president's term, has posted an average return of 7.6 percent on average, based on the Dow Jones Industrial Average.

> **Timing Tips**
>
> Most secular bear markets have begun and seen the worst part of their carnage during the first two years of a president's term. On the contrary, the second two years of a presidential term—the year prior to and the election year—have seen better returns. In fact, the third year of a presidential term, the year prior to the election, has never seen a major decline in the recent past.

For comparison's sake, it is worth mentioning that the average yearly return during this 1954 to 2001 period has been roughly 9.0 percent, based also on the Dow Jones Industrials. Thus, comparatively, the two years of the presidential cycle that have seen the best returns, and those closest to the overall return of the market, have been the third and fourth years of a president's term.

## Invest More Heavily in the Last Two Years

On average from 1978 through 2001, the return on stocks, as measured by the Dow Jones Industrial Average, has been 11.7 percent per year. On average the return on one-year Treasury Bills during this period has been 7.5 percent, as measured by a fixed one-year maturity series from the Federal Reserve.

In the 24 years studied, the Dow Jones has posted some very impressive returns. The Dow Jones has scored gains in 18 of the 24 years, though it has had some bad years. For example, in 1981, Ronald Reagan's first year as president, the Dow Jones Industrial Average declined by 9.2 percent. The heavily contested election of 2000 and the first year of G. W. Bush's presidency saw declines of -6.2 percent and -7.1 percent, respectively.

However, if we look at investing only in the two strongest years of the presidential cycle and staying out of the stock market in the other two years, then an investor would have scored an average return of +12.7 percent in those years, seeing gains in 10 of the 12 years. An investor would have missed four of the six losing years in this period and would have racked up a total return of 152.8 percent on his money.

However, our investor would have missed 127.6 percent of total gain by sitting out of the stock market for the first and second years of a presidential term. This is often seen as the Achilles' heel of stock market timing, for if an investor can truly sit through the market ups and downs, and practice a long-term buy and hold mentality, then they will beat the market timers. However, you would have had to sit through the some vicious bear markets during this period. The practitioner of investing during the last two years of a presidential election cycle would have missed four out of the six yearly declines, and garnered more than half of the total return of the buy and hold practitioner.

## Consider Bond Funds and Alternative Investments

However, when you are out of the stock market, you can consider other investments. Very rarely do investors leave money tucked under a mattress. Instead, when a market timer is out of the stock market, he or she is invested in other forms of investments, such as bond funds or Treasury securities.

Treasury securities are the safest investment in the world. As we explained earlier, these are bonds issued by the United States government, and as such are backed by the full faith and credit of such. Think of it this way, if Treasury securities are defaulted on, then the cash money (dollars) that we are investing will be worthless as well, as cash (dollar bills) are backed by the same thing Treasury securities are—the full faith and credit of the United States government. Thus, the only risk-free investment is Treasury securities.

The return on Treasury securities can be approximated by the yield to maturity. When a bond or bill is purchased, it pays out a coupon or an amount. This is usually expressed as interest rate or a yield. For example, a $1,000 Treasury bill that pays a coupon of $100 per year would have a 10 percent yield.

Thus, during the other two years, an investor could have put his or her money into the safety of Treasury bills, and garnered an average return during the 1978 through 2001 period of 7.5 percent.

**Timing Tips**

An important point to remember when considering bonds or interest rate vehicles is the longer the maturity of the vehicle, most likely the higher the rate of return. However, longer-term vehicles also carry more risk. If you were to sell a bond early, there could be a capital gain or loss in the bond, which far outweighs the coupon or interest rate.

If the investor had invested in the stock market only during the last two years of a presidential term and invested in one-year Treasury bills each of the other two years, then the average return during this period would have been 10.1 percent, which is less than the 11.7 percent achieved by buy and hold.

However, you have to remember that for half of the period you are invested in T-Bills, an extremely safe investment. You could have chosen a longer-term bond series, which would have more sporadic returns, but also a higher return. Or you could have gone into corporate bonds, which yield a higher return than do Treasuries, because corporations can default on their debt.

Thus, with a little ingenuity, and applying a little more timing on the stock market and a little more risk on the debt market side, you can probably match the returns of a simple buy and hold, if not beat it.

# Trend Following and the Best Months

Remember back several sections where we highlighted the investment calendar and where we highlighted the basic premise of trend following using a moving average?

**Timing Tips**

The basic tenet behind trend following is that strength in a market will continue longer than most people think and weakness will also continue longer than most people think. Or as Wall Street lore holds "The trend *is* your friend, until it bends or ends."

The basic premise behind the investment calendar is that the best time of the year to invest in stocks is the period from November through April.

Having followed this simple strategy of buying at the end of October and selling out at the end of April, since 1950, $1,000 invested in the Dow Jones Industrial Average would be worth $46,668.82 at the end of April 2001. By timing the market, you have actually gained $7.48. However, this also takes into account the terrorist attacks of September 11, 2001, which saw the stock market plummet initially in its wake. Ignoring this and ending the study in

2000, you would have sacrificed a gain of $174.60 dollars by only investing during the best six months of the year.

Only two years saw the market decline by more than –10 percent. The 1969 to 1970 period saw a decline of –14.0 percent during the best six months as the conflict (war) in Vietnam escalated with the Cambodian invasion, and the 1973–74 decline of –12.5 percent caused by the OPEC oil embargo.

Thus, the best six months of the year is a good timing indicator for the stock market. However, even this can be improved upon by using a simple trend following technique.

## MACD, a Trend Following Variation

A moving average is simply the average price of the last "X" number of days, recorded versus the current days price. Moving averages tend to tell the overall trend of the market, with technical analysis lore holding that prices are bullish when they are above the trend of the market, and bearish when they are below the trend of the market.

Gerald Appel, while with Signalert Corporation, created a variation of a moving average system that looked at two moving averages and the difference between those two averages. Looking at these moving averages of the market he states that you are able to see clear buy and sell signals. By also looking at an average of the difference in the two moving averages you are able to get a more accurate signal. Mr. Appel called his creation a Moving Average Convergence Divergence Indicator, or MACD.

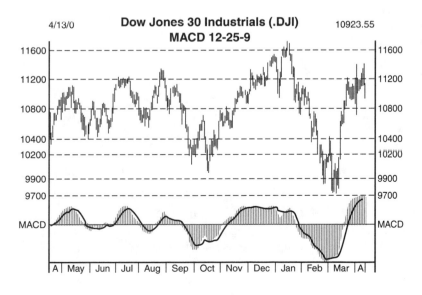

*Moving average convergence and divergence indicator and the Dow Jones Industrial Average.*

MACD is usually displayed as a *histogram*. The histogram method of MACD is read as a straight line above or below the zero baseline. This line represents the difference between the moving averages. Therefore when the moving averages move above the base line they are indicating a buy, and as the difference between the averages increases the lines will get taller.

## MACD and the Best Months

The key to using the MACD indicator is that it is best used in conjunction with other tools like the best six months strategy to confirm or assist in timing, buy and sell decisions. So once we enter April or October we begin tracking MACD.

A buy signal (positive breakout) is given when the MACD graph is in an oversold condition below the origin and the MACD line crosses above the signal line with in several weeks of November. A sell signal (negative breakout) is given when the MACD graph is in an overbought condition above the origin and the MACD line falls below the signal line, near the month of April.

**Timing Tip** _____

The performance statistics and explanations of the MACD and Best Six Months strategy are compliments of the Hirsch Organization. You can contact the Hirsch Organization at:

Hirsch Organization Inc.
P.O. Box 2069
184 Central Avenue
Old Tappan, NJ 07675-9069
201-767-4100
www.stocktradersalmanc.com

To get the latest MACD signal simply e-mail them at service@stocktradersalmanac.com to be included on their e-mail list of signals for this strategy.

Market timer Sy Harding, in his book, *Riding the Bear,* took the Hirsch Organization's November-through-April strategy, enhanced it, and termed it the "Best mechanical system ever." He simply used the MACD indicator developed by Gerald Appel to enter the best six months period up to several weeks earlier, if the market was in an uptrend. Conversely, Harding would exit up to several weeks later as long as the market kept moving up.

## MACD and the Best Months Performance

Mr. Harding was not kidding when he called this the best mechanical system ever. From 1950 through April 2001, if you had followed this system of timing purchases in the stock market during the best six months with the help of the MACD indicator, you would have seen your money grow by an amazing 500 percent, with an average yearly gain of 10.1 percent. The rest of the year actually saw declines in the stock market, with the market timer enjoying being out of the stock market as it went sideways to slightly down, losing an average of –0.78 percent.

**CAUTION**

**Trading Traps**

Mr. Harding's "best mechanical system ever" has performed amazingly over the last half of a century! However, remember the Dogs of the Dow and how its performance has deteriorated over the years as it became more and more popular? Well, the same problem can occur here. Past performance is not necessarily indicative of future results! Markets can and do change, as these cycles are ever-changing!

Of course, during the other half of the year, the speculator could have put his money into a bond fund, or Treasury securities and beaten the buy and hold bunch by fathom, with only being invested half the year.

The following table shows all the historical buy and sell dates for this indicator combination over the last 40-plus years.

| MACD Signal | Worst 6 Months May-October | | MACD Signal | Best 6 Months November-April | |
|---|---|---|---|---|---|
| Date | DJIA | % Change | Date | DJIA | % Change |
| 22-Apr-50 | 213.90 | 7.3 | 14-Nov-50 | 229.54 | 13.3 |
| 10-May-51 | 260.07 | 0.1 | 13-Nov-51 | 260.41 | 1.9 |
| 5-Apr-52 | 265.44 | 1.4 | 31-Oct-52 | 269.23 | 2.1 |
| 30-Apr-53 | 274.75 | 0.2 | 23-Oct-53 | 275.34 | 17.1 |
| 14-May-54 | 322.50 | 13.5 | 5-Nov-54 | 366.00 | 16.3 |
| 29-Apr-55 | 425.65 | 7.7 | 21-Oct-55 | 458.47 | 13.1 |
| 9-Apr-56 | 518.52 | -6.8 | 8-Oct-56 | 483.38 | 2.8 |
| 9-May-57 | 496.76 | -12.3 | 29-Oct-57 | 435.76 | 2.0 |
| 16-May-58 | 444.35 | 20.7 | 6-Oct-58 | 536.29 | 16.7 |

*continues*

*continued*

| MACD Signal | Worst 6 Months May-October | | MACD Signal | Best 6 Months November-April | |
|---|---|---|---|---|---|
| Date | DJIA | % Change | Date | DJIA | % Change |
| 5-May-59 | 625.90 | 1.6 | 6-Oct-59 | 636.06 | -3.1 |
| 22-Apr-60 | 616.32 | -4.9 | 7-Oct-60 | 586.42 | 16.9 |
| 21-Apr-61 | 685.26 | 2.9 | 9-Oct-61 | 705.42 | -1.5 |
| 23-Apr-62 | 694.61 | -15.3 | 10-Oct-62 | 588.14 | 22.4 |
| 1-May-63 | 719.67 | 4.3 | 18-Oct-63 | 750.60 | 9.6 |
| 14-Apr-64 | 822.95 | 6.7 | 9-Nov-64 | 878.08 | 6.2 |
| 19-May-65 | 932.12 | 2.6 | 26-Oct-65 | 956.32 | -2.5 |
| 2-May-66 | 931.95 | -16.4 | 17-Oct-66 | 778.89 | 14.3 |
| 12-May-67 | 890.03 | -2.1 | 21-Nov-67 | 870.95 | 5.5 |
| 8-May-68 | 918.86 | 3.4 | 14-Oct-68 | 949.96 | 0.2 |
| 21-May-69 | 951.78 | -11.9 | 16-Oct-69 | 838.77 | -6.7 |
| 15-Apr-70 | 782.60 | -1.4 | 6-Nov-70 | 771.97 | 20.8 |
| 3-May-71 | 932.41 | -11.0 | 29-Nov-71 | 829.73 | 15.4 |
| 24-Apr-72 | 957.48 | -0.6 | 25-Oct-72 | 951.38 | -1.4 |
| 26-Apr-73 | 937.76 | -11.0 | 11-Dec-73 | 834.18 | 0.1 |
| 26-Apr-74 | 834.64 | -22.4 | 10-Oct-74 | 648.08 | 28.2 |
| 1-May-75 | 830.96 | 0.1 | 17-Oct-75 | 832.18 | 18.5 |
| 5-May-76 | 986.46 | -3.4 | 28-Oct-76 | 952.63 | -3.0 |
| 27-Apr-77 | 923.76 | -11.4 | 31-Oct-77 | 818.35 | 0.5 |
| 9-May-78 | 822.07 | -4.5 | 14-Nov-78 | 785.26 | 9.3 |
| 17-Apr-79 | 857.93 | -5.3 | 5-Nov-79 | 812.63 | 7.0 |
| 20-Jun-80 | 869.71 | 9.3 | 10-Oct-80 | 950.68 | 4.7 |
| 1-May-81 | 995.59 | -14.6 | 14-Oct-81 | 850.65 | 0.4 |
| 4-May-82 | 854.45 | 15.5 | 8-Oct-82 | 986.85 | 23.5 |
| 13-May-83 | 1218.75 | 2.5 | 21-Oct-83 | 1248.88 | -7.3 |
| 11-May-84 | 1157.14 | 3.3 | 17-Oct-84 | 1195.89 | 3.9 |
| 1-May-85 | 1242.05 | 7.0 | 4-Oct-85 | 1328.74 | 38.1 |
| 25-Apr-86 | 1835.57 | -2.8 | 6-Oct-86 | 1784.45 | 28.2 |
| 13-Apr-87 | 2287.07 | -14.9 | 4-Nov-87 | 1945.29 | 3.0 |
| 10-May-88 | 2003.65 | 6.1 | 12-Oct-88 | 2126.24 | 11.8 |

| MACD<br>Signal | Worst 6 Months<br>May–October | | MACD<br>Signal | Best 6 Months<br>November–April | |
|---|---|---|---|---|---|
| Date | DJIA | % Change | Date | DJIA | % Change |
| 8-May-89 | 2376.47 | 9.8 | 14-Nov-89 | 2610.25 | 3.3 |
| 20-Apr-90 | 2695.95 | -6.7 | 22-Oct-90 | 2516.09 | 15.8 |
| 26-Apr-91 | 2912.38 | 4.8 | 17-Oct-91 | 3053.00 | 11.3 |
| 11-May-92 | 3397.58 | -6.2 | 21-Oct-92 | 3187.10 | 6.6 |
| 26-Apr-93 | 3398.37 | 5.5 | 7-Oct-93 | 3583.63 | 5.6 |
| 13-Jun-94 | 3783.12 | 3.7 | 17-Oct-94 | 3923.93 | 13.1 |
| 23-May-95 | 4436.44 | 7.2 | 23-Oct-95 | 4755.48 | 16.7 |
| 17-Apr-96 | 5549.93 | 9.2 | 17-Oct-96 | 6059.20 | 21.9 |
| 27-May-97 | 7383.41 | 3.6 | 18-Nov-97 | 7650.82 | 18.5 |
| 24-Apr-98 | 9064.62 | -12.4 | 13-Oct-98 | 7938.14 | 39.9 |
| 13-May-99 | 11107.19 | -6.4 | 20-Oct-99 | 10392.36 | 5.1 |
| 13-Apr-00 | 10923.55 | -6.0 | 23-Oct-00 | 10271.72 | 5.4 |
| 11-May-01 | 10821.31 | -17.3 | 2-Oct-01 | 8950.59 | 15.8 |
| 1-Apr-02 | 10362.70 | | | | |

*Table compliments of the Hirsch Organization, www.stocktradersalmanac.com.*

Even in the last decade, the 1990s, when stocks enjoyed a tremendous bull market, this little system outperformed the market strongly. Investing only in the best six months when a MACD signal was given, allowed an investor to rack up a 14.6 percent average gain during this period, while missing an average loss of –1.75 percent.

Hopefully this cycle will not change anytime soon!

# Adjusting Your Investments in January

As we showed in a previous chapter, January's monthly direction often acts as a precursor for the rest of the year. As Mr. Hirsch pointed out, as "January goes so goes the year."

The January barometer has its roots in the Twentieth Amendment or the "lame duck" amendment to the Constitution. This amendment states that congress will convene on January 3, including the newly elected representatives and that the presidential inauguration date will be moved from March 4 to January 20.

**Timing Tips**

Following a strong January, stocks have tended to perform well the rest of the year. Following a weak January, the market has tended to perform poorly. Thus investing in stocks at the end of January, following a strong January and holding your investment until the following January, has been an excellent idea in the last several decades. When a weak January occurs, pull out of the stock market and consider interest rate vehicles, such as bonds, or Treasury bills. Following this advice, you could have beaten a buy and hold strategy.

Thus, January has become an important month for Washington and the stock market. New representatives set laws and lobby for bills, and the president gives the all-important Sate of the Union Address. These factors set the political tone for the rest of the year, which affects the economy and the stock market. Thus "as January goes so goes the year."

The January barometer has an impressive track record. In the last 50 years, investing only in the market following a strong monthly showing would have kept you invested in all but 18 years, and would have had you beat the market by 0.5 percent on average.

**Timing Tip**

Remember back to the chapter regarding longer-term calendar anomalies, where we showed that the January barometer has an even better track record in odd numbered years, when new Congresses convene? Market timers may wish to look at these years as years to be especially aggressive in the stock market, perhaps favoring growth stocks and smaller capitalization stocks, which tend to be more volatile. As gamblers are found of saying, when the odds are in your favor, bet big!

Though you beat the market performance, this number is deceiving. First, it assumes that you are not investing in alternative investments, such as bonds or even money markets, when they are out of the stock market.

Thus, we looked at investing in stocks, only following a strong January and staying fully invested in the stock market until a weak January surfaced, then switching to one-year T-Bills until the following January.

The results, listed below, are phenomenal. If you would have invested in the Dow Jones Industrials only following a strong January and continued to hold until a down

January, then switched to one-year T-Bills until the next strong January, they would have beaten buy and hold by almost 1.5 percent.

| Year | Return | Investment |
|------|--------|------------|
| 1979 | 4.36% | Stocks |
| 1980 | 8.15% | Stocks |
| 1981 | 14.80% | T-Bills |
| 1982 | 12.27% | T-Bills |
| 1983 | 13.47% | Stocks |
| 1984 | 10.91% | T-Bills |
| 1985 | 22.09% | Stocks |
| 1986 | 37.37% | Stocks |
| 1987 | -9.26% | Stocks |
| 1988 | 19.61% | Stocks |
| 1989 | 10.60% | Stocks |
| 1990 | 7.89% | T-Bills |
| 1991 | 17.80% | Stocks |
| 1992 | 2.69% | Stocks |
| 1993 | 20.19% | Stocks |
| 1994 | -3.38% | Stocks |
| 1995 | 40.36% | Stocks |
| 1996 | 26.28% | Stocks |
| 1997 | 16.05% | Stocks |
| 1998 | 5.05% | T-Bills |
| 1999 | 16.90% | Stocks |
| 2000 | 6.11% | T-Bills |

Following this system, you would have only been invested in stocks about two thirds of the time. Though you would have had to suffer through two losing years in the stock market, they would have avoided two years that they buy and hold crowd would have had to weather.

Investors following the simple January barometer approach of investing at the end of January is stocks are up, and T-Bills if stocks are down and holding until the following January, would have avoided the losing years of 1981 and 2000, the two worst years in the period studied.

# When Things Don't Agree

We presented three very useful tools for timing the market. By combining these indicators, you may be able to improve upon the results even more, though each is an extremely valid approach for the time being.

> **CAUTION**
>
> **Trading Traps** _____
>
> Many market timers or financial gurus follow so many different patterns and cycles that they can always appear to be correct. However, when it comes down to making decisions, they suffer from "paralysis through analysis," meaning that so many things are pointing in so many different directions, that they can't see the forest for the trees. Do yourself and your finances a favor, and don't fall into this trap. Keep it simple, and invest for the longer term, you will be better off.

For example, follow the January indicator, but consider investing more heavily in the third or fourth year of the election cycle, especially the third year. Perhaps, adding a MACD indicator to the January barometer, and the best six months could improve the results of the January barometer, or even switching from stocks to T-Bills at the end of the best six month period (April) following a poor showing in January may improve results.

The possible combinations and permutations of timing systems are endless. However, the key to each of these gives the market timer an approach for making a rational decision regarding his/her commitment to the stock market.

As people, we need to see some positive reenforcement for our actions. Buying a stock and getting the statement saying it has increased is a good feeling, but selling the stock at a profit and knowing that the money is no longer at risk is a better one. Thus market timing gives the investor a framework for getting this reenforcement, which is not subject to an emotional response based on fear or greed.

## If In Doubt, Get Out!

Some of the time, the market may give mixed signals. For example, a poor January early in the year followed by a MACD buy signal in October, or a strong January in the first year of a new presidency.

Dealing with these mixed signals is a problem for many market timers and the downfall of many. Just as the old saying goes "too many cooks spoil the soup" is applicable, an expression from the world of short-term traders is just as applicable. *"If in doubt, get out!"*

When you are unsure of how the market is going to behave—not like you can ever be totally sure—but different patterns and cycles which you follow are pointing in different directions, consider putting on less, or even switching to another asset class, such as bonds.

> **Trading Traps**
>
> Take a few moments, go back and reread the chapter on contrarian thinking! My major goal in writing this book is not give away the holy grail of beating the market, because that does not exist. The tricks we show that have worked in the past may not work in the future, as the market place is ever-changing. Though the timing tricks may not continue to work phenomenally well in the future, they do provide discipline upon the decision-making process. Many investors buy in and sell out at the wrong time, reacting to the news, which appears to point in the opposite direction of the markets next primary trend. Make sure when you plan for investing and managing your portfolio, because in the long run a well-developed plan for rational decisions will serve you better than emotionally reacting to the latest news.

In the next chapter, we are going to discuss a method for beating the market with bonds, which may be an approach you may wish to take when such mixed signals occur.

Remember, a key feature of market timing is to reduce risk.

## The Least You Need to Know

- ◆ You can very closely match the performance of the market by simply investing only in the last two years of a presidential term—the year prior to an election and the election year. If you would have followed this strategy for the last two decades, investing in stocks along with the presidential cycle, and investing in T-Bills in the first two years of a presidential term, you would have closely matched the market's performance with only half the risk.

- ◆ You could have actually beaten the markets performance in the last 50 years by simply investing only in the strongest six month period—November through April—as indicated by the Moving Average Convergence Divergence Indicator (MACD).

◆ By simply following Yale Hirsch's sound advice of "As January goes, so goes the year" you could have outperformed the stock market in the last two decades by simply buying stocks only following a strong January and holding them until a weak January when the investment is switched to a one-year Treasury bill.

◆ By combining some or all of these market timing systems, you may be able to strongly outperform the stock market. However, when they are flashing incongruent signals, it is probably best to avoid being fully invested in the stock market.

◆ The true power of market timing is not in beating the performance of buy and hold, though that is nice when it happens, but in giving investors a disciplined approach to follow so that they don't react emotionally to the latest headlines, and make irrational decisions based on fear and greed.

# Part 8

# Be Your Own Financial Guru

This part covers some broad topics, not specifically about market timing but still very important, such as how to pick a qualified investment advisor, work with them, and still think independently about your finances and your financial decisions as well as tips and tricks about your personal finances that can help with your investing.

# Chapter 21

# Think Independently

## In This Chapter

- ◆ Contrarian thinking revisited
- ◆ Analysts and brokers: use 'em, don't worship 'em
- ◆ The news, rumors, and the media
- ◆ Buy bad times, sell good times

It has been said that people spend more time researching a new appliance purchase than they do investigating stock picks or their finances. Hopefully, as a reader of this book you are taking an active involvement in your finances and your financial future.

In this chapter, we are going to expound further on some ideas we have presented, to help you steer a solid course with your finances. They key point we will make here and hopefully have made throughout this book is that you need to have a plan of action and that plan should be tailored to your own risk tolerance. The plan you are going to operate under should also be unique and separate from the crowd, because acting like everyone else will most likely lead to financial ruin.

# Going Against the Crowd

One of the key themes throughout our research thus far into market timing has been that the crowd is generally wrong. Charles Dow noticed this back at the turn of the previous century and it will probably be true at the turn of the next century.

> **Timing Tips**
>
> Despite the vast amounts of knowledge available to investors today as compared to a century ago, the mass psychology of the crowd and the habits of investors have changed little. People tend to get excited and overly aggressive at market tops and overly fearful at market bottoms, because the market doesn't just react to today's news, but the future as well. Don't react to the news, which will most likely to emotional decisions, but instead have a well-thought-out timing strategy and implement it.

This is a fact of the markets. Basically, people tend to believe what is comfortable to believe. They enter the stock market not when it represents a great value, but when it is the acceptable thing to do. We are ruled by conventional wisdom, which does serve to make us good members of society and helps us all to get along, but in the field of investing tends toward our own detriment.

These same impulses and group thinking tend to make us financially in the market act like sheep, with the wolves baying at the door. We are going to present a few examples from history to show this and as you read these examples, think about how similar they sound to some of our modern day markets and the hysteria which surrounded them.

## Classic Market Manias

Probably the best-known market mania historically is the crash of 1929 and the ensuing economic depression of the 1930s. Going back and looking at the events surrounding the 1929 is an extremely interesting lesson in mass psychology.

Following the sharp market panic of 1921, the stock market soared from 1921 through 1929. The engine of this growth was primarily the automobile.

The automobile was an epoch-making invention, as it changed the very nature of society. Before the automobile, people used to live near where they worked. But with the advent of the automobile, people could move farther away from places of employment.

**Trading Traps**

Usually the story to explain a major bull or bear market is very logical and quite apparent at the end of the move, which is why investors often get overly bullish or bearish at the wrong times. Remember, stock prices are a reflection of what is going to happen, not what has happened. Thus by the time we understand a situation, the marketplace may have already priced it into the market. Ask yourself before buying a hot stock or market sector that if prices have already "doubled" will the expectations of the future quadruple, because that is the bet being made. Don't concentrate on yesterday's winners, look for tomorrow's.

Think about the landscape before and after the automobile. Though roads existed in the horse-and-buggy days, the invention of the automobile and its popularity necessitated the building of roads. This in turn led to the production of more concrete and asphalt, the building materials of roads.

Construction crews were hired to build these roads. Equipment had to be manufactured to assist in building these roads. We also saw a boom in residential construction, following World War I and the influx of immigrants.

As populations moved out of the cities and into the countryside, new businesses were started. Each suburb needed a grocery store, clothing stores and such, right?

The simple automobile pushed employment far beyond Ford Motor Company, and changed the landscape. Couple that with the widespread use of electricity, and—*voilà*—you see changes to the very fabric of our society.

This was true in 1921, when the Dow Jones Industrial Stocks stood at 71. A decade later, the Dow Jones had soared to 380, gaining roughly 535 percent. This equates to 66 percent a year. Could the economy continue to grow indefinitely at this rate?

The fever of speculation had captured the American public. One noted commentator at the time said " The traditional theory is that business corporations issue stocks and bonds only when they need additional capital … During this period, however new securities were manufactured almost like cakes of soap, for little better reason than there was a gain to be made out of their manufacture and sale." This statement can be backed up in historical

**Timing Tips**

Large numbers of initial public offerings are usually a sign of a market top. Before investing in an IPO, ask yourself a simple question … "If the company is so great, why do the current owners wish to sell it?"

fact. Between 1925 and 1929, the number of shares listed on the New York Stock Exchange more than doubled.

Looking at paper of the day, stock exchange listings became more prevalent. Subscriptions to the Dow Jones *Wall Street Journal* increased precipitously and books on investing and stock speculation became popular.

The advice of the day was that to create money, you had to invest in the stock market. A new era of economic prosperity had gripped the nation, and that old rules regarding valuation did not take into account the changes that had occurred and were rendered useless.

Of course, we all know what happened. Stocks topped out in 1929, and crashed, coinciding with an economic depression that lasted a decade. When stocks finally hit bottom in 1933, more than 83 percent of all the value had been lost. All the way down, major financial analysts proclaimed that the break was merely a correction within a major up trend.

Predictions of a radio in every house eventually came true, but sadly investments in the technology stocks of the day, like RCA, are worth little and never again reached their 1929 highs.

**Timing Tips**

Often predictions regarding new technology do come true, just like every house will have a radio and the expectations that most people in America and the world will be on the Internet. However, remember that new technology has a very wide profit margin—once it becomes commonplace, it becomes a commodity. Though every house did eventually get a radio, or even three if you count the ones in our cars, the profit margins in producing them dropped and competition increased, so no company really benefited. Look at the computer industry, and the Internet service providers of today. See the parallel?

But, of course, that was then and this is now. We are much smarter, and better educated with more information available.

## The Wonder of the 1990s

The same conventional wisdom that led the public lock, stock, and barrel into the stock market in the 1920s and saw fortunes reversed in the 1930s, is being repeated before our eyes in recent years.

Instead of the automobile, our epoch-making invention was the personal computer. The PC may not have changed the very landscape of our society like the automobile, but it did change the way we do business.

With the PC came software companies, and investment in them. Afterward, came the Internet, a promising new technology that would further change the way we do business. Some early companies on the Internet, like America Online or Yahoo!, really showed promise and fantastic gains for those who invested in them.

> **Timing Tips** _____
>
> Just like with the fall television line-up, in which many of the new shows each season are simply different twists on last season's popular shows, the stock market is very similar. Before investing in the latest fad or breakaway new popular stock or market sector, ask yourself if the current companies can continue to post the same impressive results if they have to sell their product at half the price with twice the competition. This is usually what happens, as nothing breeds imitation and competition like success.

However, as their fortunes became well known, and the fortunes of those who invested in them, other wished to repeat the process. New stocks were being issued at a surprising rate, as the word IPO (initial public offering) became a household word, as "new securities were manufactured almost like cakes of soap, for little better reason than there was a gain to be made out of their manufacture and sale."

New cultural icons were born. CNBC moved from a cable business channel to a widely watched media force, contending with the major networks. The best-sellers list was crammed with books about investing and speculating in stocks.

The best advice anyone could get was to be fully invested in stocks. Want to double your money in a hurry, buy an IPO.

Take a moment to reflect upon the mass mood changes and such that were present both in recounts of the 1920s and the 1990s, at least as far as the stock market was concerned. A new technology offered much hope and incredible amounts of money being were made. Investors, many of whom had avoided stocks for an extremely long time, flocked to he markets and made oversized returns, to eventually have their money taken away.

> **Timing Tips** _____
>
> Most people are not aware that the 1930s saw some excellent investing opportunities. Typically after excessively long bull markets, the bear markets are long as well as quite painful. However, in the rubble of what once was, many gems and valuables can be found. Remember, markets react to tomorrow's news not today's.

Now, it is doubtful that we will enter into a decade-long economic depression, but many of the market's similarities may occur. It is interesting to note that of the 15 strongest years in stock market—as measured by the Dow Jones Industrial—since 1928 to present four of them occurred in the 1930s: 1933 up 66.7 percent, 1935 up 38.5 percent, 1938 up 28.1 percent and 1936 up 24.8 percent.

Just as the cycle of excess optimism and overindulgences creates the bull market and the eventual substantial drop in prices, a wave of pessimism also occurs that causes excessive selling and incredible values. However, as most investors react without a plan or in an undisciplined fashion, they tend to buy during the heady raging bull markets and sell during the excessive pessimism of the bear markets, either losing a tremendous amount of their capital in the process, or substantially reducing their overall returns.

Hopefully by providing you with some rational framework upon which to base your decisions, you can time the market more effectively to better benefit from the longer-term opportunities that stock market investing has provided historically and should continue to provide.

# Professional Advice

One of the major problems with being a contrarian is you will most likely be early. It was obvious to many pundits of this school of thought that stocks, especially the NASDAQ stocks were extremely overpriced during the later 1990s.

Alan Greenspan, the chairman of the Federal Reserve, noticed this around 1997 when he delivered his now infamous "Irrational Exuberance" speech. However, being early can be just as dangerous as not seeing the handwriting on the Wall.

> **CAUTION**
>
> **Trading Traps**
>
> One of the major problems with being a contrarian is that you will most likely be early, just as Mr. Greenspan warned of the "irrational exuberance" years ahead of the marketplace finally coming crashing down. The legendary hedge fund manager George Soros once said that "all major trends are based on lies at the end." The trick he found is not in noticing the lie, but in what will bring it to light. Learn not to spot the excesses of the marketplace, but what will most likely rein them in or bring them to the surface.

Many professional speculators began shorting stocks in 1998, especially NASDAQ stocks. They saw the NASDAQ index rise from around 2,000 to over 4,000 before the mania eventually came to a close.

The mania was widely propagated by professionals in the industry. Brokerage firms continued to put out bullish reports as NASDAQ stocks plummeted, calling each break a tremendous buying opportunity and continued to bring new issues to market.

Now, just as in the 1930s following the crash of 1929, the government is getting involved and passing tougher regulations on the industry and calling for steep separations between the analysts and the investment banking sides of the industry, as many brokerages firms are being accused of abusing their fiduciary duties toward the client by ratcheting up ratings on stocks to secure investment banking relationships.

Just as many of the changes were needed in the 1930s, many of the changes I am seeing look to be well-served and in the public interest. However, this does not change the basic relationship an investor should have with his/her investment advisor.

An investment advisor, broker, financial planner or whatever route you wish to go can be a great benefit to you. These people are paid to understand the affect that an investment will have on your entire portfolio, and many can also be beneficial in helping you set up tax-deferred accounts and to meet your own financial goals.

The investment climate has come a long a way since the days when brokers were nothing more than "pitching the stock of the week" guys and gals, who made their livings writing stock tickets. Today's financial advisors, are up on the changing tax laws, as well as asset allocation, and a whole host of other things.

**Timing Tips**

Today's investment advisors are becoming more and more just that. They are highly trained and can be of great assistance in helping you to reach your financial goals. Just like the rest of us, they can't predict where the market is going, and will probably be much worse at market timing than you are. However, they can offer excellent advice on asset allocation, risk reduction, taxes, and estate planning. Use their knowledge and guidance, as that is what you are paying for. But remember, the ultimate fate of your investments is your responsibility.

The key thing for you to remember when dealing with a financial advisor is that they work for you. You pay them and the ultimate responsibility lies with you, not them.

Go over your plan for your account, why you are making the decisions you are making. They may be able to help with several things. If they understand your goals and what you expect from them, they can then service your account better.

Your investment advisor can keep track of your asset allocation and alert you when you have deviated from your plan. Your advisor can also help you in structuring your savings into tax-deferred accounts to meet your specific goals, such as special account types for saving for college educations, as well the whole host of retirement account available.

Remember, though we pay these people, today's financial advisors are mostly extremely reputable professionals, who are more and more being compensated on how your account performs instead of how often you trade. Take advantage of this knowledge, but remember that you are the one in charge and as such the decisions as to how your account is handled are yours. They are paid to advise you, as well as to execute your wishes.

# Don't Be Swayed by the News

As we have stated several times throughout this book, the markets are forward-thinking vehicles. They do not react to just what is happening today, but also to all the hopes, fears, rumors, and expectations about what tomorrow will bring.

This is why Hamilton, Charles Dow's predecessor, called the stock market a business barometer. Remember one of the tenets of the Dow Theory, "The fluctuations of the daily closing prices of the Dow Jones rail (transportation) and industrial averages afford a composite index of all the hopes, disappointments, and knowledge of everyone who knows anything of financial matters, and for that reason the effects of coming events (excluding acts of God) are always properly anticipated in their movement."

**Timing Tips**

Participating in the stock market are some of the greatest and most informed people in the world. They know the news and world events long before we do, and they act on it. Their buying and selling changes prices, and as such the market discounts news long before it is news. Don't waste your time on the latest news, or earnings estimates, concentrate more on the long-term picture as that is what the marketplace reacts to anyway.

However, on a daily basis we are confronted by the current news. The Federal Reserve did this; a leading economist predicted that. However, the marketplace is not only reacting to these current factors, but is also reacting to the likely future. This is so true that the U.S. government uses the price change of the S&P 500 as one of its "leading economic indicators" to predict changes in the economy.

Thus, the news today is not nearly as important as the new tomorrow. However, none of us has a crystal ball, and as such we have to make educated guesses as to what tomorrow will bring. In doing such, we are much better off not paying too close attention to the news, but instead on developing a consistent plan that removes much of the emotion from investing, as emotional reactions based on fear and greed will most likely be to our own detriment.

# Contrarian Thinking Yet Again

I am sure by now you are sick of hearing that the crowd is often wrong and how "no tree grows to the sky" and that it is always "darkest before the dawn" but the point of these platitudes is so important to the investor that they bear repeating.

Investors have to learn to think apart from the crowd. This need not be taken to extremes, but should be used as a filter in your own investing.

Think of the financial markets for a moment in the context of the greater fool theory. Under this market model, you buy a stock knowing that somebody else will come along and buy the stock at a higher price—the greater fool. However, once everyone already owns a stock, or is fully invested in the stock market—where does the greater fool come from?

Stock prices can only do one of three things. Go up, go down, or remain unchanged. After buying a stock, you have three choices, sell it, continue to hold it, or buy more. If everyone has already bought a lot of stocks, then they only have two choices, continue to hold or sell it. As long as prices continue to go up, opt for continued holding. However, as prices start to level off, or drop, the selling begins. As selling progresses, prices will fall farther under that pressure, and some investors will simply bury their heads in the sand and wait out the market correction.

However, what usually happens is they plan on waiting it out, but eventually the losses are so great, they panic and sell their positions so that they will at least have something left. This last selling drives prices down to bargain prices, as the current news is bad, and the future does not look bright to most. However, as this selling stops pressuring prices lower, some investors are snapping up bargains and the cycle begins fresh.

**Timing Tips** _____

When you buy a stock you hope that you can sell it at a later time at a higher price. Basically, what you are doing is seeing value and hopefully holding the stock until it reaches an excessive value and selling it to a greater fool? Learn to think ahead of the crowd, for when the fools rush in and buy, who is left to buy what you have to sell if they are already fully committed.

Basically, what happens is that many public investors buy after a prolonged rally when the future looks bright and conventional wisdom says that is the thing to do. Usually, short-term they are right as their buying drives prices up. However, when their buying stops, prices fall with the lack of support. Eventually panic sets in and the investor throws in the towel at or near the bottom, suffering market losses or at least very substandard returns. After the market has bottomed and rallied for a while, they jump back in now that the market is safe again, and the cycle replays itself.

**Trading Traps**

> Have you ever done this or heard someone say that a current stock holding is too far below water or the losses are too great to sell? Usually when this is said, it is a precursor to the stock or market dropping another 20 percent, at which time the begrudged investor sells his stock hoping to keep some of his money. Don't get married to a position. When wrong, admit it and get out, as a stock is never too cheap to sell when it is showing a loss, and those funds may be more useful somewhere else.

This can be seen time and time again, as the tale is told in public ownership of stocks being extremely high at market tops and extremely low at market bottoms. Magazine headlines and covers exalt the virtues of the stock market at highs, and the utter hopelessness of the market at bottoms.

By being aware of this cycle, hopefully you can learn to avoid it. You can't buy the market at the exact bottom ad you can't sell it at the exact top, but by being aware of this cycle you can hopefully spot when the cycle is near an extreme and capitalize on it by having a disciplined approach to making your decisions regarding market participation, instead of being tossed about by the cycle as it unfolds.

# Buy Bad Times and Sell Good Times

Timing the stock market is very important, as most who set out to be long-term investors invariably make the wrong decisions along the way. These decisions, which are usually made under duress, after watching portfolio values plummet and seeing constantly declining prices for periods of time after aggressively buying prices near the highs, can be avoided by having a plan.

For example, in much of this book we have discussed the relationship between Wall Street and Washington, and showing how the stock market appears tied to the presidential cycle. Usually as we enter into the first years of a presidential administration, times are good and the economy is strong.

However, the new administration will most likely make its tough decisions in the first years of the administration. For example, George Bush Sr. raised taxes in his second year in office, while President Clinton tried to overhaul national health care in his first year in office, while President Bush Jr. had to fight the war on terrorism in his first year, as well as deal with the fact that his election was widely contested.

Going into each of these, the economy was strong, and all of them saw stock prices correct to a certain degree. However, as they rolled out the punches to seek reelection, both of these former presidents managed to turn around the economy and the stock markets.

When things looked the most dismal, prices turned higher and when things looked the brightest, they turned as well.

# Thinking Ahead of the Crowd

The presidential cycle forces you to learn to think ahead of the crowd. Though not a perfect indicator—as there is no such as that—it does tend to put the process of market cycles from bullish to bearish and back to bullish into perspective.

Basically, as market timers we have to think of the market in terms of secular bull and bear markets or cycles. By doing so, we can learn to invest less heavily following strong advance and excessive public enthusiasm toward stocks, and to look to invest more aggressively following severe breaks and excessive pessimism.

**Timing Tips** _____

We tend to think of Wall Street professionals as being omnipotent regarding the market. Nothing could be further from the truth! Usually when all the analysts and the media agree upon something, they are almost universally wrong. It is not just the public that gets caught up in the emotions of the day, the professionals on Wall and Broad are just as human as we are ... don't be fooled into thinking otherwise.

This is a common theme throughout the indicators that we highlighted. For example, the volatility index (VIX) timing model showed us that not only does the public show excessive in enthusiasm, but so do the professionals and the sophisticated investors and users of options. Basically, when the market was pricing put options—or contracts which benefit from lower prices—excessively, the market was due for a rally. The opposite occurs when the market is underpricing these options, showing that sophisticated investors were discounting risk, a sure sign of excessive enthusiasm.

Magazine covers and feature newspaper articles also serve as a warning of a major turn in the market as these are representative of a consensus of public opinion. And though President Lincoln "couldn't fool all of the people all of the time," the market sure has a tendency to do so.

Thus, instead of getting caught up in this roller coaster of emotions, sit down with your financial advisor or planner and set goals for your investment and take an active role in reaching those goals by establishing a solid plan for making commitments to either the stock or bond markets. Don't follow the latest fads of investing, but instead try to think what the majority are doing and learn to try to do the opposite.

## The Least You Need to Know

- ◆ In market timing and investing, typically the majority is often wrong, especially at major turning points because their decisions are the result of acting from fear or greed. Avoid being overly emotional in your investing by setting a plan, and sticking to it.

- ◆ The majority of people tend to have repeated the same basic market timing mistakes historically. Just as the 1920s stock market was seen as a classic mania or overspeculation, the market of the 1990s may go down in history as the same thing. Learn to think away from the crowd and not to react to mass hysteria and prosper in the long run.

- ◆ One way to help establish a disciplined approach to your investment decisions is to work with a qualified professional investment advisor. Seek out a professional to offer guidance in implementing your goals, but always remember they work for you, so carefully explain your goals, and listen to their advice but remember the ultimate decision is yours.

- ◆ Learn to think ahead of the crowd and not to follow accepted wisdom. The mass media and analysts are usually wrong at major market turning points because the market doesn't react to today's news, but future prospects. No trends last forever, invest that way.

# Chapter 22

# Taking Care of Your Finances

## In This Chapter

- ◆ It's your money—remember that
- ◆ Dealing with mistakes
- ◆ Paying off debt, pay yourself

There is much more involved in being financially independent one day than investing right. It involves a lot of steps to eventually take, like making a budget, foregoing some things today for a better tomorrow, and learning to think of money not as the end all, be all of everything but as a tool.

In this chapter, we are going to discuss a bit about being a good shepherd with your finances. We will start off with choosing a financial consultant, and go into dealing with eventual mistakes, then off to paying down your debt, and finally end with thinking about money in its proper perspective.

## It's Your Money—Remember That!

Life is what you make of it. How many times have we heard this trite expression, or others like "when life hands you lemons, make lemonade"? Though it is sometimes difficult to look on the brighter side of things, it becomes easier when you realize that you are in control of your own destiny, especially financially.

In the last chapter we touched on the subject of choosing a financial consultant. For most people, this may be a broker, as today's financials consultants are highly trained and able to help in a lot of areas. The financial services companies of today offer a one-stop-shopping approach to many of your financial needs, and are able to help you plan financially for all of life's major events, like sending your kids off to college, weddings, opening a business, or simply being able to save enough to eventually stop working one day.

> **Timing Tips**
>
> Today's investment professionals are very knowledgeable. As such, they can be an asset to you in reaching your investment goals. However, always remember that they work for you and the ultimate decisions on your portfolio and investments are yours and yours alone. Use their counsel but make the decisions yourself, as no one cares more about your money than you do.

If you are the president of your household—or for us men, the junior vice president, because we all know that our wives make all the really important decisions—your financial advisor should be your most trusted advisor, your first lieutenant.

Choosing the right financial advisor is very important. Here are some tips on choosing the right advisor for you.

## Do I Trust Him or Her?

The most important part of your relationship with your financial advisor is trust. After all, you are counting on their expertise in matters, and will be hesitant to take their advice if you don't trust them.

> **Timing Tips**
>
> When interviewing a prospective financial advisor, ask them questions. Learn about their investment philosophies and see if they mesh well with yours. Pick someone who has the same basic beliefs that you do, as they will be better suited to help you meet your goals.

One of the first things that I have always done before using any financial advisors or professional services is to meet the person face to face. A telephone conversation is nice, but actually sitting down with someone and talking with them in person is quite a different matter.

We usually trust people who are similar to ourselves or from similar backgrounds. Ask them what school they went to and what type of experience they have. Just as none of us want to be the first patient of a surgeon, do you really want to be a new financial advisor's first client?

Get to understand their basic philosophy about the markets before offering yours. If they view the stock market as a wonderful casino, similar to Las Vegas but without the drinks, and think people should trade heavily, and you feel differently, then perhaps this relationship will never work out.

On the other hand, many financial experts have been through the wringer enough times and are a bit pessimistic about the market. They think that doing business with them entails following the recommendations of the firms analysts, and our job as investors or clients of the firm is to follow this advice.

**Timing Tips**

Avoid financial advisors who have a know-it-all attitude. No one is smarter than the market, and anyone who thinks they are is a fool. Look for someone who is knowledgeable and willing to help you reach your goals, not someone who is going to command you. They work for you, don't forget that!

Look for an individual you could be friends with. Look for an advisor who shares your views of the market, as well as your goals for investing in the market.

The best way to get their views is to ask them their views before offering yours. Many professionals hold very strong opinions about the markets, and they are very good at convincing people about their opinions. As such, they may be able to change your mind about things, even if unintentionally.

Look for a like-minded individual, whom you like and whose company you enjoy. In investing, we will not always make the right decisions, and as such it is usually easier to hear this news from a friend than not. Also, it is usually much easier to make the difficult decisions, those that aren't popular at the time, when the person from whom you seek counsel thinks in a fashion similar to you.

## Get Down to Brass Tacks

Early in my career, I was flown halfway across the country for a job interview. After being picked up at the airport, and treated to a very nice lunch, we discussed what the firm did and how I would fit into it. We had a wonderful day together, talking shop as well as swapping stories, and eventually had a wonderful dinner at the firm president's home, with his family.

The next day, after being taken to a wonderful brunch, we continued talking casually. Eventually, as the day wore on, I finally broached the subject of salary and benefits and the nuts and bolts of working for them.

What a shock! The level of compensation was not even close to what I was expecting and had received as other offers for similar positions. Though the trip was wonderful, a nice little mini-vacation, I could have cut it short and returned home a day earlier had I only gotten down to brass tacks sooner.

Though it is important to get to know your financial advisor and to trust him or her, it is also extremely important to understand how they make their money and what you receive in return.

Be sure to get to brass tacks when choosing a financial advisor. If they are evasive about commissions and fees, then run for the hills. After all, if you are surprised when you get a statement about the level of fees, how much will you trust them?

Understand all of their fees. Some firms may charge a management fee for smaller accounts, while others may have additional fees for research, or for buying non-firm products.

Sit down and explain to your prospective financial advisor what you are looking at doing, the type of assets and allocation you are looking at, and ask them what types of fees would be involved.

Remember, the more you pay them the less you will have for yourself. Good, solid and professional services do not always come cheaply, but also there is no point in overpaying for a service. Thus, understand how he or she makes their money and see if the level of service you expect fits in with your budget.

## Get Referrals and Take Referrals

**Timing Tips**

Get referrals from prospective investment advisors. Seek out individuals who are similar to yourself in circumstances, who are happy with his services. References are a standard of most job applications, and should be a standard part of seeking investment advice. After all, you are hiring this person to help you manage your money.

Usually, one of the best ways to find a great service is to ask your friends. Ask them whom they use, if you are unhappy with yours or are looking. It is much easier to trust somebody if they come referred by a friend.

If you follow your friend's advice, and meet with the financial consultant, be sure to tell them you are a friend of another client. This not only is beneficial for the financial professional to know, but may also help your friend out as well. It will also help to break the ice in initially meeting with him or her. But it also has another side effect. The financial professional knows that when they are dealing with you, or your friend, they have to worry about making two clients happy.

Be sure to ask the professional for references from other happy clients. Just like a perspective employer asks for personal and professional references before hiring a new employee, it is not out of the question to ask for professional references from someone whom you are looking to hire.

## Look Before You Leap

You can also check out your personal broker/financial advisor with the state. If they or the firm they work for handles securities (stocks and bonds) then they have to be registered.

Before you invest, make sure your brokers, investment advisers, and investment adviser representatives are licensed to sell securities. Always check and see if they or their firms have had run-ins with regulators or other investors.

This is very important, because if you do business with an unlicensed securities broker or a firm that later goes out of business, there may be no way for you to recover your money—even if an arbitrator or court rules in your favor.

People or firms that get paid to give advice about investing in securities generally must register with either the SEC or the state securities agency where they have their principal place of business. Investment advisers who manage $25 million or more in client assets generally must register with the SEC. If they manage less than $25 million, they generally must register with the state securities agency in the state where they have their principal place of business.

Some investment advisers employ investment adviser representatives, the people who actually work with clients. In most cases, these people must be licensed or registered with your state securities regulator to do business with you. So be sure to check them out with your state securities regulator.

> **Timing Tips**
>
> Be sure to check the regulatory background of any investment advisor you are considering doing business with. Ask them for a Form ADV, which is available from the Securities and Exchange Commission (SEC) or your state. Check out their background before doing business with them; it builds trust.

To find out about advisers and whether they are properly registered, read their registration forms, called the "Form ADV." The Form ADV has two parts. Part 1 has information about the adviser's business and whether they've had problems with regulators or clients. Part 2 outlines the adviser's services, fees, and strategies. Before you hire an investment adviser, always ask for and carefully read both parts of the ADV.

You can view an adviser's most recent Form ADV online by visiting the newly launched Investment Adviser Public Disclosure (IAPD) website at www.adviserinfo. sec.gov/IAPD/Content/IapdMain/iapd_SiteMap.asp.

At present, the IAPD database contains Forms ADV only for investment adviser firms that register electronically using the Investment Adviser Registration Depository. In the months ahead, the database will expand to encompass all registered investment advisers—individuals as well as firms—in every state.

You can also get copies of Form ADV for individual advisers and firms from the investment adviser, your state securities regulator, or the SEC, depending on the size of the adviser. You can find out how to get in touch with your state securities regulator through the North American Securities Administrators Association, Inc.'s website at www.nasaa.org/nasaa/abtnasaa/find_regulator.asp.

> **Trading Traps**
>
> Almost all investment advisors and financial professionals have to be registered with some regulatory body, be it the SEC or the state they are doing business in. Beware of totally unregistered advisors and firms. If problems arise, you will have little protection in dealing with them, and may never see your money again. Be sure you check them out before investing money with them.

If the SEC registers the investment adviser, you can get the Form ADV at a cost of 24 cents per page (plus postage) from the SEC at:

Office of Public Reference
450 5th Street, NW, Room 1300
Washington, D.C. 20549-0102
phone: 202-942-8090
fax: 202-628-9001
e-mail: publicinfo@sec.gov

Because some investment advisers and their representatives are also brokers, you may want to check both the CRD and Form ADV.

## Now Ask the Tough Questions

Just like a job interview, you are interviewing your prospective financial advisor. We have all had those tough questions asked of us in interviews, the ones that really make us think.

Here are some questions to ask a prospective financial advisor, compliments of the Securities and Exchange Commission, the government body that regulates the sale and distribution of securities to the public

- What experience do you have, especially with people in my circumstances?

- Where did you go to school? What is your recent employment history?

- ◆ What licenses do you hold? Are you registered with the SEC, a state, or NASD?

- ◆ Are the firm, the clearing firm, and any other related companies that will do business with me members of SIPC?

- ◆ What products and services do you offer?

- ◆ Can you only recommend a limited number of products or services to me? If so, why?

**Timing Tips** _____

Before opening an investment account or using the services of an investment professional, fully understand what all the fees are associated with the relationship you are entering. It is always a good idea to understand what it is you are buying before you buy it!

- ◆ How are you paid for your services? What is your usual hourly rate, flat fee, or commission?

- ◆ Have you ever been disciplined by any government regulator for unethical or improper conduct or been sued by a client who was not happy with the work you did?

- ◆ For registered investment advisers, will you send me a copy of both parts of your Form ADV?

This may seem a bit uncomfortable to do, but I have personally witnessed several fraudulent activities by financial services firms in the past, and 99 percent of these could have been avoided if the clients of the firm only took the time to check out the representatives and the firm a bit more closely and not have been scared to ask some tough questions. After all, it's your money!

**Timing Tips** _____

Interview a prospective investment advisor just as you would any new hire in your company or business. These people will be working for you and you deserve to know about them before putting your money with them. Be sure to check on licenses and do not be afraid to ask tough questions.

# Dealing with Mistakes

A common mistake people often make is choosing the wrong financial advisor. This is the easiest mistake to remedy ... get a new one. Do not be afraid to switch firms and financial advisors. The harder and often more costly mistakes have to do with making poor decisions in the marketplace. These mistakes can lead to more mistakes and are often much more costly.

At one previous employer I worked for, they offered a very limited 401(k) package. The package was limited to five mutual funds: an S&P 500 fund, a NASDAQ fund, a growth and income fund, a special situation fund, and an overseas fund. The package also included a bond fund and a money market fund.

In order to increase employee participation in the fund, the management decided to have a contest. The employee who had the best performance in their 401(k) fund, based on percentage gain, received an additional 5 percent bonus to their performance.

This worked like a great football pool, after all an additional 5 percent could be a lot of money. The results each month were posted, and people would frantically rearrange their portfolios to get the best performance.

> **Timing Tips** _____
>
> Some of the best advice ever offered about the stock market is do not ask for advice nor offer any. Make your own decisions based on your feelings, regardless of what your next-door neighbor is doing. Usually hot stock tips will lead you to the poor house faster than to easy street.

Some of the older employees who started off with well-balanced portfolios of stock and bond funds, soon switched the weightings of their portfolios to almost exclusively being in the NASDAQ fund to keep up with the younger employees who were winning the pool. Very soon, as the stock market, especially the NASDAQ was skyrocketing, they were heavily invested in stocks in search of the prize money.

The funny part about this was that after about six months, almost everyone had the same weightings and the prize money was split across the majority of the employees.

I shudder now to think about what happened to several of the employees' 401(k) plans now as the stock market has corrected and entered into a primary secular bear market. Think about it this way, if they gained 35 percent one year and lost –26 percent the next year, then at the end of the second year they would have seen no appreciation at all in their investment portfolio.

> **Timing Tips** _____
>
> As we have shown you throughout this book, when an investment idea becomes extremely popular it is usually the end of that idea outperforming the market. Do not follow the latest fad because usually by the time we see it and it is a fad, it is almost over.

Though most of you probably have not seen a situation exactly like this one, it is very similar to what goes on everyday around the water cooler, or at cocktail parties. One guy or gal is talking about how well their portfolio is performing, and the money they are making. We get a bit envious and call our financial advisor to buy some of that stock or that group as well, after all they are no smarter than we are.

What is most likely to happen is that we are being the greater fool, and chasing performance. We will most likely end up buying near the top, and sadly watching as the market or the sector comes crashing down.

This is what causes manias, be they the crash of 1929, or the Internet boom of the 1990s. We see easy money being made by those less deserving than ourselves and line up to get a piece of the action.

Avoid this. Investing is a long-term proposition. Think of a roller coaster. If you ride in the car, the rises and falls and twists and turns are exciting and scary, but at the end of the ride you are right back to where you started. However, if instead of jumping onto the roller coaster, you simply started walking, the journey wouldn't be nearly as exciting, but you would get a lot farther. In the tale of the rabbit and the tortoise, the turtle won by simply plodding along at his own pace. Be the turtle and plod along, for in the end you will be much happier.

# Paying Down Debt Is Investing

The average return from the stock market has been about 11 percent per year historically. I have credit cards in my wallet that let me borrow money at 21 percent. If I get 11 percent a year on my investments, and am paying my credit company 21 percent a year, I am in effect losing –11 percent.

Debt can be a good thing. For example, I purchased a very nice laser printer for my business. This printer, financed along with the purchase of a new computer, allowed me to save money on printing costs for some of the publications that I write on a monthly basis.

For example, to have 1,000 two-sided research reports printed for a client, the printer may charge me $350 for paper and his time. Now the printer cost me about $1,500 and I am paying it off at 6 percent interest over five years, for a total cost of $2,007.33 for the printer plus interest. The cost of 1,000 sheets of paper is about $10. Since I can work on the computer while the laser printer is pumping out sheets, I do not count my time as an expense, thus I can save $340 every month by purchasing the laser printer. In other words, by incurring this debt—as I could not budget the additional $1,500 for the printer at the time

**Timing Tips**

Consider debt as good or bad. If the cost of the debt is greater than the return you expect on your investments, then pay it down. However, if debt will yield a greater return than the cost of incurring it, by all means take that proposition. This is how business handles debt, and is how we as individuals should also.

of starting my own business—I actually saved $340 a month and the printer paid for itself in six months.

Businesses operate this way all the time. They borrow money to buy new equipment or expand. If their investment pays a greater return than the cost to borrow money, then they have a positive return on the debt. However, when the cost of borrowing is too much, then they loose money.

It is very hard to beat credit card debt as a rate of return. As such, consider paying down your credit card and other high interest debt ahead of your investing. In the long run it will pay off.

## The Least You Need to Know

- ◆ Your investment advisor should be a trusted lieutenant to your finances. This trust should be based on knowledge of him or her as a professional, which comes from understanding what they are expected to do, as well as what you pay them. Clarify both before entering into a relationship with an investment professional.

- ◆ You can get complete background checks regarding their work history and educational history as well as their regulatory history in Form ADV, which is available from the Securities and Exchange Commission (SEC) or your state. Check out their background before doing business with them. It builds trust.

- ◆ Do not judge your investment performance as successful or not based on comparisons with others. Your investment decisions should not be made to keep up with the Joneses, but based on your own goals and risk tolerances.

- ◆ Consider paying down or off any debt that is causing more money to leave your wallet than you are getting back in returns from the market. This is a form of investing that more people should practice.

# Appendix A

# Glossary

**accumulation**   The first phase of a bull market. While most investors are discouraged with the market, and earnings are at their worst, some investors start buying shares.

**alpha**   The premium an investment earns above a set standard. This is usually measured in terms of the Dow Industrials or the S&P 500. How the stock performs independent of the market.

**arbitrage**   The simultaneous buying and selling of two or more different, but closely related securities, in different markets to take advantage of price disparities.

**asset allocators**   Differ from market timers in that they usually try to keep a constant allocation mix, while market timers tend toward a more variable allocation mix.

**at-the-money**   An option whose strike price is equal to the price of the underlying security.

**back testing**   Optimizing a trading strategy on historical data and applying it to fresh data to see how well the strategy works

**bear trap**   A false signal that indicates that the rising trend of a stock or index has reversed when in fact it has not.

**bear market**   A series of lower prices, punctuated by a series of minor price advances; a 20 percent decrease in prices from a high point, without a subsequent 20 percent advance in prices.

**bear spread**   An option strategy with maximum profit when the price of the underlying security declines. Maximum loss occurs if the underlying security rises in price. The strategy involves the purchase and simultaneous sale of options. Puts or calls can be used. A higher strike price is purchased and a lower strike price is sold. The options have the same expiration date.

**beta**   The degree of sensitivity of a stock in relation to swings in the market.

**beta (coefficient)**   The degree of risk that cannot be decreased by diversification. A stock with a beta greater than one will rise faster or decline faster than the overall market. A stock with a beta lower than one will rise slower or decline slower than the overall market.

**Black Scholes option pricing model**   A model used to estimate the price of an option.

**blue chips**   Typically refer to the stock of a large, national company with a solid record of stable earnings and/or dividend growth and a reputation for high quality management and/or products. The term originated from gambling, when the blue chips were worth more than the red, or the white ones, signifying quality and assurance.

**bond**   A debt security, similar to an I.O.U. When you purchase a bond, you are lending money to a government, municipality, corporation, federal agency or other entity known as the issuer. In return for the loan, the issuer promises to pay you a specified rate of interest during the life of the bond and to repay the face value of the bond (the principal) when it "matures," or comes due.

**breadth (market)**   Relates to the number of issues participating in a market move. The move can be either up or down. As a rally develops, and the number of advancing issues is declining, the rally is suspect. As a decline develops, and the number of declining issues falls, the decline becomes suspect.

**bullish**   Generally a longer period of time in which prices rise.

**bull market**   A series of higher prices punctuated by a series of minor price corrections; a 20 percent increase in prices from a low point, without a subsequent 20 percent break in prices.

**bull spread**   An option strategy in which the maximum profit is attained if the underlying security rises in price. Either calls or puts can be used. The lower strike price is purchased and the higher strike price is sold. The options have the same expiration date.

**bull trap**   A false signal that indicates that the price of a stock or index has reversed to an upward trend, but that proves to be false.

**buy and hold**   The term used to describe long-term investing, as long-term investors are said to buy and hold a stock indefinitely.

**call option**   A contract which gives the purchaser the right not the obligation to purchase the underlying security at a specific price within a specific time frame.

**call price**   The price at which a bond or preferred stock can be called in by the issuing authority.

**candlestick charts**   A charting method originally developed in Japan. The high and low are described as shadows and plotted as a single line. The price range between the open and close is plotted as a rectangle on the single line. If the close is above the open, the body of the rectangle is white. If the close of the day is below the open, the body of the rectangle is black.

**capitalization weighted index**   A stock index that is computed by adding the capitalization of each individual stock and dividing by a predetermined divisor. The stocks with the greatest market values have the greatest impact on the index.

**contingent order**   An order given to a trading desk to buy stock and sell a covered call option. It is given as one order.

**channel**   Used in charting, it allows the user to draw parallel lines connecting the low points and the high points. It can be ascending or descending

**convertible security**   One security that is convertible into another. It is generally used with convertible preferred stock and convertible bonds. There is a specific rate at which the security can be converted.

**cover**   The act of buying back in a closing transaction an option which was originally written.

**covered**   Writing an option when the writer also owns the underlying security on a one-to-one ratio. A short call is covered if the underlying security is owned. A short put is covered if the underlying security is also short in the account. A short call is covered if a long call of the same underlying security is owned in the same account with the same or lower strike. A short put is covered if a long put of the same underlying security is owned in the same account with a strike price equal to or greater than the strike of the short put.

**confirmation**   At least two indicators or indexes corroborate a market turn or trend. In the case of the stock market, with respect to the Dow Theory, it would be the Dow Industrials and the Dow Transports.

**congestion area**   At a minimum, a series of trading days in which there is no or little progress in price.

**correction**    A price reaction of generally ⅓ to ⅔ of the precious gain.

**daily range**    The difference between the high and low during one trading day.

**delta**    The amount an option will change in price for a one-point move in the underlying security.

**delta neutral**    An options strategy designed so that the position is insensitive to movements in the underlying security. It can be composed of options/options or options/ underlying security. It is a careful calculation of offsetting long and short positions.

**discount**    An option is trading at a discount if it is selling for less than its intrinsic value. If a future is trading for less than the price of the underlying security, it is considered to be trading at a discount.

**discount rate**    The rate the Federal Reserve charges for loans from its discount window; considered largely a symbolic rate, much less important than the federal funds rate.

**discount window**    Often referred to as the window of last resort, and most banks will avoid routinely borrowing from it for fear it could give the impression that they are in trouble.

**dollar cost averaging**    The term used to continually buy a stock as its stock prices changes. When prices decrease, you are able to buy more, and when it increases you buy less, thus the cost of the stock is averaged over time.

**double bottom/ double top**    These are reversal patterns. It is a decline or advance twice to the same level (plus or minus 3 percent). It indicates support or resistance at that level.

**drawdown**    Reduction in account equity from a trade or series of trade. It happens to all of us some of the time.

**early exercise**    Early exercise prior to expiration, the exercise or assignment of an option.

**efficient market theory**    Holds that all market participants receive and act on all of the relevant information available as soon as it becomes available; if true, no investment strategy would be better than a coin toss.

**Elliot wave theory**    Originally published by Ralph Nelson Elliot in 1939. It is a pattern recognition theory. It holds that the stock market follows a pattern of five waves up and three waves down to form a complete cycle.

**ex-dividend**   The day when the dividend is subtracted from the price of a stock. The ex-dividend date is the date on which this takes place. Investors who own the stock are paid their dividend on that date. Investors who are short the stock must pay the dividend on that date.

**exercise**   The right granted under the terms of a listed options contract. Call holders exercise their right to buy the underlying security. Put holders exercise their right to sell the underlying security. There is generally an exercise limit placed by the options exchange. This is to prevent a group of investors or an individual investor from cornering the market on an underlying security.

**fair value**   Describes the worth of an options or futures contract. On a daily basis, fair value is published pertaining to the S&P futures. When fair value falls below a predetermined value, traders sell the cash index and buy futures. When fair value rises above a predetermined value, traders buy the cash index and sell futures.

**Fibonacci ratio**   The relationship between two numbers in the Fibonacci sequence. The sequence for the first three numbers is 0.618, 1.0, and 1.618. In general terms the Fibonacci series is 1, 1, 2, 3, 5, 8, 13, 21, 34, 55, 89, etc.

**first notice day**   The first day a buyer of a futures contract can be called upon to take delivery.

**float**   The number of shares outstanding for a particular common stock.

**floor broker**   A trader on the floor of an exchange who executes orders for people without access to the trading area.

**fundamental analysis**   Analysis of a security which takes into consideration sales, earnings, assets, etc.

**gamma**   It measures the amount the delta changes for a one-point move in the underlying security.

**good till canceled**   An order placed with a broker that is good until either filled or canceled. In practice, this order has to be reconfirmed twice annually.

**head and shoulders pattern**   One of the more common and popular patterns. It is comprised of a rally that ends a fairly extensive advance. It is followed by a reaction on less volume. This is the left shoulder. The head is comprised of a rally up on high volume exceeding the price of the previous rally. And the head is comprised of a reaction down to the previous bottom on light volume. The right shoulder is comprised of a rally up that fails to exceed the height of the head. It is then followed by a reaction down. This last reaction down should break a horizontal line drawn along the bottoms of the previous lows from the left shoulder and head. This is the point in which the major decline begins. The major difference between a head and shoulder top and bottom is that the bottom should have a large burst of activity on the breakout.

**implied volatility**   A measurement of the volatility of a stock. Current price rather than historical price is used. Generally, if the price of an option rises without a corresponding rise in the underlying equity, implied volatility is considered to have risen.

**index option**   An option whose underlying security is an index. An example would be the S&P 100 (OEX). A trader can buy index options and bet on the direction of the OEX.

**in-the-money**   A call option with a strike price below the underlying equity. A put option with a strike price above the underlying equity.

**inside day**   A day in which the total range of price is within the range of the previous days price range.

**leaps**   Long-Term Equity Anticipation Securities. Currently, these are long term options with expirations up to two and a half years.

**limit order**   An order to buy or sell at a fixed price. A person can also place a limit order with discretion. This enables the broker to buy or sell within a small range, usually ⅛ or ¼ of a point.

**limit up/ limit down**   Commodity exchange restriction on the maximum amount of movement up or down that a commodity can trade in a given day.

**local**   A futures trader in the pit of a commodity exchange who buys or sells for his own account.

**lognormal distribution**   A statistical distribution often applied to stock prices. It implies that stock prices can rise infinitely but can not fall below zero.

**margin**   The minimum amount of money required to buy or sell a security. The investor is using borrowed money.

**margin call**   The demand by a broker to an investor to put up money because his security(s) have declined in value. There are minimum amounts of capital required by the exchanges or the broker.

**market capitalization**   The market size of a company. Market capitalization equals the share price of the company multiplied the number of shares outstanding.

**market if touched**   An order with the floor broker which becomes a market order if a trigger price is reached.

**market maker**   An exchange member who makes a market by buying and selling for his own account when the public is not buying and selling.

**market order**   An order to buy or sell a security at the present market price. As long as there is a market for this security, the order will be filled. This type of order takes precedence over all other orders.

**market not held order**   This is a market order. However, the investor is giving the floor trader the discretion to execute the order when he feels it is best. If the floor trade feels that the market will decline, he may hold the order to try to get a better fill. This order may not get filled.

**market timing**   The belief that you can improve upon long-term performance of investments by moving their investments between different asset classes, such as stocks and bonds. For example, switching assets from the bond market to the stock market.

**momentum**   The strength behind an upward or downward movement in price. Graphically, momentum is represented as a horizontal line that fluctuates above and below an equilibrium line.

**money market account**   A savings account that shares some of the characteristics of a money market fund.

**moving average**   An average of the number days previous closes, usually plotted on the current day.

**moving average convergence/divergence (MACD)**   The crossing of two exponentially smoothed moving averages. They oscillate above and below an equilibrium line.

**odd lot**   A block of stock consisting of less than 100 shares. When odd lots trade, a premium is usually tacked on by the specialist or market maker. These receive the least favorable price and trade last.

**options clearing corporation (OCC)**   The issuer of all listed options on all exchanges.

**out of the money**   A call whose strike price is above the current market price of the underlying equity. A put whose strike price is below the current price of the underlying security.

**overbought**   Market prices that have risen too steeply and too quickly.

**oversold**   Market prices that have declined too steeply and too quickly.

**portfolio insurance**   In order to protect a portfolio of stocks an investor may sell index futures or buy index put options for downside protection.

**premium**   The price an investor pays the writer of an option above the options intrinsic value.

**price earnings ratio**   The ratio of the price of a stock to the earnings per share. Or total annual profit divided by the number of shares outstanding.

**program trading**   Trades based on signals from computer programs. These are usually entered directly from the trader's computer to the market's computer system. Program trading accounts for an increasingly larger and larger portion of all trades throughout the day. Additionally, these large trades may be hedged by an offsetting position in index futures.

**put option**   A contract which gives the purchaser the right, not the obligation, to sell a security at a specific price in for a specified period of time.

**put call ratio**   The ratio of put trading volume divided by the call trading volume. Moving averages can be used to smooth this chart out.

**random walk theory**   States that market prices follow a random path up and down, making it impossible to predict with any accuracy which direction the market will move at any point.

**ratio write**   Buying stock and selling calls against the stock. It can also be constructed by shorting stock and then selling puts against the short stock.

**relative strength**   A comparison of an individual stock's performance to that of a market index. Most times the S&P 500 or the Dow Jones Industrial Index are used for comparison purposes. It is calculated by dividing the stock price by the index price. A rising line indicates that the stock is doing better than the market. A declining line indicates that the stock is not doing as well as the market.

**resistance**   A price level where a security's price stops rising and moves sideways or downward. It indicates an abundance of supply. Because of this, the stock may have difficulty rising above this level. There are short-term and longer-term resistance levels.

**return on assets**   Net earnings of a company divided by its assets.

**return on equity**   Net earnings of a company divided by its equity.

**secondary market**   A market available to trade securities after their initial public offering. The New York Stock Exchange is an example of a secondary market.

**selling short**   Selling a security and then borrowing the security with the intention of replacing that security at a lower price than it was borrowed. The short trader is betting that the price of the security will go down.

**specialist**   An exchange member who keeps the public book, maintains an orderly and efficient market, buys and sells for his own account.

**short interest**   Shares that have been sold short and not yet repurchased.

**short interest ratio**   A ratio that tells how many days it would take to buy back all the shares that have been sold short. A short interest ratio of 2 would indicate that it would take 2 trading days to buy back all the shares that have been sold short. This is based on the current volume.

**slippage**   The difference between estimated and actual transaction costs. The difference is usually comprised of commissions and price differences.

**spread strategy**   An option strategy having both long and short options on the same underlying security.

**spot month**   The current trading month. Also known as the front month in commodity trading.

**spot price**   The current cash price for which a commodity is trading at a specific time and place.

**standard deviation**   The statistical term used to describe the distribution of data. In the stock market, the standard deviation is about 15.7 percent historically, meaning that most price moves over a 12-month period of time will fall within +/- 15.7 percent of the average about two out of three years.

**stock**   An instrument that signifies an ownership position, in a corporation, and represents a claim on its proportionate share in the corporation's assets and profits. When you buy a stock you are buying a piece in the ownership of that company.

**stock exchange**   Provides or maintains a marketplace where securities (stocks) can be traded.

**stock indexes**   Groups or baskets of stocks used to represent a segment of the stock market. A stock index is a proxy used to describe the behavior of the entire market.

**stop order**   An order placed that is not at the current market price. It becomes a market order once the security touches the specified price. Buy stop orders are placed above the present market price. Sell stop orders are placed below the present market price.

**stop limit order**   This is similar to a stop order. It is an order that becomes a limit order once the specified price is touched.

**stop and reverse**   A stop that when hit is a signal to close the current position and open an opposite position. A trader holding a long position would sell that position and then go short on the same security.

**straddle**  An options strategy where the purchase or sale of an equal number of puts and calls is made. The same strike price and expiration date is the same for all.

**strangle**  An options strategy that is a combination involving a put and a call with different strike prices with the same expiration.

**support**  A price level at which declining prices stop falling and move sideways or upward. It is a price level where there is sufficient demand to stop the price from falling.

**synthetic stock**  Using options, it is equivalent to the stock. A long call and a short put is a synthetic long stock. A long put and a short call is a synthetic short stock.

**theta**  A measurement of how much an options price decays for every one day that passes.

**Treasury Bill, or T-Bill**  A short-term debt instrument issued by the U.S. Treasury that will mature in less than two years.

**trending market**  Price moves in a single direction and it usually closes on an extreme for the day.

**trendline**  Constructed by connecting a series of descending peaks or ascending troughs. The more times a trendline has been touched increases the significance of a break in the trendline. It can act as either support or resistance.

**uncovered option**  This is sometimes referred to as a naked option. It is when a trader writes an option without owning the underlying security. It is a position with large risk.

**vega**  A measurement of how much an options price changes for a 1 percent change in volatility.

**volatility**  The measurement of how much an underlying security fluctuates over a period of time.

**warrant**  A long-term security that is similar to an option. A stock warrant usually allows a trader to purchase one share of stock at a fixed price for a certain period of time.

**whipsawing**  Frequent in and out trading.

**write**  To write an option is to sell an option. The person who sells the option is considered to be the writer.

# Resources

Here's a list of websites, books, and other resources that you may find helpful in your market timing and investing. By no means is this list complete, but it's a good resource for finding information about the markets.

## Exchanges

The exchanges are an excellent resource for investors. They contain lots of information regarding specific companies, as well current news and any pending legal matters that may affect trade.

The exchanges also have a plethora of free market research and investing tips. Take a few moments and visit their websites; it's time well spent.

The New York Stock Exchange
11 Wall Street
New York, NY 10005
212-656-3000
www.nyse.com

The NASDAQ Stock Market, Inc.
80 Merritt Boulevard
Trumbull, CT 06611
203-375-9609
www.nasdaq.com

The Pacific Stock Exchange
115 Sansome Street
San Francisco, CA 94104
415-393-4000
www.pacificex.com

Chicago Stock Exchange
One Financial Place
440 South LaSalle Street
Chicago, Illinois 60605
312-663-2222
www.chicagostockex.com

For more information on derivatives, puts and call options, as well as futures contracts, visit these exchanges. They contain great information about these derivative markets.

Chicago Board Options Exchange
400 South LaSalle Street
Chicago, IL 60605
1-877-THE-CBOE
www.cboe.com

Chicago Board of Trade
141 West Jackson Boulevard
Chicago, Illinois 60604-2994
312-435-3500
www.cbot.com

Chicago Mercantile Exchange
30 South Wacker Drive
South Tower
Chicago, Illinois 60606
312-930-3480
www.cme.com

# Government and Regulatory Agencies

Regulatory bodies are an excellent resource for information about investing, offering tips and tricks on how to invest safely, as well as how to avoid financial scams. They are also an excellent place to look up information on investment companies you are considering doing business with:

The Securities and Exchange Commission (SEC)
450 Fifth Street, NW
Washington, DC 20549
202-942-7040
www.sec.gov

The National Association of Securities Dealers (NASD)
One Liberty Plaza
New York, NY 10006
212-858-4000
www.nasd.com

For economic information, such as Gross Domestic Product, employment levels, inflation, or even the rates on various government securities, try these agencies or their websites:

The Federal Reserve Board
www.federalreserve.gov
Information about the Fed, calendar of upcoming meetings, copies of reports and speeches by Fed governors and much more.

The United States Treasury
www.ustreas.gov
The United States Treasury is responsible for many things from printing money and stamps, to collecting taxes and managing the nation's public debt. Excellent resource for bond investors with the latest information on government bonds, bills, and notes.

The following is a list of additional government agencies:

Department of Agriculture: www.USDA.gov
Department of Energy: www.doe.gov
Department of Commerce: www.doc.gov
Department of the Interior www.doi.gov
Department of Labor: www.dol.gov

# Advisory Services

Contrarian Investing Association (www.contrarian-investing.com): A website and service dedicated to looking outside the mainstream for clues about market performance.

Dow Theory Forecasts (www.dowtheory.com): Since 1946, *Dow Theory Forecasts* investment newsletter has been devoted to achieving superior returns by recommending market-beating stocks that do not involve undue risk. The weekly newsletter holds one of the nation's oldest and most respected investment performance records.

Dow Theory Letters (www.dowtheoryletters.com): Richard Russell began publishing Dow Theory Letters in 1958, and he has been writing the Letters ever since. Dow Theory Letters is the oldest service continuously written by one person in the business.

The Motley Fool (www.fool.com): Don't let the casual style of their advice and the silly hats fool you! The Motley Fool contains excellent information for the beginning investor and market timers alike.

Q Insight Group (www.qinsight.com): investment advice, research and financial consulting services for institutions, investment professionals, and individuals. Their products and services are based on a rigorous quantitative approach, and their investment advice is keyed to the U.S. business cycle.

Sector Fund Timer (www.timing.net): Publishers of the Sector Fund Timer, this website provides a plethora of useful information regarding market timing through different stock market sectors.

The Speculator (http://moneycentral.msn.com/content/newtoday.asp): The speculating duo of Victor Niederhoffer and Laurel Kenner put out a free weekly article that covers many of the principles covered in this book. The emphasis of their work is on quantifying market performance and separating the "hoo doo" of investing from the practical. A great, free resource that should be on every market timer's weekly reading list.

Standard and Poor's (www.spglobal.com): The inventors and keepers of the S&P, Standard and Poor's is a well-respected research and data provider. A plethora of data and market insights awaits the investor at this website.

*Stock Trader's Almanac* (www.stocktradersalmanac.com): Published for almost 40 years, the *Stock Trader's Almanac* and its useful website contain many of the theories and observations made in this book.

The Prudent Bear (www.prudentbear.com): Unconventional look at the stock market and why the returns of the 1990s will not be repeated in the near future. Though this site and their funds are devoted to the downside of the stock market, they offer an excellent insight into the risks of the stock market.

Tulips and Bears (www.tullipsandbears.com): An informational site dedicated to contrary investing for thinking individuals. A wonderful collection of unconventional analysis based on the theory of contrarian investing.

Value Line (www.valueline.com): Home to the oldest and most respected independent research firm in the nation. Value line's number one picks for timeliness and growth have outperformed the stock market for over 50 years.

# Great Books

The following are some excellent books and periodicals that we highly recommend that investors read to further their education. Remember, knowledge is power and you can be a master investor with the knowledge contained in these pages:

Anthony M. Gallea, William Patalon, Jim Rogers. *Contrarian Investing: Buy and Sell When Others Won't and Make Money Doing It* (Prentice Hall Press, 1999). How to succeed and profit by *not* following conventional trends, that is the secret to Contrarian investing: buy assets that are out of favor. Contrarian Investing gives readers the investing tips and techniques used by a portfolio manager overseeing $600 million in assets, with a track record for focusing on increasing returns while attempting to reduce risk. Written in a conversational style with exciting stories about big name but (at one time) out-of-favor stocks like Chrysler, IBM, Citicorp, and Xerox.

The Hirsch Organization. *Stock Trader's Almanac.* (Hirsch Organization, 2002) An up-to-date reference and planning book for the serious investor and market timer. This book is a must buy for anyone who wishes to time the stock market, as it covers in much more detail many of the topics touched on in this book as well as many more.

Peter Lynch, John Rothchild. *One Up on Wall Street: How to Use What You Already Know to Make Money in the Market* (Fireside, 2000). The former star manager of Fidelity's multibillion-dollar Magellan Fund, Lynch reveals how he achieved his spectacular record. Writing with John Rothchild, Lynch offers easy-to-follow directions for sorting out the long shots from the no shots by reviewing a company's financial statements and by identifying which numbers *really* count. He explains how to stalk great investment opportunities and lays out the guidelines for investing in cyclical, turnaround, and fast-growing companies.

Victor Niederhoffer. *Education of a Speculator* (John Wiley and Sons, 1998). This book draws material from disciplines as varied as biology, music, cards, and sports. Written with humor and verve, it offers readers a chance to see the world through lenses of a true speculator, Victor Niederhoffer. This is a terrific, rewarding book.

Victor Niederhoffer, Laurel Kenner. *Practical Speculation in an Uncertain World* (John Wiley and Sons, 2002).

Along with co-author Laurel Kenner, Niederhoffer explains his new theme of "old-hearted investors vs. new-hearted investors" and reveals some unique ideas for profiting in volatile markets. This sequel to "Education of a Speculator" is sure to satisfy both old and new readers alike, and will lead investors to finding market opportunities in the most unlikely places.

Brett N. Steenberger, PHD. *The Psychology of Trading: Tools and Tactics for Minding the Markets* (John Wiley and Sons, 2002).

A solid look at the investor instead of the investing method, Steenberger looks at the individual and how they fit into the process of investing, offering tricks to improve your performance and discipline in your own market timing.

Christy Heady. *The Complete Idiot's Guide to Making Money on Wall Street* (Alpha Books, 2000).

A well-written and easy-to-follow guide to the basics of how Wall Street works. This title is an excellent primer on the various investments available in today's financial markets.

Edward T. Koch. *The Complete Idiot's Guide to Investing Like a Pro* (Alpha Books, 1999).

A classic from the Idiot's collection, Investing Like a Pro takes the reader through the ins and outs of trading from A to Z. This book is a must read for anyone seriously looking at taking an active role in their own financial decisions.

Scott Barrie. *The Complete Idiot's Guide to Options and Futures* (Alpha Books, 2001).

This book offers complete coverage of the futures and options markets from cattle to crude oil, as well as the S&P futures and soybeans. It explains the workings of the futures and options and futures markets so that potential speculators can make an informed decision as to whether this high risk, high potential reward investment niche is for them.

# Index

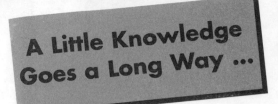
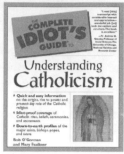

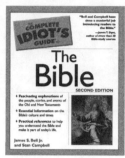